Sexism and Sin-Talk

Sexism and Sin-Talk

*Feminist Conversations
on the Human Condition*

Rachel Sophia Baard

© 2019 Rachel Sophia Baard

First edition
Published by Westminster John Knox Press
Louisville, Kentucky

19 20 21 22 23 24 25 26 27 28—10 9 8 7 6 5 4 3 2 1

All rights reserved. No part of this book may be reproduced or transmitted in any form or by any means, electronic or mechanical, including photocopying, recording, or by any information storage or retrieval system, without permission in writing from the publisher. For information, address Westminster John Knox Press, 100 Witherspoon Street, Louisville, Kentucky 40202-1396. Or contact us online at www.wjkbooks.com.

Scripture quotations from the New Revised Standard Version of the Bible are copyright ©1989 by the Division of Christian Education of the National Council of the Churches of Christ in the U.S.A., and are used by permission.

Scripture quotations marked (NIV) are taken from the *Holy Bible, New International Version®*, NIV®. Copyright © 1973, 1978, 1984, 2011 by Biblica, Inc.™ Used by permission of Zondervan. All rights reserved worldwide. www.zondervan.com. The "NIV" and "New International Version" are trademarks registered in the United States Patent and Trademark Office by Biblica, Inc.™

Book design by Sharon Adams
Cover design by Lisa Buckley Design

Library of Congress Cataloging-in-Publication Data

Names: Baard, Rachel Sophia, author.
Title: Sexism and sin-talk : feminist conversations on the human condition / Rachel Sophia Baard.
Description: First edition. | Louisville, Kentucky : Westminster John Knox Press, 2019. | Includes bibliographical references and index. | Summary: "Early feminist theologians criticized the Christian doctrine of sin for its focus on female sexual purity and its enabling of the marginalization and oppression of women. Others have questioned whether the entire theological category of sin should be abandoned in favor of other ways of talking about the human predicament. In this new book, Rachel Baard argues for a feminist critique of traditional sin-talk alongside a constructive reinterpretation of the doctrine of sin—one that can be life affirming for all persons. She claims that the Christian idea of sin—that tragic flaw at the core of human experience—provides one of the best tools for understanding the evils of sexism, patriarchy, and traditional sin-talk itself. She likewise provides a new rhetoric of sin-talk, one that accounts for the diverse experiences of the human family, not simply those of powerful men"—Provided by publisher.
Identifiers: LCCN 2019040189 (print) | LCCN 2019040190 (ebook) | ISBN 9780664234430 (paperback) | ISBN 9781611649819 (ebook)
Subjects: LCSH: Sin—Christianity—History of doctrines. | Sexism—Religious aspects—Christianity—History of doctrines. | Sex—Religious aspects—Christianity—History of doctrines. | Feminist theology.
Classification: LCC BT715 .B24 2019 (print) | LCC BT715 (ebook) | DDC 241/.3—dc23
LC record available at https://lccn.loc.gov/2019040189
LC ebook record available at https://lccn.loc.gov/2019040190

♾ The paper used in this publication meets the minimum requirements of the American National Standard for Information Sciences—Permanence of Paper for Printed Library Materials, ANSI Z39.48-1992.

Most Westminster John Knox Press books are available at special quantity discounts when purchased in bulk by corporations, organizations, and special-interest groups. For more information, please e-mail SpecialSales@wjkbooks.com.

Contents

Acknowledgments	vii
Introduction	1
1. Rhetoric	**9**
Rhetorical Theory	11
Rhetorical Theology	18
Feminist Rhetorical Strategies	24
Outline	28
2. *Kairos*	**31**
The Rhetorical Situation	31
Naming the *Kairos*	35
Gender Violence	44
Gender Violence and the Church	49
3. Mary	**57**
Historical Overview	58
The Feminist Rhetoric of Difference	64
The Feminist Rhetoric of Oppression	69
The Patriarchal Rhetoric of Life-Denial	73
4. Eve	**83**
Historical Overview	84
The Feminist Rhetoric of Oppression	90
The Feminist Rhetoric of Reason	97
The Patriarchal Feminine and the Rhetoric of Death	102

5. Grammar	**109**
Toward Critical Retrieval	110
The Doctrine of Original Sin	112
Patriarchy as Original Sin	115
Feminist Sin-Talk and the Grammar of Original Sin	121
6. Life	**127**
Ethos: The Cry for Life	128
Pathos: Embracing the Diversity of Life	133
Logos: Denouncing Death	141
Affirming Life	151
Bibliography	155
Index	167

Acknowledgments

I am very grateful to the many, many people who have played a direct or indirect role in the journey this book represents. Primary among these is my spouse, Cobus Greyling, whose commitment to human dignity played a significant role in my own theological journey, and who has been very patient and supportive as I wrote this book. My precious daughter has often had to forgo my time and attention as I struggled to finish a footnote or a paragraph. My mother, Wiena Baard, has had to listen to me complain and explain about my book during her visits to our home. My theological mentors and friends have been many, and I owe them thanks and appreciation: to my former dissertation adviser, Mark Lewis Taylor, for his wisdom and guidance as I originally worked on the themes of this book; to my former teacher, Dirkie Smit, for always reminding me what the task of the theologian is; to my brilliant friend, Alice Yafeh, for always being willing to offer insights and ideas from her perspective as an Afro-womanist-feminist biblical scholar; to my friend Julie Claassens, for traveling a long road from South Africa to Princeton and beyond with me; to my friend Don Compier, for his work on rhetorical theology and the doctrine of sin, as well as his wonderful Christian example; to my friend Elna Mouton, for patiently listening to me as I figured out what I was trying to say; to the wonderful Nico Koopman, whose grace and kindness remind me what a Christian ought to be; to teachers at Princeton Theological Seminary who taught and inspired me, including my dissertation committee members, Nancy Duff and Stacy Johnson, as well as my teacher, Daniel Migliore; to teachers and friends at Stellenbosch University who helped and influenced me, in particular the late Flip Theron and Willie Jonker, who taught me about grace; to my colleagues in the Colloquium on Redeeming Sin, led by Ernst Conradie, who offered helpful criticisms; to my former colleagues at Villanova University, from whom I learned a deeper appreciation of Augustine; and to my colleagues at Union Presbyterian Seminary, for their encouragement during the final phase of this book process. I also owe special thanks to my editors at Westminster John Knox Press, in particular Robert

Ratcliff, who was very patient with me despite the fact that I took so long to finish this manuscript. There are of course many other people who deserve thanks, and even if their names are not included here, I want to express my gratitude for the words of encouragement and kindness that I have received over the years from so many people. The South African concept of *Ubuntu* reminds us that each individual is embedded in a community: "I am because we are." I am lucky to be embedded in many different communities that have played a role in my life, and for that, I am grateful.

Introduction

> She speaks with wisdom, and faithful instruction is on her tongue.
> —*Proverbs 31:26 NIV*

This book explores the language of theology and the power it has over human lives. Specifically, it treats the classical rhetoric of the church on the sinfulness of humans, and how this classical rhetoric often becomes deadly to women. As such, it is a book about the rhetoric of feminist theologians, relative latecomers to the language game known as theology, who, after centuries of negative and often deadly rhetoric about women, are creating narratives of critique and reimagination with an eye toward life and the flourishing of women. Moreover, this book shows how feminist critiques of classical sin-talk speak with the grammar of classical sin-talk, but also create a new narrative with it.

Delwin Brown talks about theology as the creative reconstruction of inherited symbols, the construction of a tradition's future from the resources of its past.[1] This definition of theology expresses the fact that a living religious tradition is both continuous with the past and open to change in new times and contexts. The temptation might be to want to make a choice between these two aspects: either you are for tradition and resist change, or you embrace change to the extent that the tradition is seen as irrelevant or wholly harmful. However, the first option gives rise to dead (and often deadly) traditionalism, and the second forgets that traditions exist because they have given people life. The art of constructive theology is that of discarding that which is dead and death-dealing and finding that which is alive and life-giving.

---

1. Delwin Brown, *Boundaries of Our Habitations: Tradition and Theological Construction*, SUNY Series in Religious Studies, ed. Harold Coward (Albany: State University Press of New York, 1994), 148.

This perspective shapes my approach to feminist conversations on sin. I develop here a rhetorical approach to this conversation, which leads me to use the terminology of "sin-talk" rather than "doctrine of sin," since the focus is on how we speak about sin, and what kind of praxis that speech encourages. Feminist theologians criticize those aspects of classical sin-talk that are death-dealing, especially for women. However, the very criticism of some classical forms of sin-talk is itself already a form of constructive sin-talk, as notable feminist theologians have remarked. This is, moreover, not new to the Christian tradition, which every now and then has engaged in sin-talk against its own sinful teachings—even against the sinfulness of some forms of sin-talk. Therefore, the thesis in this book is that the feminist rejection of some forms of classical sin-talk is not merely critical, but in fact itself already constitutes, and forms the foundation of, constructive sin-talk, and that this is in fact not entirely new, but is a classical Christian theological move, characterized by a prophetic rhetorical tone aimed at human flourishing, albeit now with a specific focus on women.

To be sure, the Christian concept of sin is one that is often seen as negative, moralistic, and increasingly irrelevant. One of my theological mentors once said to me that a theologian should not focus on the doctrine of sin too much, and should focus on God's love instead. He had a point, of course. Christian theology is faith seeking understanding of the good news as presented by the Gospel writers, which makes the "bad news" of sin a secondary theological concern. In fact, as theologians from Augustine to Luther taught, an obsessive focus on sin can indeed be sinful!

Nevertheless, the Christian gospel does not bypass sin, and the Christian theologian therefore needs to take the concept of sin very seriously, even if we are not to dwell on it. After all, the good news of the gospel logically correlates with the perception of something-that-is-not-as-it-ought-to-be, that is, sin.[2] The English word "sin" corresponds to the Greek term *hamartia*, which carries the connotation of "missing the mark."

Furthermore, there is an ethical responsibility to speak of sin, since sin is that which is harmful to human flourishing. We cannot reduce the gospel of grace to one of cheap grace, as Dietrich Bonhoeffer so famously remarked.[3] What Bonhoeffer meant was that costly grace calls us to discipleship, implying that faith is not only a matter of believing, but also of doing, including responding to things-that-are-not-as-they-ought-to-be. Therefore, I would argue that the love command that is central to Christian ethics requires us to take the question of sin seriously, since sin is that which harms human life.

---

2. See especially Cornelius Plantinga Jr., *Not the Way It's Supposed to Be: A Breviary of Sin* (Grand Rapids: Eerdmans, 1995).

3. Dietrich Bonhoeffer, *Discipleship*, Dietrich Bonhoeffer Works 4 (Minneapolis: Fortress Press, 2001), 43–56.

British theologian Alistair McFadyen points out that the trivialization of the concept of sin in modern Western culture reflects the fact that "sin" has ceased to function as a way of talking about the pathological in human affairs. The aim of sin-talk, he says, is to speak of *concrete* pathologies in relation to God.[4] Reflection on sin, when it transcends moralistic blame games, is reflection on the human condition, on human misery in all its concreteness. It is reflection on our alienation from our true selves, from each other, from the Source and Ground of Being and of our being. However, it is also reflection on the ills that are expressions of this alienation: violence, war, racism, oppression, sexism, heterosexism, greed, abuse, and much more. In short, although a sickly dwelling on sin has to be avoided, God-talk and grace-talk cannot bypass sin-talk, since God speaks the word of grace into the concrete pathologies we encounter in human existence and is heard from within those experiences. The theologian therefore cannot bypass reflection on the painful matters that go by the name of "sin."

What feminist theologians have been saying, however, is that if we are to speak of sin, we need to be mindful of possible distortions in our rhetoric on sin that become harmful in the lives of human beings. Stephen Ray speaks of this phenomenon as the "sins of sin-talk."[5] This book seeks to trace the continuing conversation among feminist theologians on sin-talk, its sins, and its potential, and to show what the contributions of feminist theology as a field have been and can be with regard to the Christian conversation on sin. The book is premised upon the recognition that words have power, and perhaps more so when those words have doctrinal status, that is, speaking with the authority of religious tradition. In the words of Serene Jones, "doctrines function like loose but nonetheless definitive scripts that persons of faith perform; doctrines are the dramas in which we live out our lives."[6] The feminist conversation on sin-talk is therefore centered on the question, how does sin-talk create a script that people perform?

In short, the guiding question in this book is: what are the dynamics of feminist theological conversations on sin-talk, particularly in light of its rhetorical function? This is a deceptively simple question, and many a student who has sat through an introductory class in theology will raise their hand and mention something about the feminist critique of the classical focus on the sin of pride. The slightly more clever ones will add that feminist theologians

---

4. Alistair McFadyen, *Bound to Sin: Abuse, Holocaust, and the Christian Doctrine of Sin* (Cambridge: Cambridge University Press, 2000), 3–5.

5. Stephen G. Ray Jr., *Do No Harm: Social Sin and Christian Responsibility* (Minneapolis: Fortress Press, 2003), 1–35.

6. Serene Jones, *Feminist Theory and Christian Theology: Cartographies of Grace*, Guides to Theological Inquiry (Minneapolis: Fortress Press, 2000), 17.

are critical of the ways in which women have been associated with sin. The more critical ones will complain that feminist theologians want to do away with the doctrine of sin and replace it with fuzzy concepts that take out the sharp edges of Christian theology. While all of these hypothetical students would have a point, I contend that the answer to this simple question might include all these responses, and yet also is more complex than that, and that feminist theologians do not in fact want to do away with sin-talk. Indeed, I even contend that when some feminist theologians reject sin-talk they do so because they deem it to be too sinful, which paradoxically affirms the very concept of sin.

A few general notes about my approach. I do not pretend to include every feminist theologian who has said something about sin, but focus for the most part on some "classical" feminist voices. While the term "classical" might be stretched here a bit, it is worth remembering that Christian feminist conversations on sin and sin-talk have been going on for nearly sixty years at this point, and there are indeed "classical" voices and perspectives within that conversation. So the analytical part of this book aims to trace those voices and perspectives. Primary among these are Valerie Saiving, Judith Plaskow, and Susan Nelson Dunfee on the "pride critique," and Mary Daly and Rosemary Radford Ruether on the theme of women-blaming. I also include the voices of female (and sometimes male) scholars who may or may not self-identify as feminist theologians, but who add important insights to this conversation. I furthermore try to keep in mind that feminism is not the domain of white North American women, and that it is also not the only kind of female voice in the theological conversation. I am aware of the very valid critiques lodged against classical feminist theology by womanist and *mujerista* scholars, and also of the multicultural expressions of feminism claimed by women around the globe. I do not pretend to be sufficiently aware of all voices and perspectives out there, and present this book as an invitation to further conversation, even as I trace the "classical" feminist conversation on sin while offering some constructive proposals of my own. In the constructive chapters at the end of the book I push toward two things: a deep retrieval of the tradition, on the one hand, and a global, intersectional feminism, on the other hand. These arise from two broad characteristics of my theological approach in general.

My approach to feminist theology is in part the result of the history of my native country of South Africa, and my opposition to apartheid, which I perceived to be incompatible with my Christian faith at the young age of thirteen (this was in the early 1980s, a time when South Africa was being torn apart by violence as a result of racial oppression). This religious-political awakening shaped my life decisions in multiple ways. Awareness of the reality and pain of racism continues to shape my feminist perspective, prompting me to remember that even when feminist scholarship demands analysis of gender oppression, such scholarship should keep in mind that gender alone is not sufficient as an analytical focus. From my experience of how white women, while themselves subjugated within a patriarchal culture, also "bossed about" women (and men) of color as a result of racial hierarchy, I know all too well that women are not only victims but often perpetrators in the oppression of others. I therefore also know that sisterhood is complex and fragile as a result of the intersection of gender with race (as well as other factors).

My intersectional, global approach to feminist theology is furthermore shaped by the fact that, as a white South African woman now living in the United States, I occupy a hybrid social space: I do not quite share the world of white North American feminists, but of course would not presume to share the world of black African feminists and womanists either. Instead I find myself in a strange intersection of whiteness, Africanness, "immigrant-ness," and Americanness. Postcolonial theorist Homi K. Bhabha uses the phrase "interstitial perspective" to speak of this kind of complexity, while other postcolonial thinkers speak of hybridity or liminality, although, as Sang Hyun Lee notes, the latter also "includes the meaning of being located at the periphery or edge of society," and given the reality that my whiteness largely precludes such liminality I don't claim that term for myself. My experience is perhaps best expressed by Vietnamese American theologian Peter C. Phan, who speaks simply of being "betwixt and between," that is, being "neither here nor there, to be neither this thing nor that."[7] In this book, the interstitial perspectives of African, Asian, and other global scholars shape my perspectives on the issue of gender violence, which is so central to this book, and continue to inform my perspective on theology.

My feminist theology was furthermore shaped by earlier work I did on the thought of American Catholic feminist theologian Elizabeth A. Johnson, whose theology combines serious critique with deep retrieval of the Christian tradition. Her approach can be seen, for example, in her brilliant retrieval of Thomas Aquinas's insights on God in her book *She Who Is*. From her I learned that serious critique of the tradition does not preclude deep retrieval of the life-giving elements in it. In this book I primarily retrieve elements of the thought of John Calvin and Augustine of Hippo, albeit amid serious critique of the androcentrism in their thought.

---

7. Homi K. Bhabha, *The Location of Culture* (London: Routledge, 1994); Sang Hyun Lee, *From a Liminal Place: An Asian American Theology* (Minneapolis: Fortress Press, 2010), x; Peter C. Phan, "Betwixt and Between: Doing Theology with Memory and Imagination," in *Journeys at the Margin: Toward an Autobiographical Theology in American-Asian Perspective*, ed. Peter Phan and Jung Young Lee (Collegeville, MN: Liturgical Press, 1999), 113.

Elizabeth Johnson is not the only feminist theologian whose work has influenced me. Serene Jones's work on the rhetoric of John Calvin, but especially her use of feminist theory as conversation partner for theology, both play a role in my analysis here. Elisabeth Schüssler Fiorenza's insights on how texts both reflect and shape praxis influenced the development of my rhetorical model for doing theology. María Pilar Aquino's liberationist-feminist emphasis on the human cry for life and the affirmation of God as the God of life shaped the final conclusions of this book. But I need to especially honor the work of Rosemary Radford Ruether, whose analysis of dualism has deeply shaped my work in general and this book in particular. It should also be noted that the title of my book was partly inspired by the title of Ruether's famous *Sexism and God-Talk*. My title, *Sexism and Sin-Talk*, also of course expresses the book's focus on sin, and my use of the term "talk" instead of "doctrine" reflects the book's rhetorical perspective.

In this book I utilize both classical and modern rhetorical concepts. The first chapter, "Rhetoric," develops my critical-constructive model for doing rhetorical theology, in conversation with both rhetorical theory and other rhetorical theologians. It also introduces the classical and feminist rhetorical tools that I use to trace the feminist conversation on sin. Chapter 2, titled "*Kairos*," covers the crisis context within which feminist conversations on sin occur, with specific recognition that there is a dialectical relationship between context and theological rhetoric. This second chapter also recognizes the term "feminism" as an intersectional concept, in recognition of womanist, *mujerista*, and global feminist perspectives. These two introductory chapters are followed by chapters titled "Mary" and "Eve," which analyze the two major criticisms lodged by feminist theologians against classical sin-talk. In chapter 3, I trace the development of the so-called feminist pride critique from a mode of naming difference to a mode of naming oppression, and I show how the classical emphasis on pride ties in with an oppressive ethic that is ultimately life-denying for women as it participates in encouraging women to emulate the example of Mary, understood primarily in terms of humility and self-sacrifice. In chapter 4, I examine the feminist critiques of the classical theme of blaming women for sin and the ways in which this blaming of women for sin forms a patriarchal rhetoric of death centered on the symbol of Eve, which contributes to various forms of violence against women. In chapters 5 and 6, "Grammar" and "Life," I start to move toward the more constructive work done by feminist theologians in their discussion of sin-talk, and make some constructive proposals of my own. I do so in chapter 5 by first pointing to ways in which feminist theologians, even amid serious criticism of classical sin-talk, are already (sometimes only implicitly) retrieving the concept of sin, in particular the inner logic or "grammar" of the doctrine of original sin. In the final chapter, I make use of classical Aristotelian rhetorical elements, which are first introduced in chapter 1, to outline the contours of constructive feminist sin-talk: the prophetic *ethos* that drives it, the complex *pathos* (broadly understood as situation) of women, and the death-denouncing and life-affirming *logos* (arguments) at the heart of it. So, in short, the book consists of three parts and six chapters: two introductory chapters ("Rhetoric" and "*Kairos*"), two chapters focused on criticism of classical sin-talk ("Mary" and "Eve"), and two chapters focusing on constructive sin-talk ("Grammar" and "Life").

1

Rhetoric

> The tongue has the power of life and death.
> —*Proverbs 18:21 NIV*

The twentieth-century linguistic turn brought attention to the fact that language is not merely descriptive of reality but also helps to bring reality into being. This has led, among other things, to a revival in the field of rhetoric, that is, the study of the persuasive nature of language. This development has also influenced theology: many modern theologians are interested in the question of how theological language functions practically in the lives of people, that is, how it shapes their worldview and inspires their actions. Within such a perspective, theological symbols are seen not only as truth-expressions but also as language actions that shape the ideas and praxis of human beings. This emphasis on praxis is not new to theology, which has always been interested in persuading people to virtuous action. But the linguistic turn helps us see that theological language need not be deliberately persuasive (as in a sermon or ethical treatise) in order to be praxis-shaping. It also helps us to see that rhetoric is always embedded in social realities, and often, whether inadvertently or deliberately, serves to either undermine or support those social realities. As such, a rhetorical approach to theology is not primarily interested in asking about the purity of a doctrine or its coherence with other doctrines (although those are important emphases), but rather in the praxis and power with which it is intertwined. This would call for a rhetorical-theological approach that is focused not only on deliberate persuasion but also on critical examination of power and praxis. Rhetorical theology should therefore take both a constructive and a critical form, and these are often intertwined.

Rhetorical theology in *constructive* mode has variously been described as aimed at a "rhetoric of piety" (Serene Jones), "faithful persuasion" (David Cunningham), or "emancipatory discourse" (Rebecca Chopp), that is, expressions of doctrine that specifically aim at shaping praxis.[1] Rhetorical theology in *critical* mode, on the other hand, launches what Elisabeth Schüssler Fiorenza calls a "critical rhetorical inquiry" aimed at exposing problematic practical implications of doctrinal symbols.[2] In combined mode, therefore, rhetorical theology is focused on both the power relations reflected in doctrinal symbols and the praxis to which doctrines lead—that is, it is both a critical rhetorical inquiry, and it aims at emancipatory discourse (faithful persuasion or rhetoric of piety). One can therefore define *rhetorical theology* as *a critical-constructive form of theology that focuses on the way the symbols of a faith reflect as well as reinforce power relations, and thereby shape human behavior.*

In this book I adopt such a critical-constructive approach to the feminist conversation on sin, both in my analysis of what other feminist theologians have said and in my own contributions. In this chapter, I develop this critical-constructive rhetorical approach to the analysis of doctrine by examining the shift in rhetorical theory in the twentieth century and then correlating that with methodological debates in the field of theology itself. In subsequent chapters, I then show that feminist theologians have subjected the doctrine of sin to critical rhetorical inquiry, and I add my own analysis of that critical rhetorical inquiry by linking it to the classical patriarchal-feminine symbols of Mary and Eve. I furthermore show that feminist theological conversations aim at constructing emancipatory discourses on sin (even though this constructive aim is sometimes hidden within critical denunciations of patriarchal forms of sin-talk). And I show that such a critical-constructive move is a classical theological move, before adding my own constructive proposal in this regard. Given the rhetorical rather than the "purely" doctrinal approach taken here, the language of "sin-talk," rather than "doctrine of sin," is more appropriate here and I therefore use it in most cases.

Sin-talk has been a matter of significant concern in modern feminist theology since the latter's inception in the 1960s, due to both the androcentric

---

1. Serene Jones, *Calvin and the Rhetoric of Piety*, Columbia Series in Reformed Theology (Louisville, KY: Westminster John Knox Press, 1995); David S. Cunningham, *Faithful Persuasion: In Aid of a Rhetoric of Christian Theology* (Notre Dame, IN: University of Notre Dame Press, 1991); Rebecca S. Chopp, "Theological Persuasion: Rhetoric, Warrants, and Suffering," in *Worldview and Warrants: Plurality and Authority in Theology*, ed. William Schweiker (Lanham, MD: University Press of America, 1987), 17–31; and *The Power to Speak: Feminism, Language, God* (New York: Crossroad, 1989).

2. Elisabeth Schüssler Fiorenza, *But She Said: Feminist Practices of Biblical Interpretation* (Boston: Beacon, 1992), 40–50; Schüssler Fiorenza, "Challenging the Rhetorical Half-Turn: Feminist and Rhetorical Biblical Criticism," in *Rhetoric, Scripture, and Theology: Essays from the 1994 Pretoria Conference*, Journal for the Study of the New Testament, Supplement Series 131, ed. Stanley E. Porter and Thomas H. Olbricht (Sheffield, UK: Sheffield Academic Press, 1996), 28–53.

assumptions classically at work in diagnosing human ills, and the sins of marginalization and violence that are part of the feminist rhetorical situation. Sin-talk is also, and perhaps somewhat paradoxically, a tool used by feminist theologians to name the oppression of women. To trace the contours of this rather complex and multifaceted conversation, and to push toward emancipatory sin-talk, rhetorical theory can be immensely helpful. Utilizing feminist rhetorical theory, we can see that feminist theologians employ a variety of different rhetorical strategies and expose several problematic rhetorical practices in classical sin-talk. I furthermore employ classical rhetorical categories to highlight the specifics of the problematic rhetoric that feminist theologians expose, and I use those same categories to present a constructive proposal for emancipatory sin-talk. This critical rhetorical inquiry is driven by the concern that classical sin-talk has often functioned as a rhetoric of death for women, and therefore any suggestions for emancipatory sin-talk would aim at developing sin-talk that denounces death and death-dealing rhetoric, prompting sin-talk that is life-giving rhetoric aimed at human flourishing.

In this chapter I introduce multiple concepts from classical, postmodern, and feminist rhetorical theory, which I use throughout the rest of the book. For the purposes of this book, two sections of this chapter are of paramount importance. The first of these is the discussion of Aristotle's rhetorical categories of *ethos, pathos,* and *logos* in the next section, since it plays a role in both my feminist analysis of patriarchal classical sin-talk and in my constructive proposals toward the end of the book. The second crucial section of this chapter is the discussion of feminist rhetorical strategies, since it is central to my analysis of feminist critiques of classical sin-talk. The rest of this chapter, where I develop a critical-constructive model for doing rhetorical theology, is important for the sake of understanding my approach in general but is not directly necessary for understanding the argument in the book itself. I develop this critical-constructive approach to rhetorical theology by first tracing the shift in twentieth-century rhetorical theory from a classical constructive focus on "how to speak well" to a critical focus on how language masks power. I then argue that rhetorical theology ought to reflect both of these emphases, the classical and the modern, that is, the constructive and the critical, and how they are often intertwined in theological reflection.

RHETORICAL THEORY

Long considered the "dangerous Other" of philosophy, reduced to merely a question of literary style, or at the very least made subordinate to the rational mode of dialectical thinking, rhetorical theory experienced a revival in the twentieth century. However, modern rhetorical theory, the so-called New Rhetoric, differs significantly from Classical Rhetoric, and these differences inform my understanding of rhetorical theology and of the inherent dynamics of feminist sin-talk.

In ancient Greece, the Sophists tended to see all language use as rhetorical—that is, as persuasive—and argued that what is called "truth" is a social arrangement, not a glimpse into ultimate reality. Socrates and Plato famously rejected this as dabbling with mere opinion dressed in discursive finery, instead of the real knowledge attained by reflection on that which transcends human sensory experience.[3] Aristotle, on the other hand, while privileging the quest for universal truth through dialectic (the art of logical reasoning), saw rhetoric (the art of public speaking) as its counterpart (*antistrophos*).[4] Aristotle's rhetorical theory, which played a central role in twentieth-century revivals of rhetoric, has been influential both in and of itself, and through appropriations of his thought by classical Roman orators. The Roman rhetorical tradition, represented most famously by Cicero and Quintilian, did not merely channel Aristotle, however, but built up a formidable rhetorical theory of its own, characterized by a holistic anthropology and a strong emphasis on praxis.[5] Overall, classical rhetorical theories emphasized the contextual over the universal, the practical over the philosophical. They also all emphasized the use of rhetoric for the good of the polis, seeing it as an instrument to educate and persuade the public to virtuous action.

The twentieth century's renewed emphasis on the idea that language does not merely describe reality but also helps to create it led to the birth of the New Rhetoric, which differs in emphasis from Classical Rhetoric.[6] Kenneth Burke, one of the key figures in this rhetorical revival, argues that while the key term for Classical Rhetoric was *persuasion*, and its stress was upon deliberate design, the key term for the New Rhetoric was *identification*, which can

---

3. Plato, *Gorgias and Phaedrus*, trans. James H. Nichols Jr. (Ithaca, NY: Cornell University Press, 1998).

4. Aristotle, *On Rhetoric: A Theory of Civic Discourse* 1.1.1, trans. George A. Kennedy (New York: Oxford University Press, 2007).

5. For a helpful introduction to, and selection from, Cicero's rhetorical theory, see Patricia Bizzell and Bruce Hertzberg, eds., *The Rhetorical Tradition: Readings from Classical Times to the Present* (Boston: Bedford Book, 1990), 195–250. For further helpful discussions of Roman oratory and specifically its implications for rhetorical theology, see Don H. Compier, *What Is Rhetorical Theology? Textual Practice and Public Discourse* (Harrisburg, PA: Trinity Press, 1999), 3–9, and George A. Kennedy, *Classical Rhetoric and Its Christian and Secular Tradition from Ancient to Modern Times* (Chapel Hill: University of North Carolina Press, 1980), ch. 5.

6. Seminal texts include Chaim Perleman and Lucie Olbrechts-Tyceta, *The New Rhetoric: A Treatise on Argumentation*, trans. John Wilkinson and Purcell Weaver (Notre Dame, IN: University of Notre Dame Press, 1969); Kenneth Burke, *A Rhetoric of Motives* (Berkeley: University of California Press, 1969); and Raymie E. McKerrow's now-classic award-winning essay "Critical Rhetoric: Theory and Praxis," *Communication Monographs* 56 (1989): 91–111.

include a partially unconscious factor in appeal.[7] Identification points more explicitly than persuasion to the effects of discourse in everyday language. Correspondingly, Burke's work is characterized by an emphasis on symbolic action, which shifts the focus from deliberate arguments aimed at persuasion to the question of how symbols evoke shared meaning—that is, create social worlds. The understanding of rhetoric as identification is foundational to Burke's theory of scapegoating, an issue that is of some concern to feminist theologians: by identifying some as members of the dominant group, language simultaneously creates the Other, who is not part of the group. This is often exacerbated by a more explicit "rhetoric of othering."[8] As we shall see, feminist critical rhetorical analysis shows how classical sin-talk has often functioned as a rhetoric of scapegoating and othering of women.

In Burke we see the union of hermeneutics and rhetoric: he holds that where there is meaning, there is persuasion, and where there is persuasion, there is rhetoric.[9] More particularly, the New Rhetoric, as a critical mode of inquiry into power relations, is the union of rhetoric and critical hermeneutics: thus, for example, the work of thinkers such as Michel Foucault on the intertwining of knowledge and power, or Antonio Gramsci on the ways in which hegemony operates with persuasion, are of some significance for the New Rhetoric. Critical rhetoric is not primarily interested in the "truth" or "falsity" of symbols, but in the way they "come to possess power—what they 'do' in society as contrasted to what they 'are.'"[10] The public functioning of symbols should not be understood in terms of direct causality, but rather in terms of the ways in which language shapes the concepts that organize much of our everyday existence by generating the conditions that shape our identities and agency. Critical rhetoric sets itself the task of exposing and undermining the discourses of power; as such, it shares the concern for the life of the polis found in Classical Rhetoric.

In short, the New Rhetoric shifts the focus away from Classical Rhetoric's constructive mode of "how to speak well in order to persuade" to a critical inquiry into the way everyday language constitutes character, community, and culture. Rhetoric is now reenvisioned as symbolic action rather than delivered speeches. Rhetorical theory is no longer primarily preoccupied with the inventions of the speaker and the conventions of speech, but with interpreting the audiences of discourse and the way language influences them. This

---

7. Kenneth Burke, "Rhetoric—Old and New," *Journal of General Education* 5 (1951): 203–5.
8. Stephen Harold Riggins, "The Rhetoric of Othering," in *The Language and Politics of Exclusion: Others in Discourse*, ed. Stephen Harold Riggins (Thousand Oaks, CA: Sage, 1997), 1–30.
9. See Walter Jost and Michael J. Hyde, eds., *Rhetoric and Hermeneutics in Our Time: A Reader* (New Haven, CT: Yale University Press, 1997).
10. McKerrow, "Critical Rhetoric," 104.

implies a shift from studies of single texts to critiques of bodies of discourse. Critical rhetorical inquiry is not uninterested in truth—it just does not reduce truth to transcendent ideas, but examines the realities of power and the practical effects of language as part of the overall question of truth.

The New Rhetoric does not leave Classical Rhetoric behind entirely, but instead translates it for the purposes of critical rhetorical inquiry. Among the translated classical categories are the concepts of *ethos*, *pathos*, and *logos*, which refer to Aristotle's insight that the rhetor's spoken words (*logos*) will be interpreted in interaction with his perceived moral character (*ethos*) and the audience's frame of mind (*pathos*).[11] In the New Rhetoric, however, these heuristic categories are transformed into hermeneutical ones, as the focus shifts from persuasive speech to critical analysis of texts. Let us briefly look at each concept in a bit more detail, since they play a role in both tracing feminist critical rhetorical inquiry and shaping the contours of constructive feminist sin-talk.

First, Aristotle used *ethos*, or "character," to refer to the ways in which the perceived attributes of a speaker are persuasive. Aristotle limited *ethos* to the attributes of the speaker as manifested in the discourse, whereas the New Rhetoric broadens the scope of *ethos* by suggesting that attributes of the rhetor's character not present in the speech/text will have an impact on the ability to persuade an audience. The appropriation of this concept by critical rhetorical inquiry should not be seen as trying to find meaning in authorial intent, nor as a return to the Cartesian subject, but rather as serious consideration of the fact that audiences will perceive and judge a rhetor's interests.[12] More specifically, as Susan Jarratt and Nedra Reynolds point out, *ethos* (within the New Rhetoric) "theorizes the positionality inherent in rhetoric," that is, it points to "a constant awareness that one always speaks from a particular place in a social structure."[13] Within a critical rhetorical inquiry, then, the notion of *ethos* is rendered an aspect of the hermeneutic of suspicion that would ask about the power relations that lie behind certain discourses. We shall see in the next two chapters that feminist theologians lodge such a hermeneutic of suspicion against the interests of classical theologians who operated in a system of systemic religious and social domination of women, thereby implicitly questioning the *ethos* that drives classical sin-talk. In the final chapter I point to the specific *ethos* that drives feminist sin-talk in turn.

The second concept in Aristotle's triad, the speech utterance or *logos*, refers to appeals to reason and argument, as opposed to appeals either to the rhetor's

---

11. Aristotle, *On Rhetoric* 1.2.3.
12. Cunningham, *Faithful Persuasion*, 111.
13. Susan C. Jarratt and Nedra Reynolds, "The Splitting Image: Contemporary Feminisms and the Ethics of Êthos," in *Ethos: New Essays in Rhetorical and Critical Theory*, ed. James S. Baumlin and Tita French Baumlin (Dallas, TX: Southern Methodist University Press, 1994), 47.

character or the audience's emotions. In the New Rhetoric this concept goes well beyond both "rational" argument in the Enlightenment sense, and the classical categories of deductive reasoning (*enthymemes*), inductive reasoning (examples), and topics. Instead, as Wayne Booth notes, the New Rhetoric operates with synthetic, contextual judgments about the issues at stake.[14] This judgment is also communal, thereby operating with the intersubjectivity that hermeneutical thinkers (e.g., David Tracy) argue for in their efforts to steer clear from both the hegemony of false universals and the chaos of sheer relativism. In the following chapters I examine what feminist critical rhetorical inquiry reveals about the *logos* (stories, argumentation, or values) of classical sin-talk, and outline the kind of *logos* that would be part of sin-talk as emancipatory discourse.

Aristotle's third element of persuasive argument, *pathos*, is an appeal to the emotions or passions of the audience. As is the case with *ethos* and *logos*, *pathos* has become a hermeneutical concept in the New Rhetoric, indicating ways in which states of mind that audiences and authors share determine the acceptance of texts.[15] The meaning of *pathos* has therefore become broader, referring "more generally to the audience's state or condition: *everything* that the audience brings to the rhetorical situation."[16] It is here that we note the importance of introducing women's experiences into the conversation on sin-talk: given the experiences that women bring to the rhetorical situation, how might they hear the rhetoric of sin? Is their specific *pathos* addressed? These are among the questions that this rhetorical category enables us to ask of classical sin-talk.

In summary, whereas *ethos* refers to the audience's judgment about the character and social positioning of the speaker, *logos* refers to the audience's judgment about the kinds of arguments forwarded in the texts they analyze, and *ethos* expresses the reality that such judgments cannot be separated from the audience itself, which is involved not as disembodied interpreters but as situated human beings. In other words, in the New Rhetoric, the *pathos* of the audience, the *ethos* of the rhetor, and the *logos* of the discourse are all firmly set within the broader social matrix. As a result, the concept of *pathos* now overlaps somewhat with the classical rhetorical emphasis on what is appropriate (*prepon* in Greek and *decorum* in Latin). *Decorum* refers to the idea of adjustment in the orator's speech in light of what is appropriate for a particular audience; it is, in other words, contextually

---

14. Wayne C. Booth, *The Company We Keep: An Ethics of Fiction* (Berkeley: University of California Press, 1988), 70–73.
15. The major contribution on this theme was Chaim Perelman and Lucie Olbrechts-Tyceta's *The New Rhetoric*. Although their work was done separately from that of Gadamer, it occurred at the same time, and indeed shares many of the latter's emphases. See, in this regard, Richard E. Palmer, "What Hermeneutics Can Offer Rhetoric," in Jost and Hyde, *Rhetoric and Hermeneutics in Our Time*, 108–31.
16. Cunningham, *Faithful Persuasion*, 43.

sensitive speech.[17] In Classical Rhetoric *decorum* is quite distinct from the concept of *pathos*, which focuses more on putting the audience in a certain state of mind than in reading their existing state of mind. But in the New Rhetoric, where these concepts are translated into hermeneutical categories, *decorum* and *ethos* overlap significantly. Attention to *decorum* risks reducing rhetoric to something that says what the audience wants to hear, to mere flattery (Plato's main charge against rhetoric), and not what the audience needs to hear from an ethical or political standpoint. Yet in its emphasis on *kairos*, the sophistic concept denoting the relationship between truth and context, which points to the importance of seizing the right moment, the notion of *decorum* indicates an awareness that truth cannot be reduced to uniform and universal ideas. Instead, *decorum* is an integral part of a theory of language as strategic action, as opposed to merely "knowing" a transcendent "truth." In contrast to the somewhat amoral attitude of the Sophists, Aristotle interprets *prepon* (*decorum*) as having to do with a sense of tact, or as he states it, the *lexis* (i.e., the delivery of words) "will be appropriate if it expresses emotion and character and is proportionate to the subject matter."[18] In the Roman rhetorician Cicero's thought, *decorum* is a humanistic concept that is integral to the process (and duty) of human development. In this understanding of *decorum*, tact is elevated to the level of justice: "It is the function of justice not to do wrong to one's fellow-men; of considerateness, not to wound their feeling; and in this the essence of propriety is best seen."[19] Thus, in Cicero, *decorum* is the aesthetic sensibility that grounds moral life. After Cicero, already starting with Quintilian, the notion of *decorum* increasingly became a purely aesthetic, as opposed to political, concept, and its ethical implications did not really come to the fore again until its revival in the New Rhetoric. In the following chapters, the concept is used in conjunction with the concept of *pathos* to point to a problematic lack of awareness of women's gendered contexts in classical sin-talk, and to contrast that with the concrete and holistic focus on women's lives that we see in feminist sin-talk.

One of the reasons why the ethical aspects of *decorum* have resurfaced in the New Rhetoric is the emergence of a new emphasis on the concept of *kairos* in rhetorical theory, especially thanks to the work of James L. Kinneavy. According to Kinneavy, *kairos* is "the appropriateness of the discourse to the particular circumstances of the time, place, speaker, and audience involved."[20]

---

17. See Compier, *What Is Rhetorical Theology?* 6.
18. Aristotle, *On Rhetoric* 3.7.1.
19. Cicero, *De Officiis*, trans. Walter Miller, Loeb Classical Library 21, ed. G. P. Goold (Cambridge, MA: Harvard University Press, 1975), 1.99.
20. James L. Kinneavy, "*Kairos*: A Neglected Concept in Classical Rhetoric," in *Rhetoric and Praxis: The Contribution of Classical Rhetoric to Practical Reasoning*, ed. J. D. Moss (Washington, DC: Catholic University of America Press, 1986), 84.

Kinneavy's definition of *kairos* goes beyond the usual definition of it as "the right time" to include a broader contextual perspective. As such, *kairos* is related to *decorum*. For our purposes, what he says about the ethical dimension of *kairos* is most significant. Among the Sophists (particularly Gorgias), justice was determined by circumstance, that is, justice was grounded in *kairos*.[21] Plato and Socrates were concerned by the relativism of such a position, yet Platonic ethics were also grounded in *kairos*—as can be see especially in the *Phaedrus*. Plato, says Kinneavy, used *kairos* in the double sense of proper measure and right time to construct the idea of virtue as the mean between two.[22] Kinneavy's main contribution has been his tracing of the *kairos* concept in the rhetorical theory of Aristotle, however. He notes that, as in Plato, in Aristotle the rhetorical act is situationally determined. The general rules of rhetoric therefore need careful adaptation within specific situations. One can see this principle at work in the legal aspects of the *kairos* concept: Kinneavy writes that "*kairic* law" is "law when it is applied in particular circumstances, at specific times, to specific situations not foreseen by the legislators."[23] As such, the *kairos* concept enables us to see that true justice is situation-specific (although one should nevertheless emphasize that this does not mean it is determined by the situation alone). Kinneavy notes that this insight is expressed in the Christian idea that the letter of the law is to be distinguished from the spirit of the law.

A related aspect of *kairos*, one that is often encountered in theological appropriations of the concept, most elaborately in the theology of Paul Tillich, is the epistemological perspective that *kairos* brings that which is timeless into historical time. Biblical references to *kairos* suggest that it has to do with the fulfillment of time (see Mark 1:14) but also with the discerning of the present time (see Luke 12:56). In general, therefore, the biblical and theological concept of *kairos* is related to the religious concept of revelation, both in the objective sense of the entering of eternity into the moment (fulfillment of time) and in the subjective discerning of the moment.

In the next chapter we revisit the *kairos* concept with specific reference to the revelatory and situational justice aspects of the concept as we ask the question: what is the rhetorical situation within which feminist critical-constructive rhetoric on sin occurs? I point to certain aspects of "women's experience" (and the complexities of that concept), and particularly to the widespread phenomenon of gender violence, which is of particular relevance

21. James L. Kinneavy, "*Kairos* in Classical and Modern Rhetorical Theory," in *Rhetoric and Kairos: Essays in History, Theory, and Praxis*, ed. Phillip Sipiora and James S. Baumlin (Albany: State University of New York Press, 2002), 61.
22. Ibid., 62.
23. Ibid., 68.

within feminist discourses on sin. I also use the concept in developing the driving *ethos* of feminist sin-talk in chapter 6.

But first we turn to a brief overview of the historical relationship between rhetoric and theology, followed by an introduction to some relevant feminist rhetorical theory, which is integral to my analysis of feminist critical inquiry into sin-talk.

RHETORICAL THEOLOGY

Christian theology's traditional focus on truth that transcends sensory human experience has led it to generally view rhetoric with Platonic distrust. To the extent that theology appropriated Aristotle, it privileged his dialectical reasoning rather than his rhetorical theory. Yet rhetoric nonetheless retained a minor presence in classical theology. For example, Augustine, despite his postconversion disdain for his former field of study, saw a limited use for rhetoric in conveying religious truth and encouraging morality.[24] This attitude remained the status quo throughout the Middle Ages. There was a revival of interest in rhetoric in the Renaissance period, and the Protestant Reformers followed suit by making use of classical Roman rhetoricians like Quintilian and Cicero.[25]

But a serious appropriation of rhetoric for theology has had to wait until modern times. It is especially theologies of praxis and liberation that have shown an (implicit) interest in rhetorical perspectives on theological language. If one were to work with Gustavo Gutiérrez's threefold classification of theology as theologies of spirituality, reason, and liberation, it would appear that the concrete focus of rhetorical reasoning makes it as logical a companion for theologies of liberation, as Platonic philosophy has been for theologies of spirituality, or Aristotelian philosophy for theologies of reason.[26] Liberation theologies, including feminist theologies, often engage in critical rhetorical inquiry, that is, a mode of theology that is highly critical of

---

24. Augustine, *Teaching Christianity* (*De Doctrina Christiana*), trans. Edmund Hill, O.P., *The Works of Saint Augustine*, ed. John E. Rotelle, O.S.A. (New York: New City Press, 1996), 4.2.3, 4.6.

25. Gregory Kneidel, "Rhetoric in the Age of Reformation and Counter-Reformation," in *Encyclopedia of Rhetoric*, ed. Thomas Sloane (New York: Oxford University Press, 2001), 690–94. The rhetorical nature of Calvin's theology has received much attention in recent years. See, for example, Don H. Compier, *John Calvin's Rhetorical Doctrine of Sin*, Texts and Studies in Religion 86 (Lewiston, NY: Edwin Mellen Press, 2001), and Serene Jones, *Calvin and the Rhetoric of Piety*, Columbia Series in Reformed Theology (Louisville, KY: Westminster John Knox Press, 1995).

26. Gustavo Gutiérrez, *A Theology of Liberation: History, Politics, and Salvation*, trans. Sister Caridad Inda and John Eagleson, rev. ed. (Maryknoll, NY: Orbis Books, 2001), 3–11.

the practical effects of many aspects of the classical theological heritage. It is also, of course, aimed at emancipatory praxis. It would therefore (implicitly) appropriate both the critical mode of the New Rhetoric and the persuasive mode of Classical Rhetoric.

Although most theologians of praxis do not engage in explicit rhetorical theorizing, one can describe all theologians who share an interest in praxis as rhetorical theologians. To this end, rhetorical/praxis theologians often refer to Clifford Geertz's definition of religion as "a system of symbols which acts to establish powerful, pervasive, and long-lasting moods and motivations in men," as a theoretical basis for their emphasis on the way religion shapes social reality.[27] For example, feminist theologian Carol P. Christ uses this definition of religion in her argument that women should embrace the Goddess since religious worship of a male God creates "moods" and "motivations" that keep women in a state of psychological dependence on male authority. She explains that a "'mood' for Geertz is a psychological attitude such as awe, trust, and respect, while a 'motivation' is the social and political trajectory created by a mood that transforms mythos into ethos, symbol system into social and political reality."[28] Although operating with a different feminist theological approach that aims to broaden God-talk rather than replace it with Goddess-talk, Catholic feminist theologian Elizabeth A. Johnson similarly refers to Geertz's definition of religion as an anthropological basis for her argument when she says that the classical male symbol of God functions to support a patriarchal culture.[29] From yet another place on the theological map, that of the "Yale school" of thought, we see the use of Geertz's definition of religion as a theoretical underpinning for understanding doctrines in terms of persuasion to pious action. In particular, George Lindbeck sees doctrines as operating like grammatical rules to shape the life of the religious community, as opposed to seeing doctrines as either informative propositions about objective realities or noninformative symbols of inner experiences or attitudes.[30] These three examples, representing quite different theological approaches, nevertheless show a very similar use of Geertz. Lindbeck's understanding of doctrine has been particularly influential in the work of theologians such as David Cunningham and Serene

---

27. Clifford Geertz, "Religion as a Cultural System," in *A Reader in the Anthropology of Religion*, ed. Michael Lambek (Malden, MA: Blackwell, 2002), 63.

28. Carol P. Christ, "Why Women Need the Goddess: Phenomenological, Psychological, and Political Reflections," in *Womanspirit Rising: A Feminist Reader in Religion*, ed. Carol P. Christ and Judith Plaskow (San Francisco: Harper & Row, 1979), 274–75.

29. Elizabeth A. Johnson, *She Who Is: The Mystery of God in Feminist Theological Discourse* (New York: Crossroad, 1995), 36.

30. George A. Lindbeck, *The Nature of Doctrine: Religion and Theology in a Postliberal Age* (Philadelphia: Westminster Press, 1984), 16–18.

Jones, who explicitly identify their work as rhetorical theology. However, Cunningham and Jones both express some discomfort with a tendency to one-sidedness in Lindbeck's work, noting that he does not sufficiently take into account questions of context and commitment, or of power relations involved in doctrinal language.[31]

I agree with this assessment and want to argue for a form of rhetorical theology that does keep those kinds of questions in mind. Although Lindbeck uses cultural concepts to point to the rhetorical effects of doctrines, his fear that "the world" will absorb "the Christian narrative" prohibits him from taking into account that theology is itself a cultural product, rooted in the power structures and practices of the surrounding culture. Hence, while he ostensibly embraces the antifoundationalist linguistic turn of the twentieth century, he actually posits theological doctrine as a foundation—albeit a "foundation" that comes paradoxically from "above," following Karl Barth's understanding of revelation as something objective outside the human situation. This crypto-foundationalism, as Wentzel van Huyssteen calls it, leans toward an understanding of doctrine as something that may function rhetorically within a culture from its elevated vantage point, but is not subject to critical-rhetorical analysis.[32] Lindbeck's model thus neatly hijacks some of the insights of postmodern linguistic theories and their emphasis on the situatedness of subjects and texts, and tames those insights for the purposes of a protective strategy that isolates theology from their implications. This leads to a one-sided form of rhetorical theology that does not take seriously the critical rhetorical implications of these linguistic theories, because it does not leave room for suspicion about the power dynamics that led to the dominance of certain kinds of rhetoric in speaking of classical theological symbols in the first place. As such, this approach might lend itself to a "rhetoric of piety," but there is insufficient room for critical rhetorical inquiry.

In contrast to such a one-directional approach to religious rhetoric, there in fact seems to be a hint of a dialectic between symbol and concrete realities found in Geertz's thought, which is missed when rhetorical theology is built only on his "moods and motivations" language. Geertz remarks that "culture patterns have an intrinsic double aspect: they give meaning, that is, objective conceptual form, to social and psychological reality both by shaping

---

31. Cunningham, *Faithful Persuasion*, 208; Serene Jones, "Cultural Labor and Theological Critique," in *Converging on Culture: Theologians in Dialogue with Cultural Analysis and Criticism*, ed. Delwin Brown, Sheila Greeve Davaney, and Kathryn Tanner (New York: Oxford University Press, 2001), 159.

32. J. Wentzel van Huyssteen, *The Shaping of Rationality: Toward Interdisciplinarity in Theology and Science* (Grand Rapids: Eerdmans, 1999), 69–109. Van Huyssteen uses the term *crypto-foundationalism* to describe appeals to the "Christian narrative" in an isolated sense as a norm unto itself, a move that could reduce theology to fideism.

themselves to it and by shaping it to themselves."[33] In this regard, David Tracy's insistence on a more dialectical approach to the relationship between the language of faith (symbols) and extralinguistic reality seems to be closer to Geertz's view on religion. In *The Nature of Doctrine*, Lindbeck famously and erroneously described Tracy as an "experiential-expressivist," whose theology operates with the notion that religious symbols are expressions of extralinguistic experience.[34] Such a view would, of course, be incompatible with the rhetorical emphasis on how language (including religious symbols) creates or shapes experience, and hence also praxis. However, Tracy equally famously refuted Lindbeck's reading of him and pointed out that the heirs of the liberal theological tradition have been following Gadamer, Ricoeur, and other hermeneutical thinkers in rethinking the dialectical (not unilateral) relationship between experience and language.[35] In other words, Tracy rejects an understanding of language as simply expressive of nonlinguistic realities and affirms the way in which symbols shape human praxis. In contrast to Lindbeck, though, Tracy would not thereby "abandon half the dialectic by simply placing all experience under the new guardianship of and production by the grammatical rule of the codes of language."[36] This dialectical approach, I contend, is closer to Geertz's full perspective than Lindbeck's, and could help to provide the building blocks for a less one-sided rhetorical theology, if only by suggesting that a one-directional approach to rhetorical theology is not sufficient. However, even this more dialectical approach to theological symbols may not produce an adequate rhetorical theology, insofar as it still does not sufficiently recognize the role of power in the acceptance of symbols.

Anthropologist of religion Talal Asad charges that Geertz's understanding of symbol as "any object, act, event, quality, or relation which serves as a vehicle for conception" confuses cognitive and communicative questions, which makes it impossible to trace the social conditions within which they come to be constructed—in particular, the reality of power.[37] Like the classical Sophists, Asad argues that power, that is, "the effect of an entire network of motivated practices," creates the conditions for experiencing "truth." He points out that

---

33. Geertz, "Religion as a Cultural System," 65.
34. Lindbeck, *Nature of Doctrine*, 21, 37. Although Lindbeck later qualified his identification of Tracy as an "experiential-expressivist," in *Nature of Doctrine*, on 38 and 136n4, he clearly identifies Tracy as such.
35. David Tracy, "Lindbeck's New Program for Theology: A Reflection," *Thomist* 49 (1985): 463.
36. Ibid., 464.
37. Talal Asad, *Genealogies of Religion: Discipline and Reasons of Power in Christianity and Islam* (Baltimore, MD: Johns Hopkins University Press, 1993), 27–54. The Geertz quote is from Geertz, "Religion as a Cultural System," 63.

even Augustine realized the importance of laws and disciplinary practices of various kinds in experiencing the "truth" of doctrines.[38] In other words, rhetoric is intertwined with power, which could function in either a positive or negative manner. Asad's perspective goes beyond the kind of dialectic already noted in Geertz, instead pointing to a hermeneutic characterized by genealogical suspicions, since an appropriation of his critique would require an analysis of the social conditions within which doctrines were formulated and accepted as orthodoxy. This is an important insight for our purposes, since this insight enables rhetorical theology to push beyond a rhetoric of piety to also include critical rhetorical inquiry—and in fact to root its constructive rhetoric in critical inquiry.

In summary, I suggest that rhetorical theology should embrace a more explicitly dialectical approach that not only focuses on the culture created by religious symbols but also takes seriously the way in which symbols arise from culture, with specific attention paid to the issue of power. The dialectical understanding of doctrine as both rooted in and contributing to concrete realities and power relations enables us to launch a full-bodied critical-constructive rhetorical analysis of classical doctrinal symbols by allowing us to recognize the fact that doctrines are embedded in cultural realities even as they address those realities. Specifically, this dialectical approach to doctrine opens the door to a stronger hermeneutic of suspicion by asking not only how religion creates power but also how power creates religion.[39]

One feminist scholar whose method approximates such a critical-constructive rhetorical inquiry is Elisabeth Schüssler Fiorenza. She notes that "rhetorical interpretation and its theoethical interrogation of texts and symbolic worlds pays attention to the kinds of effects biblical discourses produce and how they produce them."[40] This refers to what I have earlier called the constructive or persuasive task of rhetorical theology—the task embraced by Lindbeck, that which pushes toward a rhetoric of piety, faithful persuasion, or emancipatory discourse. But Schüssler Fiorenza also recognizes that these texts not only shape social realities but reflect them, particularly their ideological interests: thus the foundational texts of Christianity are "neither reports of events nor transcripts of facts but rather rhetorical constructions that have shaped the information available to them in light of their religious or political interests."[41] This would refer to what Schüssler Fiorenza calls critical rhetorical inquiry, or what I have earlier called a hermeneutic characterized

---

38. Asad, *Genealogies of Religion*, 35.
39. Ibid., 45.
40. Schüssler Fiorenza, *But She Said*, 41.
41. Ibid., 32.

by genealogical suspicions. Schüssler Fiorenza therefore recognizes both that "language . . . creates and shapes the symbolic worlds it professes to evoke and describe," and that "language and texts are always dependent on their rhetorical situation and socio-political location."[42] In other words, in Schüssler Fiorenza's model, religious language is seen as both performative (it affects behavior) and ideological (it is rooted in existing power structures). She therefore rejects a purely intratextual analysis of texts, arguing that it must be complemented by "a critical systemic analysis of socio-political and religious structures of domination and exclusion."[43]

Schüssler Fiorenza also makes it clear that inherent in the belief that knowledge of the world is rhetorical (i.e., that texts and knowledge reflect the rhetoric of a particular group of people, for a particular audience, and with certain explicit goals or implicit interests) is also the hope that cultural mindsets and the meaning of sacred texts are changeable. Therefore, true to its contextual and practical nature, the goal of critical feminist rhetorical inquiry is not simply interpretation for interpretation's sake, but, as Rebecca Chopp puts it, "discourses of emancipatory transformation that proclaim the Word to and for the world."[44]

Echoing both the constructive mode of Classical Rhetoric and the critical mode of the New Rhetoric, a critical-constructive rhetorical theology will therefore be interested in critically examining the effective functioning of texts/symbols (including the interests served by particular rhetorical practices, the overall systemic matrix within which they function, and a particular audience's location within that matrix), and it will also make constructive proposals for how the texts/symbols might function with an eye toward human flourishing. These are the kinds of concerns that drive feminist critical rhetorical inquiry into Christian discourses on sin. How does the symbol of sin function in the lives of women and gendered Others (or, to put it in Foucault's terms, how does sin-talk regulate social life)? Whose interests are served by certain kinds of rhetoric? What is the systemic matrix within which sin-talk occurs? But also, in a more constructive mode, what kinds of vision do feminist theologians conjure up with their own sin-talk?

In order to examine these questions and concerns, I employ various rhetorical strategies over the course of the next few chapters. Below I briefly introduce these feminist rhetorical strategies, and then conclude with an outline of the overall argument.

---

42. Schüssler Fiorenza, "Challenging the Rhetorical Half-Turn," 41.
43. Ibid.
44. Chopp, *The Power to Speak*, 3.

FEMINIST RHETORICAL STRATEGIES

It is common to distinguish among "radical" feminist theologians who leave the tradition behind to embrace a Goddess spirituality, more conservative/reformist feminist theologians who focus on including more women in the tradition, and reconstructionist/revisionist feminists, who are more critical of classical traditions but maintain a presence within it. Other classifications of feminist theologies point to the theoretical differences that separate liberal, radical, socialist, or psychoanalytical feminists. For our purposes, those kinds of distinctions are not particularly relevant, although my rhetorical approach obviously shares a basic perspective on the importance of critical-constructive retrieval of the tradition with reconstructionist/revisionist feminist theologies. Feminist theorist Mary Hawkesworth offers us a more helpful way to look at different emphases in feminist discourses by distinguishing among different feminist rhetorical strategies. Feminist theologies, when looked at through this lens, are therefore not distinguished by looking at their use of a particular theory or their degree of loyalty to classical theological traditions, but rather by the kind of rhetoric they use. Hawkesworth distinguishes four feminist rhetorical strategies: the rhetoric of oppression, the rhetoric of difference, the rhetoric of reason, and the rhetoric of vision.[45]

The tactic of the feminist *rhetoric of oppression* is that of supplanting civilization's self-description with the image of a (monolithic) patriarchy characterized by conquest, domination, hierarchy, and so forth. This strategy risks depicting women only as victims (and even disempowering women in the process), and of viewing men as completely irredeemable and the eternal enemies of women. However, its strength lies in its shock value: by reading history as a record of atrocities, it aims at breaking through denial by "providing a pitiless description that forces its own acceptance."[46] We see examples of the rhetoric of oppression when feminist scholars point to the history of Christianity as steeped in the blood of women. The feminist theologian most associated with this kind of rhetoric is Mary Daly, who speaks of patriarchy as the prevailing "religion" of the entire planet, and calls all religions "parts of the male's shelter against anomie," that is, women as the projected personifications of "The Enemy."[47] Daly also refers to violence against women as "the various manifestations of Goddess-Murder on this patriarchal planet," the "deep and universal intent to destroy the divine spark in women."[48]

---

45. M. E. Hawkesworth, *Beyond Oppression: Feminist Theory and Political Strategy* (New York: Continuum, 1990), 111–29.
46. Ibid., 113.
47. Mary Daly, *Gyn/Ecology: The Metaethics of Radical Feminism* (Boston: Beacon, 1978), 39.
48. Ibid., 315.

The feminist *rhetoric of difference*, on the other hand, is rooted in claims of women's specific moral endowments and the value of women's traditional activities. Those using this rhetorical strategy are sometimes wary of the notion of "equality," if that means women are to be measured by male standards. Instead, the rhetoric of difference tends to operate with the French feminist concept of *différence*, which states that "the sexed embodiedness of women repressed by the phallic order must be reclaimed by the creation of a place for the feminine in language."[49] Another version of this kind of rhetoric can be seen in the work of scholars such as Carol Gilligan, whose landmark book, *In a Different Voice*, argues that the relationality traditionally associated with women should form the basis of ethics.[50] The goal of the feminist rhetoric of difference is therefore to capitalize upon women's traditional strengths. This strategy risks an essentialist and romanticized view of womanhood, working with an almost metaphysical conception of "woman," ignoring the social construction of gender, and thereby understating the scope of possible social change. On the other hand, in its positive valuation of women's traditional activities and bodies, the rhetoric of difference promises wholeness through the recovery of the repressed. This strategy as presented so far is not central to the critical rhetorical inquiry in this book, but a reversed version of it comes into play. Such a reversed feminist rhetoric of difference can be seen when feminist theologians such as Valerie Saiving, Judith Plaskow, and Susan Nelson Dunfee emphasize the particular sins to which women are prone.[51] In short, the (reversed) rhetoric of difference employed here focuses not on women's traditional strengths but on the weaknesses to which women's traditional strengths may give rise.

Perhaps the most commonly used feminist rhetorical strategy is that of the *rhetoric of reason*, which focuses on exposing and correcting misinformation about women contained in classic texts, and often emphasizes the principle of equality.[52] Premised on the idea that reason will ultimately triumph, some versions of this strategy may not necessarily be able to go deeply enough into the causes of misogyny. However, the strength of this strategy lies in its intellectual rigor and its use of the tools of academic analysis, which has developed

---

49. Hawkesworth, *Beyond Oppression*, 116.
50. Carol Gilligan, *In a Different Voice: Psychological Theory and Women's Development* (Cambridge, MA: Harvard University Press, [1982] 2016).
51. Valerie Saiving, "The Human Situation: A Feminine View," in *Womanspirit Rising: A Feminist Reader in Religion*, ed. Carol Christ and Judith Plaskow (San Francisco: Harper & Row, 1979), 25–42; Judith Plaskow, *Sex, Sin, and Grace: Women's Experience and the Theologies of Reinhold Niebuhr and Paul Tillich* (New York: University Press of America, 1980); Susan Nelson Dunfee, "The Sin of Hiding: A Feminist Critique of Reinhold Niebuhr's Account of the Sin of Pride," *Soundings* 65 (Fall 1982): 316–27.
52. Hawkesworth, *Beyond Oppression*, 121.

a body of evidence that counters unwarranted stereotypes about women. An example of this rhetorical strategy would be Rosemary Radford Ruether's focus on the underlying dualistic patterns in Western thought, which contribute to the devaluing of the body and as such to the oppression of women.[53]

Hawkesworth favors a fourth feminist rhetorical strategy, which she calls the *rhetoric of vision*. This strategy combines many aspects of the other feminist rhetorical strategies, such as the recognition of language as a powerful ideological weapon, and the simultaneous recognition of women's unique contributions and their equality to men in worth and human dignity. Although the idea of a "rhetoric of vision" can be accused of lacking concreteness, this strategy combines the more critical strategies with a constructive aim, which targets the imagination as the primary site of ideological struggle. In targeting the imagination as the site of struggle, the rhetoric of vision recognizes that misogyny is rooted in more than ignorance, and as such, it goes beyond the critiques and corrections of the other rhetorical strategies. Because it sees the recoding of dominant cultural symbols as the key to social transformation, the rhetoric of vision is consciously engaging in the literary production of reality. Specifically, it aims to create some space in our conceptual and perceptual worlds "within which women can expand their subversive activities."[54] Although I do not here employ this strategy in quite the way Hawkesworth defines it, the two final chapters indeed, in their delineation of constructive feminist sin-talk, develop a variant of the rhetoric of vision. Specifically, in chapter 5 we shall see that feminist theologians, precisely as a result of their critical rhetorical inquiry, already (sometimes implicitly) engage in the recoding of the symbol of sin. This recognition in turn forms the basis for my suggestions regarding a constructive feminist form of sin-talk in chapter 6. These constructive proposals can be seen as proposing a "vision" for sin-talk in light of feminist concerns, and as such would be similar to Hawkesworth's rhetoric of vision. The main difference lies in the more concrete, practical focus of sin-talk, compared to Hawkesworth's more aesthetic rhetoric of vision (even though the latter still is, as rhetoric always is, aimed at praxis).

In summary, Hawkesworth's analysis of different feminist rhetorical strategies is helpful insofar as it enables us to analyze the mechanisms and ends of seemingly opposing types of feminist discourse, and to see their shared goals despite their different rhetorical approaches. In short, Hawkesworth's analysis enables us to weave together the varying strands of feminist discourses on sin in order to see the feminist conversation on sin as a whole. More specifically

---

53. Rosemary Radford Ruether, *Sexism and God-Talk: Toward a Feminist Theology* (Boston: Beacon, 1983).
54. Hawkesworth, *Beyond Oppression*, 125.

for our purposes here, in the following chapters, we shall see that these categories are useful in tracing the different rhetorical practices adopted by feminist theologians in their critiques of classical sin-talk. Using a rhetoric of difference that exposes the androcentric assumptions of classical sin-talk, feminist theologians bring women's experiences into the realm of sin-talk to remind us that the persuasive effects of sin-talk are partially dependent on the audience's situation. Using a rhetoric of reason, aimed at deconstructing the dualistic thought patterns that contributed to the depiction of women as denigrated body and symbol of sin, feminist theologians critique the sexist philosophical arguments found within much of classical sin-talk. Using a rhetoric of oppression, which aims at unsettling the positive self-image of classical traditions by reciting their history of atrocities against women, feminist theologians retell the history of sin-talk as one of misogyny and violence against women, and attack the *ethos* that lies behind this history. A rhetoric of oppression is also used to point to the destructive effects if the situation of the audience is not sufficiently kept in mind. These different feminist rhetorical strategies expose two misogynist rhetorical practices present in classical discourses on sin: a patriarchal rhetoric of life-denial, which emphasizes the sin of pride in such a way that it becomes particularly destructive in the lives of women; and a patriarchal rhetoric of death, which justifies gender violence by associating women with sin who are therefore worthy of punishment. Feminist theologians expose these misogynist, patriarchal rhetorical practices by implicitly focusing on the various rhetorical dimensions in classical sin-talk: by asking about the interests of classical (male) theologians when they talk about sin in certain ways (the *ethos* question); by asking about the kind of logic and values present in classical sin-talk (the *logos* question); and by asking about the audience presupposed in classical sin-talk, and the consequences if that sin-talk is inappropriate for some audience members who receive it (the *ethos/decorum* question).

Furthermore I explore how the critical rhetorical strategies of feminist theologians form part of a constructive, rhetorical, prophetic mode of sin-talk, aimed at addressing the very concrete evils that follow in the wake of patriarchal classical sin-talk, in particular gender violence. Finally, in constructing a death-denouncing, life-affirming rhetoric of sin, I refer to elements in the thought of two classical theologians, Augustine of Hippo and John Calvin, in order to show how feminist concerns, even where they would critique these very same classical theologians, nevertheless also align with certain elements in the classical traditions of Christianity. As I show in more detail, these two theologians are chosen for specific reasons: Augustine because of his central presence in classical Christian sin-talk, and Calvin because of his particular prophetic mode of sin-talk at the time of the Reformation.

OUTLINE

The next chapter, "*Kairos*," offers a brief examination of the rhetorical situation in which sin-talk occurs, with specific reference to women's situations and experiences. Two chapters ("Mary" and "Eve") follow that analyze prominent feminist voices who engage in critical rhetorical inquiry into two specific harmful patriarchal rhetorical practices found in classical Christian sin-talk. The final two chapters ("Grammar" and "Life") push toward a constructive discourse on sin, aimed at human flourishing, by first analyzing the already-existing constructive elements in feminist sin-talk, and then offering a rhetorical outline for further constructive feminist sin-talk. Throughout the process of this critical-constructive rhetorical inquiry, we shall see that the central practical effect in light of which classical sin-talk is interrogated is the widespread phenomenon of gender violence. I use the language of "gender violence" to refer to all forms of violence against women, including not only violence against cisgender women but all violence that targets people based on gender role expectations and/or associations, which includes violence against all who are seen as transgressing gender norms, including gay men and transgender individuals. As the next two chapters show, feminist critical rhetorical inquiry unearths two patriarchal rhetorical practices that contribute to a culture of gender violence. I call these, respectively, the patriarchal rhetoric of life-denial (which I link to the Mary symbol) and the patriarchal rhetoric of death (which I link to the Eve symbol). In the two final, more constructive chapters, sin-talk is once again correlated with the issue of systemic gender violence. However, despite the centrality of the issue of gender violence, this book is not an ethical examination of the phenomenon of gender violence per se, but rather a critical interrogation of Christian sin-talk in light of concrete female experiences of the world, in which gender violence is a central concern, aimed toward a construction of sin-talk that may instead contribute to human flourishing.

The task of this book is therefore to map the feminist conversation on sin through a rhetorical analysis that performs the following tasks:

1. It uses classical rhetorical concepts to name various rhetorical dimensions of classical Christian sin-talk that feminist theologians critique.
2. It identifies different rhetorical strategies that feminist theologians use to critique classical sin-talk.
3. It describes the problems in classical sin-talk as two destructive rhetorical practices, namely the rhetoric of life-denial and the rhetoric of death, which in combination are symbolized by the Mary-Eve dichotomy.
4. It argues that what we encounter within these feminist critiques of classical sin-talk is not so much a rejection of the notion of sin, but rather the

emergence of a constructive feminist rhetoric of sin that utilizes the same "grammar" as the classical doctrine of original sin.
5. It outlines the contours of a constructive feminist rhetoric of sin, making use of classical rhetorical concepts to do so, and centering this final proposal on a hermeneutic of life.

In short, in feminist theology's *critical mode*, we shall see three feminist rhetorical strategies (oppression, reason, difference), which critically examine classical sin-talk in its three rhetorical dimensions (*ethos, logos, pathos*), which yields a feminist critical exposé of two destructive rhetorical practices: the patriarchal rhetoric of life-denial (symbolized by Mary) and the patriarchal rhetoric of death (symbolized by Eve). This critical deconstruction enables the development of feminist constructive sin-talk, which consists of a retrieval of the inner pattern of the doctrine of original sin, and a counter-rhetoric characterized by a prophetic *ethos*, a decorous recognition of the *pathos* of the audience of sin-talk, and a *logos* focused on denouncing death and affirming life.

2

Kairos

The sufferings of this present *kairos* are not worth comparing with the glory about to be revealed to us.
—*Romans 8:18 NRSV, alt.*

Before we can move on to feminist theologians' various criticisms, retrievals, and constructions of sin-talk, we need to ask the question: Why? What drives feminist critical-constructive sin-talk? What is the context in which feminist critical-constructive sin-talk originates? This chapter aims to respond to these foundational questions by, first, briefly returning to rhetorical theory to examine the concept of "rhetorical situation," that is, the context of rhetoric. I then proceed to look at the rhetorical situation within which feminist rhetoric engages the Christian tradition. In other words, this section lays the contextual foundation for my analysis of feminist conversations on sin. I center the discussion of the rhetorical situation around the concept of *kairos*, understood in the terms already hinted at in the previous chapter, that is, as encompassing both a time and a situational element. The chapter then goes into the specifics of what drives feminist rhetorical sin-talk by revisiting key feminist concepts, and by examining gender violence as a key element of the feminist rhetorical situation.

THE RHETORICAL SITUATION

In rhetorical theory the concept of "rhetorical situation" refers to the context within which rhetoric arises. So let us examine what this concept means by briefly returning to the field of rhetorical theory, before examining what the feminist rhetorical situation is that gives rise to feminist theological rhetoric. In the field of rhetorical theory, the concept of "rhetorical situation" first received serious attention in a 1968 essay by Lloyd Bitzer, who argued that, just as an answer responds to a question, so rhetoric responds to a rhetorical situation, defined as "a natural context of persons, events, objects, relations, and an exigence which strongly invites utterance." Of particular importance in this definition is the term "exigence," that is, "an imperfection marked by urgency . . . a defect, an obstacle, something waiting to be done, a thing which is other than it should be."[1] This is the crisis element of the rhetorical situation, and it is particularly significant for our purposes, since the feminist rhetorical situation is marked by crisis, that is, it rhetorically engages the exigence of gender oppression.

In a 1973 critique of Bitzer, Richard Vatz argued that it is not so much the case that rhetoric is situational, as that situations are rhetorical. In other words, the rhetorical situation is not an externally existing phenomenon to which rhetoric responds, but is rather a product of the rhetor's perspective and subsequent rhetoric. This approach has ethical implications, since to "view rhetoric as a creation of reality or salience rather than a reflector of reality clearly increases the rhetor's moral responsibility."[2] However, since it is not clear what would drive the rhetor to create the rhetorical situation, Vatz's perspective invokes the specter of ethical relativism. Vatz is not wrong when he recognizes that rhetorical situations are (at least partially) created by rhetors, as they create, through language, a sense of urgency about a specific situation. But if rhetoric is to be more than just the cynical use of language to create crises for personal or ideological gain, the question needs to be asked about the presence of concrete concerns within the rhetorical situation even prior to speech. It is clear that this debate echoes to a large extent the theological method debate between Tracy and Lindbeck (and similar debates in philosophy, even going back to the days of Plato and the Sophists), and here too, I argue (following Tracy) for the need to find a third way out of the impasse.

Scott Consigny attempted to bridge the Bitzer/Vatz divide by embracing an Aristotelian perspective on rhetoric as an "art." Defining the rhetorical situation as an "indeterminate context marked by troublesome disorder which the rhetor must structure so as to disclose and formulate problems," he argues that the rhetor must work through the *pragmata* of the situation until an issue emerges from the rhetor's interactions with the situation.[3] He therefore suggests that the real question is not whether the situation or the rhetor

---

1. Lloyd Bitzer, "The Rhetorical Situation," *Philosophy and Rhetoric* 1 (January 1968): 5–6.
2. Richard E. Vatz, "The Myth of the Rhetorical Situation," *Philosophy and Rhetoric* 6 (Summer 1973): 154–61, 159.
3. Scott Consigny, "Rhetoric and Its Situations," *Philosophy and Rhetoric* 7 (1974): 178.

is dominant, but whether the rhetor is engaged in the "troublesome" situation with the goal of making sense of it. To this end the rhetor should possess two things: integrity, that is, the skill to function rhetorically in any situation (the universal element), and receptivity, that is, the ability to become engaged in specific situations without predetermining the exigence of the situation (the particular element).[4] The rhetor as "artist" is therefore somewhat objective in the sense of having the ability to function rhetorically in any situation as well as in the sense of being open to the *pragmata* of the situation (i.e., not being completely agenda-driven), but the rhetor is also somewhat subjective, in the sense of being engaged in the situation without the pretense of complete objectivity. The emphasis on engagement here echoes the feminist theological insight that theology does not just derive from "above" but from the lived situations of human beings—what feminist theology has classically referred to as "women's experiences." In biblical terms, one might speak of "discerning the spirits" within the situation.

Theology, especially the existential theology of Paul Tillich, as well as various liberation theologies, has used the term *kairos* to speak of this "discerning of the spirits." Rhetorical theorist James L. Kinneavy has argued that this previously neglected concept was central to the rhetoric of the Sophists, as well as Plato and especially Aristotle, and he posits this as a richer concept than Bitzer's "rhetorical situation" in explaining "*how* rhetoric was born."[5] I use it as the key concept in expressing what Consigny means when he speaks of the discerning engagement of the rhetor as the starting point of rhetoric. We saw in the previous chapter that Kinneavy defines *kairos* more broadly than just in terms of "the right time," which is the usual connotation, but in terms of time, place, speaker, and audience involved in a situation. Other scholars similarly suggest that "*kairos* refers to a struggle, at the point of rhetorical intervention, between situational factors."[6] In these perspectives, *kairos* emerges as a dynamic concept that has to do with reading the situation carefully, or as I suggested above in response to Consigny's third way of understanding the rhetorical situation, *kairos* is a matter of "discerning the spirits."

The Bitzer/Vatz debate is in many ways a modern version of the Plato/Gorgias debate on *kairos*: for Plato, *kairos* was the means to the end of transcendent truth, while for the Sophists like Gorgias, *kairos* was the end itself, and

---

4. Ibid., 181.
5. Roger Thompson, "Kairos Revisited: An Interview with James Kinneavy," *Rhetoric Review* 19 (Autumn 2000): 73.
6. David Sheridan, Tony Michel, and Jim Ridolfo, "*Kairos* and New Media: Toward a Theory and Practice of Visual Activism," *Enculturation: A Journal of Rhetoric, Writing, and Culture* 6, no. 2 (2009), http://enculturation.net/6.2/sheridan-michel-ridolfo.

as such, notes Kinneavy, the cornerstone of ethics, aesthetics, and rhetoric.[7] Kinneavy also suggests that *kairos* can be seen as those aspects of the rhetorical act that are beyond the rhetor's control.[8] He interprets this uncontrollable element in the rhetorical situation as the presence of the universal, that is, the transcendent idea being applied within the particular situation, although he rejects any theological perspectives on this. In theology, of course, this "uncontrollable" element of *kairos* is understood as the eternal breaking into the temporal, that is, as revelation in concrete situations. This perspective on *kairos* bridges the Plato/Gorgias divide by viewing *kairos* as neither the means to an external truth, nor truth itself, but instead the situation and moment in which truth emerges in part as the result of the work of the artist-rhetor. Following Consigny's embrace of the idea of rhetoric as an art practiced by the skillful and engaged rhetor, I see the rhetorical theologian's task, then, as discerning the *kairos* as the starting point of rhetorical theology. Not only does this help us bypass the Bitzer/Vatz impasse in understanding the origins of rhetoric, but it could help us avoid the risk of ethical relativism present in Vatz's recognition of the rhetorical nature of the situation itself. After all, as Kinneavy also notes, *kairos* brings the ethical/political element to the concept of the rhetorical situation, noting that "one of the most significant components of *kairos* had to do with its close relation to justice."[9] From the perspective of *kairos*, justice is situation-specific, but also rooted in transcendent truth.

In summary, rhetorical theology is rooted in the rhetorical situation. The latter, however, is not an objective reality outside of discourse that is merely interpreted or responded to by rhetoric. Instead, the situation qua rhetorical situation is in part created by the rhetorical theologian. She does not, however, create a rhetorical situation simply out of whim or self-interest, but is driven by the epistemological and ethical imperatives of the *kairos* situation in which she is engaged. As a concept that is related to time, albeit not chronological time, *kairos* points to moments of heightened crisis and opportunity. But as a concept that is also intimately connected to *decorum*, *kairos* also suggests proportionality, a careful reading of the context. It thus transcends the time metaphor to become a more broadly situational, even relational one. As such, *kairos* is central to a sensitive interpretation of time and context as the starting point for rhetorical theology.

---

7. James Kinneavy, ""*Kairos:* A Neglected Concept in Classical Rhetoric," in *Rhetoric and Praxis*, ed. Jean Dietz Moss (Washington, DC: Catholic University of America Press, 1986), 80.
8. Thompson, "Kairos Revisited," 74.
9. James L. Kinneavy, "*Kairos* in Classical and Modern Rhetorical Theory," in *Rhetoric and Kairos: Essays in History, Theory, and Praxis*, ed. Phillip Sipiora and James S. Baumlin (Albany: State University of New York Press, 2002), 61.

In its *kairos* origins, rhetorical theology affirms the ideas of divine immanence and revelation in human contexts. The foundational *kairos* of Christian theology is, of course, that of the Christ event. But Christian theology also insists that the Spirit of Christ is continuously present in the world. Theology is therefore not merely faith seeking understanding of the historical Christ event, but of recognizing the revelation of truth within the current context. The task of the engaged and informed rhetor who practices rhetoric as an art is to read the situation carefully, to "discern the spirits" and seek the divine Spirit in the situation.

The rhetorical situation as root of theological rhetoric is therefore neither an objective reality to be interpreted, nor just made up out of self-interest or whim, but is rhetoric born of the art of *kairos* interpretation. So when feminist theologians pose women's experiences as root and source of theology, this is best understood as a kairotic-rhetorical exercise, a recognition that theology does not just respond ethically to objective situations, nor elevate situations willy-nilly to the level of theological truth, but that the skilled and engaged rhetorical theologian interprets the *kairos*—the "signs of the times" in which, amid the specifics of the situation, one can discern transcendent revelatory truth and ethical demand. The classic feminist emphasis on women's experiences as theological source is therefore not a matter of positing of a second source for theology alongside revelation, but of recognizing the *kairos* within which God's will is discerned.

In the rest of this chapter, we therefore turn to some feminist descriptions of the rhetorical situation with which feminist rhetoric engages, keeping in mind that this is an exercise of interpreting the *kairos*, thereby both responding to and partially creating the rhetorical situation.

NAMING THE *KAIROS*

The usual starting point of feminist theology is women's experiences, a concept that implicitly references the rhetorical situation in which the feminist rhetorician is engaged. Here the epistemological and ethical elements of *kairos* as the central concept of the rhetorical situation become very significant. First, when understood in terms of the *kairos* concept, it becomes clear that this classical feminist starting point does not mean that human experience is placed side by side with religious revelation (which has been a charge brought against feminist theological method, especially from the side of Barthian-style theologies). The feminist starting point in women's experiences simply recognizes that religious revelation happens within human experience, including the experiences of women.

Second, apart from the above-mentioned revelatory/epistemological element of *kairos*, I have also pointed out that it contains an ethical demand. *Kairos* demands justice, and as such, it is particularly the exigence within a given situation that constitutes *kairos* and thus the origins of theological rhetoric. The fact is that feminist theology exists, and is necessary, because of the crisis of male dominance and the exclusion and indeed oppression of women and gendered Others. Within this Christian theological-rhetorical situation, there is therefore an exigence, a "thing which is other than it should be." Ironically, this description of exigence is very similar to the classical definition of sin as "missing the mark."

What women experience is partly the result of this exigence, and therefore any reference to women's experiences should be rooted in the recognition of this rhetorical reality. Such a rhetorical starting point may help us move beyond gender essentialism, since it not only already recognizes how much of our existence is linguistically shaped but may also help us recognize that all gendered Others—for example, transgender individuals—experience the negative results of the exigence within the rhetorical situation. Moreover, the justice demanded by the *kairos* concept means that identifying the exigence at the heart of the feminist rhetorical situation necessitates the recognition of the intersectionality of gender with race, class, sexuality, nationality, culture, and so on.

Therefore, in this book, as I discuss feminist critiques of rhetorical practices that feminist theologians have named as harmful to women, I do so with the recognition that many of these same rhetorical practices are also harmful to males who have been subjugated as the result of class, race, or sexuality, among other possibilities, and that, moreover, women also participate in the oppression of others (one of the clearest historical examples of this reality is the oppression of black women and men by white women). I also do so with recognition that the term "women" refers to a greater or lesser extent to a cultural construct, and that there is some measure of fluidity to the construction of gender, including differences in gender constructs across cultures. And I do so with recognition that the realities of the intersection of gender with class, race, nationality, sexuality, and so on shape the specific experience of women, which means that one cannot make assumptions based solely on one's own particular experience. Here Consigny's insistence on both the universal skill and the particular engagement of the rhetor is essential, and David Tracy's hermeneutical model based on intersubjectivity (as opposed to either objectivity or subjectivity) shapes my understanding of the theological process. Therefore, while I do not repeatedly qualify and specify the term "women" as I move forward, the intersectionality and cultural construction of gender recognized here is integral to my understanding of that term.

To name the *kairos* of the feminist rhetorical situation, feminist theologians make use of overlapping, yet distinct terms to encapsulate different aspects of women's experiences, such as *androcentrism, sexism, misogyny,* and *patriarchy*. Androcentrism is a pattern of thinking in which men (specifically, ruling men) are seen as the paradigm for humanity. This way of thinking dehumanizes women, since they cannot meet the androcentric norm. In chapter 3 we shall see that one example of androcentrism would be the assumption that the typical moral struggle of ruling males is also the typical moral struggle of women. We shall also see that while this might seem to be only a matter of exclusion, it is in fact dehumanizing and oppressive to women, contributing to a rhetoric of life-denial that plays a role in gender violence and other forms of gender oppression.

The second concept that feminists use to name the *kairos* of the feminist rhetorical situation, "sexism," refers to social values and patterns that suggest that men are superior to women on the basis of their biological differences. Specific expressions of sexism vary from culture to culture, but often rest upon some kind of gender essentialism that identifies, for example, strength with masculinity and weakness with femininity, or would assign subservient gender roles to women. Western sexism is premised upon a dualistic framework that typically identifies masculinity with traits such as reason and power, and femininity with traits such as emotion and passivity. As we shall see in chapter 4, this dualistic framework also associates women with the body, sin, and evil, and thereby contributes to a rhetoric of death that justifies gender violence.

Sexism is closely related to misogyny, which is usually used to refer to the deeply ingrained hatred of women. The most extreme way in which misogyny finds expression is in gender violence, something that, as I argue later in this chapter, is at least in part to be understood as a mechanism for enforcing control over women, and not just a matter of individual pathology. As such, one can see misogyny, as Cornell philosophy professor Kate Manne does in her book *Down Girl*, in terms of the enforcement mechanism of sexist patterns and patriarchal systems of oppression.[10] This definition suggests that misogyny is not simply a matter of individual male hatred of women, but of a response to women who step out of the roles assigned to them by sexism and patriarchy. Her reading therefore situates the "hate of women" response at the heart of misogyny in broader cultural patterns, an emphasis that resonates with classical as well as feminist perspectives on sin as simultaneously individual and systemic.

Patriarchy, which literally means "rule of the father," refers to men's broader cultural systemic domination of women. Like the feminist concept of

---

10. Kate Manne, *Down Girl: The Logic of Misogyny* (New York: Oxford University Press, 2018).

"women's experience," the concept of patriarchy has met with some criticism for being an essentialist "grand narrative" that does not pass philosophical muster and does not pay sufficient attention to differences in race, culture, and other variables. Therefore, in order to more fully define the concept of patriarchy, we need to look more closely at the feminist debate on essentialism and cultural exclusion, which can also inform our understanding of feminist rhetoric on sin as it has developed since the 1960s.

Some early feminist scholars operated with an essentialist perspective on women, which would view women's experience as rooted in a universal female nature, based on something that is everywhere uniquely female. In contrast, the constructivist position emphasizes the role of local, cultural constructs. Sometimes a distinction is made between "sex" as a biological category and "gender" as a cultural inscription of meaning upon a pre-given sex: such a view recognizes the role of culture but is still essentialist. In contrast, poststructuralist feminism has pointed out that the categories "sex" and "gender" do not correspond to nature and culture, respectively, quite as easily as previously thought. As such, feminism itself has participated in rejecting modernist claims about the universal subject and ahistorical truths, arguing instead for the contingent, partial, and historically situated character of subjects and truth claims. Indeed, as Mary McClintock Fulkerson notes, the "originating revolutionary feminist discovery was of the constructed nature of gender."[11] Furthermore, women of color have brought white Western feminism to task for its often easy assumptions about women and the issues that (should) concern them. These critiques have different emphases, and strengths and weaknesses that correspond to those emphases: the cultural critique, for example, can itself often fall prey to cultural essentialism, whereas the poststructuralist critique runs the risk of obliterating the female subject. However, both have at heart a critique of the kind of essentialism that interprets all women in terms of Western gender binaries, and point to a view of gender as a socially constructed set of behaviors with deep political roots. We see in the next two chapters how various views on gender play a role in feminist analysis of the problems in classical Christian sin-talk.

Despite the validity of these critiques of essentialism, some feminist theorists have also been quick to notice that postmodern skepticism and the emphasis on the constructed nature of personhood can be taken too far. Feminist theorist Nancy Hartsock famously asked in 1987, "Why is it, exactly at the moment when so many of us who have been silenced begin to demand the right to name ourselves, to act as subjects rather than objects of history, that

---

11. Mary McClintock Fulkerson, *Changing the Subject: Women's Discourses and Feminist Theology* (Eugene, OR: Wipf and Stock, 2001), 6.

just then the concept of subjecthood becomes 'problematic'?"[12] Relatedly, as Linda Nicholson and Nancy Fraser point out, the emphasis on the local in postmodern thought leaves no place for "critique of pervasive axes of stratification, for critique of broad-based relations of dominance and subordination along lines like gender, race, and class."[13]

In light of these observations, I would argue that feminism needs to adopt what Serene Jones calls "strategic essentialism," in the interests of liberating normative visions.[14] This is a pragmatic universalism that recognizes the validity of constructivist and cultural critiques, but also the need for collective action and normative visions of the human good. In short, feminist theology needs to engage in some form of "grand narrativizing" if it is to be politically effective. This includes talking about the "grand narrative" of patriarchy even while its complexities are kept in mind. Talking about global patriarchy does not have to mean tying feminism to universalistic assumptions, such as the idea of a global and uniform sisterhood, or an essentialist understanding of women. Nor does it suggest a uniform expression of patriarchal norms and practices around the globe. Specifically, the language of patriarchy does not have to mean universalizing the experiences of white Western women (as has sometimes been done). Kenyan feminist theologian Musimbi Kanyoro notes that feminist scholarship enables us to hear women's stories from all over the world, revealing the subordination of women across differences of race, class, creed, or nationality. She notes that the 1995 World Conference on Women in Beijing stated that there is "no single state in the world where women are safe from violence or treated as equals with men," and concludes that "despite women's diverse social, economic and political backgrounds, by virtue of belonging to the female gender, women constitute an oppressed social group."[15] The reality is that, even though oppression runs along differentiated lines, situating us in various complex spaces, it is nevertheless true that male domination is prevalent across the globe.

Therefore, although no single female situation can be sketched, the global prevalence of male dominance suggests that we would probably find some analogies between different female lives. Here the meaning of the term "analogy," as

---

12. Nancy Hartsock, "Rethinking Modernism: Minority vs. Majority Theories," *Cultural Critique* 7 (Fall 1987): 196.
13. Nancy Fraser and Linda Nicholson, "Social Criticism without Philosophy: An Encounter between Feminism and Postmodernism," in *Feminism/Postmodernism*, ed. Linda J. Nicholson (New York: Routledge, 1990), 23.
14. Serene Jones, *Feminist Theory and Christian Theology: Cartographies of Grace*, Guides to Theological Inquiry (Minneapolis: Fortress Press, 2000), 45.
15. Musimbi Kanyoro, "Feminist Theology and African Culture," in *Violence against Women: Reflections by Kenyan Women Theologians*, ed. Grace Wamue and Mary Getui (Nairobi: Acton Publishers, 1996), 4.

that which points to similarities-in-difference, needs to be kept firmly in mind if we are to avoid a cultural hegemony that merely pretends to listen to all women while in fact once again imposing white, upper-class, Western assumptions on others. The point is not to argue for the sameness of all women, or even for simplistic commonalities, but to attempt to recognize similarities and differences. Amid those differences, some pervasive features of patriarchy may be identified, even if they take different cultural forms. These features include male control over female bodies, male domination and female submission in marriage, limited education of women compared to men, the expectation that women should focus on the private sphere and men on the public sphere, restricted inheritance rights for women, economic exploitation of women, double standards when it comes to judging either the faults or merits of men and women, and widespread gender violence. Some or all of these features are present to a lesser and greater degree in the overwhelming majority of cultures around the globe and shape women's experiences alongside the variables of race, class, geography, sexual orientation, gender identity, religion, or culture.

My perspective is therefore that feminist theology, when speaking of women's situations and experiences, must take the risk of speaking of the "grand narrative" of patriarchy, while proceeding with caution in order to avoid oversimplifications and exclusions. From this perspective, patriarchy should be seen not simply as systemic male domination but as an intricate hierarchy in which ruling males have power over various groups of people—people who relate to each other according to various scripts of domination along gender, racial, and other lines. Elisabeth Schüssler Fiorenza famously coined the term "kyriarchy" (from the Greek term for "lord," *kyrios*) in order to avoid the gender binaries that are often associated with the term "patriarchy," and to better express "the domination of the lord, slave master, husband, the elite freeborn educated and propertied man over all wo/men and subaltern men."[16] However, historical formulations of patriarchy (such as that of Aristotle) already refer not only to the rule of men over women but also the rule of male heads of families of the ruling class over all women, children, and other "dependents," such as female and male slaves.[17] Therefore, while I share the anti-essentialist concerns that lie behind Schüssler Fiorenza's neologism, I prefer the term "patriarchy" for reasons of historical roots and wide usage, as well as not to obscure the reality of male dominance in the overwhelming majority of cultures in the world, even if many of these patriarchal men are themselves under the patriarchal domination of elite ruling men.

---

16. Elisabeth Schüssler Fiorenza, *Jesus and the Politics of Interpretation* (New York: Continuum, 2000), 95.

17. Aristotle, *Politics*, trans. George A. Kennedy (New York: Oxford University Press, 2007), 1.1.7, 3.1.12.

The patriarchal system is upheld by the androcentric assumption that the perspectives of ruling males are normative, and by various cultural symbols that put women and subordinate males "in their place" (sexism, racism, classism, heterosexism, etc.). Of course, women are more than victims within this patriarchal system: women are workers, parents, inventors, artists, and much more. But women occupy these roles within a patriarchal system that is characterized by various forms of gender oppression. Therefore it is necessary to speak of oppression in order to speak of women's experience of the world.

One of the most famous discussions of the various manifestations of oppression is that of Iris Marion Young, who lists "five faces of oppression": exploitation, marginalization, powerlessness, cultural imperialism, and violence.[18] *Exploitation* occurs when the people who produce social goods do not share fully in the accumulated benefits of labor: they work so that another group gains the profit. This exploitation occurs, for example, when the reproductive and domestic work of women are defined as "nonwork" and thus not worthy of compensation, or when those "public" jobs that women traditionally do (e.g., the helping professions) are deemed less worthy of compensation. The argument used is that these jobs require less skill and education, yet we see that compensation drops for all "feminized" sectors of the economy. Serene Jones points out that this labor division also strengthens the gender training that encourages women to seek safety through relationships with men—a situation that makes women vulnerable to abuse, and to poverty in the case of divorce.[19] Rosemary Radford Ruether points out that the "ideology of exploitation" rests on dualistic thought patterns that denigrate women.[20] As should be clear from my remarks in chapter 1 about a dialectical relationship between symbols and "reality," I would not want to describe the relationship between the cultural justification of women's exploitation and the material reality of it in terms of a simplistic cause-and-effect. The symbol of the defiled and hence exploitable woman, and the incarnations of that symbol in everyday life, seem to feed upon one another.

The second face of oppression in Young's analysis is *marginalization*, which can take cultural or economic form (usually the two are intertwined, although Young defines it primarily in terms of economic structures). Marginalized persons constitute a permanent underclass of the despised under- or unemployed. Marginalization often occurs along racial lines, and also often hits the elderly, persons with disabilities, single mothers, or members of the

---

18. Iris Marion Young, *Justice and the Politics of Difference* (Princeton, NJ: Princeton University Press, 1990), ch. 2.
19. Jones, *Feminist Theory and Christian Theology*, 83.
20. Rosemary Radford Ruether, "Dualism and the Nature of Evil in Feminist Theology," *Studies in Christian Ethics* 5, no. 1 (1992): 26–39.

LGBTQ+ community. This "face" of oppression is often tightly associated with problematic aspects of sin-talk. In his discussion of the "sins of sin-talk," Stephen Ray singles out marginalization as one of the primary results of a skewed understanding of sin.[21] Once again, cause and effect cannot be easily determined. Marginalized persons are associated with sin, since, as Ray notes, "the cultural discourse about sin has increasingly focused . . . on the actions of persons and groups within society who have the least social power."[22] At the same time, the language of sin often creates a social underclass as those who are associated with moral irresponsibility are pushed to the margins. An example of this is the scapegoating of persons with AIDS, which associates those who have contracted the HIV virus with particular sinfulness, thus creating and justifying their marginalization.[23] In the West, all women are marginalized to some extent through the association of women with the body, but poor women, women of color, disabled women, lesbians, or transgender women experience marginalization to a greater degree as the result of the intersection of gender constructs with other identity markers.

Third, women of all economic and racial groups also experience *powerlessness* to a lesser or greater degree. This is manifested in the degree, for example, that women have control over and power in their work environments. Here we see clearly how structural and cultural elements of oppression meet. Part of the dilemma of women is that "unfeminine" behavior is met with all kinds of censure, yet when it comes to higher-level employment, "feminine" behavior (passivity, docility, etc.) is seen as an impediment for professional advancement. For women, it is a no-win situation: when acting assertively, they are often perceived as aggressive and censured; but if they act in a more traditionally "feminine" way, they are seen as "not up to it." This perspective affects women's economic circumstances and self-esteem. Women's relative powerlessness also makes them vulnerable to abuse. The intersection of gender with race and economic status increases the powerlessness of poor women and women of color in particular. Again, the intersection of gender with other "categories of marginalization" increases the experience of powerlessness exponentially. White women, for example, while relatively powerless as a gender, nevertheless often exercise power over other women (and, indeed, men of subjugated groups). Womanist theologian Delores Williams uses the term "demonarchy" to refer to the fact that black women's oppression in white-controlled American institutions goes beyond "patriarchally

---

21. Stephen G. Ray Jr., *Do No Harm: Social Sin and Christian Responsibility* (Minneapolis: Fortress, 2003), 1–35.
22. Ibid., 3.
23. For a lengthier discussion, see Rachel Sophia Baard, "Responding to the Kairos of HIV/AIDS," *Theology Today* 65 (2008): 368–81.

derived-privileged oppression" within which white women are subjugated but in which they also share in privileges of their race.[24]

Young identifies the fourth face of oppression as *cultural imperialism*, that is, the universalization of the dominant group's experience and the stereotyping and othering of nondominant groups. Young's category of cultural imperialism evokes Antonio Gramsci's definition of *hegemony* as the manufacturing of the "consent" of the oppressed by establishing the "common sense" of a culture.[25] This category, when applied to women's situation, is closely related to the concept of androcentrism and women's concomitant dehumanization. Cultural imperialism also contributes to the development of self-esteem issues—something we see expressed, for example, in eating disorders. This face of oppression emerges in the case of sin-talk as well, especially when men's particular sins are identified and addressed as if they are universal. I discuss the problems associated with such an approach to sin-talk in chapter 4.

Young defines the fifth face of oppression, *violence*, in terms of the vulnerability of some social groups to the constant and systematic social practice of violence. What makes violence a form of oppression instead of a random occurrence is its systemic character, its existence as a social practice that targets marginalized groups for the purpose of social control. Those in targeted groups live with the constant fear of random, unprovoked attacks on their persons or property. Police shootings of black men, violence against gays, and violence against women are all examples of this kind of oppression.

Young's analysis is not without its critics. Feminist theorist Nancy Fraser, for example, argues that, as helpful as Young's "five faces" categorization might be, they really boil down to only two types of oppression: cultural and economic.[26] Exploitation, marginalization, and powerlessness all fall under the category of political oppression for Young, while cultural imperialism and violence fall under the category of cultural oppression. However, I would suggest that exploitation, marginalization, and powerlessness are as much cultural as structural, and that cultural imperialism and violence have structural elements as well.

One aspect of violence against targeted groups is the reality that violence is employed as an enforcement of the exploitation, marginalization, powerlessness, and cultural imperialism that these groups face, which can take the

---

24. Delores S. Williams, "The Color of Feminism, or, Speaking the Black Woman's Tongue," in *Feminist Theological Ethics: A Reader*, ed. Lois K. Daly (Louisville, KY: Westminster John Knox Press, 1994), 49–50.

25. Antonio Gramsci, *Selections from the Prison Notebooks*, ed. and trans. Quinton Hoare and Geoffrey Nowell Smith (New York: International Publishers, 1971).

26. Nancy Fraser, *Justice Interruptus: Critical Reflections on the "Postsocialist" Condition* (New York: Routledge, 1997), 197–200.

form of state-sanctioned violence in the name of the law.[27] Examples would include the enforcement of segregation laws in the United States until the 1960s, military patrolling of black neighborhoods in apartheid South Africa, or the enforcement of strict interpretations of sharia law in Saudi Arabia. It can also be violence that occurs outside of the law but that expresses and effects control of subjugated groups by dominant groups: one stark example would be whites' lynching of African Americans in the United States, which was "an extralegal punishment sanctioned by the community."[28] I submit that gender violence should be seen as a patriarchal control mechanism, since it is systemic and rooted in sexist cultural practices and perspectives, and it leads women to adjust behavior in order to avoid violence. As a control mechanism within the patriarchal system, I would in fact argue that gender violence, which particularly targets women, is the most significant face of oppression. Let us look at this face of oppression in more detail, since it is central to the feminist conversation on sin, and as such is at the heart of the exigence at which feminist rhetorical interrogation is directed.

GENDER VIOLENCE

Gender violence knows no class, race, religion, or nationality. Not a day goes by that one does not encounter news stories of gender violence. Yet another woman gang raped and left for dead, yet another girl forcibly married to an older man, yet another child's genitals mutilated in the name of culture and marriageability, yet another college student date raped, yet another wife beaten by the man who is supposed to love her more than anyone else ... every day the stories keep coming, like a macabre litany of suffering and death. Gender violence takes many different forms, as Elisabeth Schüssler Fiorenza notes:

> The list of abuse is endless: child-pornography, sexual harassment in schools and jobs, sex-tourism in Asia, Latin America and Africa, trafficking in women, sexual and domestic bondage, gender-specific violations of human rights, lesbian bashing, right-wing neo-Nazi terror against women, mutilation and stoning of women on grounds of infidelity, restriction of movement and exclusion from the public sphere, Purdah in its various forms, sati in India, sexual assault in the workplace, rape in war and peacetime, women refugees and displaced persons, maids and migrant workers, illiteracy, poverty, forced prosti-

---

27. Ann E. Cudd, *Analyzing Oppression*, Studies in Feminist Philosophy (New York: Oxford, 2006), 107.
28. James H. Cone, *The Cross and the Lynching Tree* (Maryknoll, NY: Orbis Books, 2017), 3.

tution, child prostitution, wife bartering, female circumcision, eating disorders, psychiatric hospitalization, battered women and children, incest and child abuse, homelessness, silencing of women, negation of women's rights, HIV infection through husbands, dowry death, isolation of widows and older women, abuse of the mentally ill, emotional violence, cosmetic surgery, cultural marginality, torture, strip search and imprisonment, female infanticide, witch burning, foot binding, rape in marriage, date rape, food deprivation, serial murder, sadomasochism, genital mutilation.... Most of these atrocities are part of women's daily lives around the globe.[29]

The statistics on gender violence are numbing. To be sure, statistics need to be interpreted because they often hide situational differences, and since many cases of gender violence are not reported, some guesswork is involved.[30] Nevertheless, these complexities cannot hide the sheer enormity of the problem.

One of the most comprehensive global surveys on violence against women (based on more than fifty population-based surveys)—conducted in the late 1990s by the Johns Hopkins School of Public Health and the Center for Health and Gender Equity (CHANGE)—indicated that around the world at least one woman in every three has been beaten, coerced into sex, or otherwise abused, or will experience one of these forms of violence in her lifetime. Globally, at least 10 percent to possibly more than 50 percent of adult women have been physically assaulted by an intimate male partner. Psychological abuse usually accompanies physical abuse. One-third to over one-half of cases also involve sexual abuse. Most women who suffer physical aggression are abused repeatedly. In many countries, wife beating is seen as justified—a husband's right to "correct" an erring wife, and women often share this notion.[31]

Little has changed since the CHANGE report in 1999. According to the most recent United Nations fact sheet, compiled from various sources, including a 2013 global review by the World Health Organization, at least 35 percent of women worldwide have experienced physical or sexual partner violence or nonpartner sexual violence. In some countries the numbers are double that. More than 700 million women alive today were married as children, that is, below the age of eighteen—a third of them before the age of fifteen. More than 120 million girls worldwide have experienced forced sexual

---

29. Elisabeth Schüssler Fiorenza, "Introduction," in *Violence against Women*, Concilium 1994/1, ed. Elisabeth Schüssler Fiorenza and Mary Shawn Copeland (Maryknoll, NY: Orbis Books, 1994), vii–viii.
30. Uma Narayan, *Dislocating Cultures: Identities, Traditions, and Third World Feminism* (New York: Routledge, 1997), 101–4.
31. Lori Heise, Mary Ellsberg, and Megan Gottemoeller, "Ending Violence against Women," in *Population Reports*, Johns Hopkins University School of Public Health, Series L, no. 11 (Baltimore, MD: Population Information Program, 1999), 5, https://vawnet.org/sites/default/files/assets/files/2016-10/PopulationReports.pdf.

activity, and 133 million girls have undergone genital mutilation. Women and girls make up the majority of the world's victims of trafficking, whether for labor or sexual exploitation.[32]

Western media and popular culture tend to focus on egregious forms of violence against women that occur in poorer nations, such as female genital mutilation, which happens largely in North Africa. But gender violence is in fact not an "exotic" Majority World problem.[33] According to a 2011 survey by the Centers for Disease Control and Prevention, 22.3 percent of American women (and 14 percent of men) have experienced severe violence at the hands of a domestic partner (including being hit hard, kicked or beaten, or burned on purpose); 19.3 percent of women (and 1.7 percent of men) have been raped; and 15.2 percent of women (and 5.7 percent of men) have experienced stalking. Most of the perpetrators—against female and male victims—are men. The CDC's conclusion is an obvious one: that a "substantial proportion of U.S. female and male adults have experienced some form of sexual violence, stalking, or intimate partner violence at least once during their lifetimes . . . and women, in particular, are heavily impacted over their lifetime."[34] Overall, although both men and women suffer from various forms of violence, in the United States and internationally, women are disproportionately vulnerable to abuse.

In its most extreme forms, violence kills women in large numbers. Nicholas Kristof and Sheryl WuDunn write that more women are killed in "gendercide" in any one decade than people killed in all the genocides of the past century, and that more women were killed in the last fifty years than men in all the battles of the last century.[35] Worldwide, an estimated 40 to 70 percent of homicides of women are committed by intimate partners, often in the context of an abusive relationship.[36]

In 1990 Amartya Sen made headlines with the claim that more than 100 million women are "missing" from the population as a result of unequal access to resources, especially in China and India, where sex ratios are significantly skewed in favor of males. Other researchers took up Sen's thesis and attempted to use more methodologically refined demographic studies in order to assess how many women are missing from the world's population—that is, how

---

32. UN Women, "Facts and Figures: Ending Violence against Women," http://www.unwomen.org/en/what-we-do/ending-violence-against-women/facts-and-figures.

33. The phrase "Majority World" is preferable to the traditional term "Third World," due to the pejorative connotations of the latter.

34. Centers for Disease Control and Prevention, *Morbidity and Mortality Weekly Report*, September 5, 2014, http://www.cdc.gov/mmwr/preview/mmwrhtml/ss6308a1.htm?s_cid=ss6308a1_e.

35. Nicholas D. Kristof and Sheryl WuDunn, *Half the Sky: Turning Oppression into Opportunity for Women Worldwide* (New York: Vintage Books, 2010), xvii.

36. Heise, Ellsberg, and Gottemoeller, "Ending Violence against Women," 19. UN Women, "Facts and Figures," mentions similar numbers.

many women have died as a result of patriarchal practices or were never born due to sex-selection abortion. This research has yielded varying results, and it is of course difficult to prove a negative. But, as Stephan Klasen and Claudia Wink note, overall there is a clear "cumulative impact of gender bias in mortality by estimating the additional number of females of all ages who would be alive if there had been equal treatment of the sexes among the cohorts that are alive today."[37] According to the United Nations Population Fund, more recent estimates indicate approximately 117 million "missing women."[38]

Important as it is to differentiate between physical violence and more "subtle" forms of violence against women, however, it is not only the "spectacular" forms of violence against women that exert a toll on women's lives. For example, nearly half of European women have experienced unwanted sexual advances or other forms of sexual harassment at work; and in the United States, 83 percent of girls in grades eight to eleven have experienced some form of sexual harassment in public schools.[39] Not only does a focus on the "spectacular" silence women who have suffered from hidden yet debilitating forms of violence, but it lets less overtly violent offenders off the hook. Focusing only on spectacular forms of violence against women might silence those women whose experience of violence is "limited" to daily humiliations, such as sexual and general harassment, the curtailing of their movements by the threat of rape, and so on. Pamela Cooper-White maintains that it is valuable to view all these forms of violence against women as a continuum, "because it demonstrates their connectedness and the cumulative effect on women's lives of so many different but related threats to their daily well-being."[40] Simply stated, what Cooper-White is pointing to is the fact that gender violence is a pervasive and systemic phenomenon.

Gender violence should therefore not be understood merely in terms of individual actions, but rather, as the authors of the Johns Hopkins/CHANGE report conclude, "within a 'gender' framework because it stems in part from women's and girls' subordinate status in society."[41] Gender violence, whether violence against women or transgender or gay people, has to do with this broad gender framework. It would appear (although cause and effect are difficult to prove with 100 percent certainty) that where a culture is more egalitar-

---

37. Stephan Klasen and Claudia Wink, "Missing Women: Revisiting the Debate," *Feminist Economics* 9 (2003): 263–99.
38. United Nations Population Fund, "Sex Imbalances at Birth: Current Trends, Consequences, and Policy Implications," August 2012, http://www.unfpa.org/public/home/publications/pid/12405, 4.
39. UN Women, "Facts and Figures."
40. Pamela Cooper-White, *The Cry of Tamar: Violence against Women and the Church's Response* (Minneapolis: Fortress Press, 1995), 44.
41. Heise, Ellsberg, and Gottemoeller, "Ending Violence against Women," 3.

ian and does not operate with strong gender binaries, gender violence is less common, whereas more patriarchal cultures lead to both greater occurrence and greater acceptance of gender violence.[42]

The complexities of the correlation between gender violence and sexism are illustrated by examining rape culture and rape myths. Various scholars have pointed to the correlation between rape myths and female subordination.[43] Correlation is not causation, of course, but history has shown that patriarchal attitudes toward women go hand in hand with the justification of gender violence. The research also clearly shows that women often react to the threat of rape by adapting their lifestyle: those who ascribe to rape myths respond by acting in traditionally feminine ways in order to keep the illusion of control, whereas those who know that any woman can be raped limit their public activities out of safety concerns. Gender violence seemingly not only stems from but also reinforces women's subordinate position in society. It is, in short, an enforcement mechanism that keeps women in a position of being exploited, marginalized, disempowered, and dehumanized.

In a world where male domination is pervasive and women are most frequently seen as members of the inferior gender, gender violence becomes a systemic phenomenon. As such, gender violence is not simply rooted in personal, individual pathology alone (although, of course, individual pathologies do play a role), nor in "natural" traits (which would declare all men aggressors and all women victims), but is instead part of the artificial and multifarious, yet pervasive, phenomena of male dominance and female subordination. Gender violence both reflects the subordinate position of women in so many societies and enforces that subordinate position by compelling women to curtail their movements or self-expression. Therefore, although gender violence takes

---

42. One fascinating example that points in this direction is anthropologist Christine Helliwell's research among the Dayak community of the Gerai in Indonesian Borneo, which suggests that where there is a lack of bodily dimorphism, there is also an absence of rape. In the absence of a view of male genitals as active and aggressive, and female genitals as inactive and vulnerable, the idea of using sex organs for violent means is apparently absent in this culture. See Christine Helliwell, "'It's Only a Penis': Rape, Feminism, and Difference," *Signs: The Journal of Women and Culture and Society* 15, no. 3 (2000): 789–816. Helliwell did not document whether other forms of violence against women occur among the Gerai.

43. See, inter alia, Alyce B. Bunting and Joy B. Reeves, "Exploring Belief Relationships in the Areas of Sex Roles, Religion, and Rape," *Journal of Pastoral Counseling* 16, no. 1 (1981): 53–64; Peggy Reeves Sanday, "The Socio-Cultural Context of Rape: A Cross-Cultural Study," *Journal of Social Issues* 37, no. 4 (1981): 5–27; Martha R. Burt, "Cultural Myths and Supports of Rape," *Journal of Personality and Social Psychology* 38 (1980): 217–30; Gerd Bohner and Norbert Schwarz, "The Threat of Rape: Its Psychological Impact on Nonvictimized Women," in *Sex, Power, Conflict: Evolutionary and Feminist Perspectives*, ed. David M. Buss and Neil M. Malamuth (New York: Oxford University Press, 1996), 173; and Frank Costin and Norbert Schwarz, "Beliefs about Rape and Women's Social Roles: A Four-Nation Study," *Journal of Interpersonal Violence* 2 (1987): 46–56.

many different forms, and is rooted in and gives expression to many different cultural expressions of sexism, it can generally be defined as systemic, continuous, and multifarious harm brought against women's bodies and psyches.

In short, feminist theorists analyze and critique gender violence as a systemic and structural component of women's oppression and not merely the product of the pathological behavior of individual men. When feminist theorists refer to this violence as "systemic and structural," they do not mean only that it is widespread; they are also pointing out how various institutions, and cultural beliefs and practices, create a social climate in which gender violence is not only imaginable but tolerated or accepted as "natural," indeed, as simply part of the human condition. The rhetoric of violence thereby becomes the "common sense" of a culture, that is, it is hegemonic. Gender violence is the central praxis of patriarchy, with *praxis* here defined as the to-and-fro movement of theory and practice. To put it in Iris Marion Young's terms, it expresses and feeds theories of female defilement and marginalization, which reinforces the exploitation of women by encouraging submission to the patriarchal status quo, and which is sustained by the cultural imperialism that feeds women narratives of powerlessness.

Part of the challenge is to think about how we construct masculinity and femininity, and distribute power and respect. Do we associate violence with masculinity, and submissiveness with femininity? Do we frown upon women who are physically strong? Do we reject intelligent women, or only allow a few intelligent women to be the exceptions that prove the rule? Do we write off postmenopausal women? Do women have the right to speak up? And if they do, are they really heard, or are they interrupted, or labeled as angry and shrill? If the answer to these and similar questions is yes, and so often it is, then the table is being set for the oppression of women, including gender violence. The Christian church, with its ideas of female submission in marriage and society, has contributed to cultural expectations that feed gender violence. However, its role in gender violence extends well beyond that, to the level of explicit justification of it, with reference to the Bible. We now turn to an examination of the church's complicity in gender violence.

GENDER VIOLENCE AND THE CHURCH

Instead of being a prophetic presence in a world in which gender violence is epidemic, the church has all too often used rhetoric that normalizes such violence. This goes back centuries, and continues to this day despite some changes in official church rhetoric. Modern Christians might be shocked to hear that Christian churches, for most of their history, justified wife beating, although some efforts were made to limit the extent of the violence. For example, Gratian's classical twelfth-century compilation of canon law said that a husband may "chastise" his wife but not beat her. Yet as Rosemary Radford Ruether notes, subsequent glosses interpreted this to mean that the husband may strike his wife in anger, although he may not "whip her like a slave."[44] She also notes that most customary and town law in the medieval and Renaissance periods gave husbands the right to beat their wives, as long as death did not result. Women in medieval times were publicly humiliated by wearing placards, and could be whipped in public for such behavior as "nagging" their husbands.[45] Ruether speculates that the contempt of celibate legislators for married women (associated with Eve) may have played a role in the church's view that husbands had the right to physically "discipline" their wives.[46]

Despite a more positive view of marriage, the Protestant Reformers were hardly better. Luther's reaction to wifely insubordination was, "When Katie gets saucy, she gets nothing but a box on the ear."[47] Although Calvin frowned on wife battering, he did exhort women who get beaten by their husbands "to bear with patience the cross which God has seen to place upon [them]."[48] To this day this advice is still sometimes directed at Christian women: indeed, the "subtle" misogyny of sending battered wives home to their abusive spouses may linger longer than the misogyny that explicitly justifies wife beating.

Part of the problem is, of course, the Bible, which reflects the patriarchal contexts in which it originated. For example, although it would be a mistake to argue that the Scriptures condone rape, some biblical injunctions require a rapist to pay a fine and marry his victim, which reflects the patriarchal idea that a rape victim is damaged goods, but which certainly does not pay attention to the feelings of the victim. Theological treatments of rape sometimes still seem to define it as first of all a sexual act gone awry instead of the act of violence and aggression that it is. The idea that rape is sinful because it harms the purity of a woman, rather than because it is an injustice against her, still lingers in some Christian circles.[49] One egregious example dates back to as recently as the 1962 Catholic *Dictionary of Moral Theology*, which depicts the

---

44. Rosemary Radford Ruether, "The Western Religious Tradition and Violence against Women in the Home," in *Christianity, Patriarchy, and Abuse: A Feminist Critique*, ed. Carole Carlson Brown and Carole R. Bohn (Cleveland, OH: Pilgrim Press, 1989), 34.

45. Adele Dingle, ed., *Domestic Violence and the Churches: Train the Trainer Manual* (Queensland, Australia: Joint Churches Domestic Violence Project), 38.

46. Ruether, "Western Religious Tradition and Violence against Women," 34.

47. Martin Luther, "Lectures on Genesis," *Luther's Works*, vol. 1, ed. Jaroslav Pelikan (St. Louis, MO: Concordia, 1955), 68–69.

48. P. E. Hughes, ed., *The Register of the Company of the Pastors of Geneva in the Time of Calvin* (Grand Rapids: Eerdmans, 1966), 345.

49. Marie Marshall Fortune, *Sexual Violence: The Unmentionable Sin* (Cleveland, OH: Pilgrim Press, 1983), 66–70.

rape of a virgin as a greater injustice than that of another woman, because "virginity is a good of greatest value, distinct from the right that she has to use of her own body according to her free choice," even adding that reparation of the rape might include marriage between the rapist and the victim, thereby echoing Deuteronomy.[50] This shows more concern for female sexual chastity (which is, at its core, a concern for male patriarchal rights) than for a woman's right to bodily integrity and autonomy. In some conservative Protestant circles in the United States, to this day, sexual assault is likewise often understood more in terms of sexual purity than of justice, and victims are even blamed for supposedly behaving in ways that led to abuse.[51]

The Bible also contains casual acceptance of wife beating. Some prophetic books, such as Hosea, Jeremiah, and Ezekiel, depict the relationship between God and Israel as that between an abusive spouse and his "headstrong, promiscuous, and disobedient" wife who brings punishment upon herself. Renita Weems concludes that "the correlation drawn repeatedly in prophetic literature between divine judgment and husbands battering their wives" shows that "there is probably more than a chance connection between patriarchy and violence against women."[52] One would seriously misjudge Weems's argument if it were read as pointing to a simple causal relationship between the metaphors encountered in this group of prophets, and the everyday practices of Israelite households of the time. These prophetic texts obviously did not introduce domestic violence in Israelite society. But in uncritically reiterating the metaphor of the erring wife who deserves punishment and the injured husband who feels "obliged" to punish her, these prophetic texts reflect and support the patriarchal system within which this practice is normal. Indeed, in lifting up the practice of wife beating to the level of the divine, it sanctifies it to some extent.

Another biblical scholar, Cheryl Exum, points out that depictions of violence against women in biblical narratives often occur within a larger framework of tribal violence, in which the woman is blamed for "causing" retributive violence between tribes because she has been raped, or, euphemistically, "seduced."[53] One finds, for example, in the story of King David

---

50. Roberto Francesco, *The Dictionary of Moral Theology* (London: Burns & Oates, 1962), 1017–18.
51. One of the most infamous examples of this is the Gothard movement. See, e.g., Recovering Grace, "How 'Counseling Sexual Abuse' Blames and Shames Survivors," April 18, 2003, http://www.recoveringgrace.org/2013/04/how-counseling-sexual-abuse-blames-and-shames-survivors/.
52. Renita Weems, *Battered Love: Marriage, Sex, and Violence in the Hebrew Prophets* (Minneapolis: Fortress Press, 1995), 3.
53. J. Cheryl Exum, *Fragmented Women: Feminist (Sub)versions of Biblical Narratives*, Journal for the Study of the Old Testament Supplement Series 163 (Guildford, UK: Sheffield Academic Press—JSOT Press, 1993).

the recurring theme of "the woman who brings death." Thus we frequently encounter a tendency in some biblical texts to blame women for the violence they either suffer or unwittingly "cause."

These examples should suffice to show that the biblical texts are problematic in their casual references to violence against women, the underlying theme in some narratives of blaming women for the violence they suffer, and the way in which rape is understood in terms of purity and a woman's value on the marriage market rather than in justice terms. This outlook played a role in the development of a strong tradition of misogyny and outright justification of gender violence in the church.

To be sure, many modern churches explicitly condemn gender violence, often by using the language of sin. The Roman Catholic Church has issued several statements stating that violence against women is sinful and never justified.[54] Many mainline Protestant churches offer resources to their congregations for dealing with domestic violence.[55] Conservative evangelical Christians, too, show concern with the problem.[56] And of course, with the exception of a few fringe groups, no Christian church would argue in favor of spousal abuse today.

Yet churches for the most part do not address the depths of the underlying theological problems that play a role in gender violence, and do not yet focus on the need for structural change, which feminist activists see as necessary to really address the issue. Indeed, many churches seem to be naïve about the rationale behind biblical injunctions about female virginity, rape, and so forth, being willing at the most to admit some "misuse" of the Bible. An example of this can be seen in Craig S. Keener's "biblical reflections" on rape.[57] He understands rape as first of all a sexual act, and not one of aggression (a tendency that is severely criticized by activists such as Marie Fortune) and shows no awareness of how the rape of women in biblical societies was

---

54. See, e.g., United States Conference of Catholic Bishops, "When I Call for Help: A Pastoral Response to Violence against Women," http://www.usccb.org/issues-and-action/marriage-and-family/marriage/domestic-violence/when-i-call-for-help.cfm.

55. A few examples: the Presbyterian Church (U.S.A.) annually issues a package with resources on dealing with domestic violence: see Turn Mourning into Dancing! A Policy Statement on Healing Domestic Violence at https://www.pcusa.org/resource/turn-mourning-dancing-policy-healing-dom/; the Evangelical Lutheran Church's list of resources is available under the title "Gender-Based Violence" at http://www.elca.org/Our-Work/Publicly-Engaged-Church/Justice-for-Women/Social-Issues/Gender-Based-Violence; to read more about the United Methodist response to domestic violence, see "Domestic Violence Awareness" at https://www.unitedmethodistwomen.org/domestic-violence.

56. See, e.g., Catherine Clark Kroeger and James R. Beck, eds., *Women, Abuse, and the Bible* (Grand Rapids: Baker Books, 1996); Mary A. Kassian, *Women, Creation, and the Fall* (Westchester, IL: Crossway), 1990.

57. Craig S. Keener, "Some Biblical Reflections on Justice, Rape, and an Insensitive Society," in Kroeger and Beck, *Women, Abuse, and the Bible*, 117–30.

primarily interpreted in terms of the infringement of property rights of men and not as a violation of women's bodily integrity. Keener seems more anxious to insist on how biblical rape victims like Tamar were sexually innocent than in criticizing power relations in the Bible that left women vulnerable. His lack of awareness of how rape was blamed on a victim such as Tamar in ancient Israelite society shows clearly in his assumption that "there must have been hundreds of virgin men in Israel eager for her hand, but Tamar chose to avoid intimacy," even adding that "she did not consent to rape, but unlike many rape victims, she did consent to a life of failing to come to terms with what had happened to her." He thus ends up blaming Tamar—if not for the rape itself, then for "failing to come to terms with" it and thus "allowing" it to destroy her life—instead of putting the blame where it belongs, namely on the rapist, and on cultural gender inscriptions that blamed the victim for the rape if she "did not cry out" (Deut. 22:23–29) and marked her as defiled because she had "lost her virginity." This naivety about the historical background to biblical texts and unwillingness to read the texts in their broader literary context contribute further to a lack of focus on structural issues that is unfortunately typical of many religious responses to gender violence. In contrast to Keener, Pamela Cooper-White, in her discussion of the same story, shows that Tamar's rape made her ineligible for marriage in her society, and that her father and brother's response to her rape was not primarily out of concern for her, but had to do with the power politics of the Davidic royal house.[58]

Aside from such problematic perspectives on biblical material, few churches are willing to critically examine the traditional hierarchical marriage relationship, and many still prescribe female submission in marriage. The reality is that female submission in marriage is deeply problematic, and that it serves a paradigm in which gender violence becomes normalized. Evangelical author Carolyn Holderread Heggen writes that, the more she listens to stories of family abuse, the more she is convinced that "we cannot both support patriarchy and stop domestic abuse.... We must teach that the subordination of woman to man's dominance is the result of sin and not an expression of God's intentions."[59] As Elisabeth Schüssler Fiorenza notes, while Christian theology "overtly condemns oppressive forms of exploitation and victimization such as incest, abuse, femicide or rape," the "politics of submission and its attendant virtues of self-sacrifice, docility, subservience, obedience, suffering, unconditional forgiveness, male authority and unquestioning surrender to God's will covertly advocate patriarchal practices of victimization as Christian revelation

---

58. Pamela Cooper-White, *The Cry of Tamar*, 1–14.
59. Carolyn Holderread Heggen, "Religious Beliefs and Abuse," in Kroeger and Beck, *Women, Abuse and the Bible*, 18.

and faith-tradition."[60] In other words, it is not just the gender violence itself that is sinful and worthy of theological-ethical condemnation but also the church's own teachings that create the kind of power relationship in which such violence becomes normalized. Indeed, even where more serious biblical criticism and more egalitarian marriage relationships are advocated, there is often much resistance to feminism and its critiques of the Christian tradition in the church, so that these professions often do not amount to much more than lip service.

In short, the churches that do respond to gender violence for the most part do so without a serious look at structural and theological issues in the church. But by far the most damaging Christian response to gender violence is the churches' overwhelming silence on the issue. This, says prominent activist and theologian Marie Fortune, is probably the most important contributing factor in perpetuating the problem in the church.[61] Fortune's research shows that many victims and abusers hesitate to go to their clergy for fear of the response: they fear talking to yet another person who either does not know how to help or whose "help" may in fact be detrimental. Ironically, she says, "the church has failed to hear the suffering of violent families because, in general, it has failed to speak out."[62]

Without a doubt the church has come a long way toward addressing gender violence. But the analysis of the theological problem needs to go deeper. It is clear that when churches do break their silence on this issue, the response generally does not go much further than support groups or general condemnation. Elizabeth Gerhardt is right when she notes that the churches generally treat gender violence as an ethical issue somewhat separated from the work of theological reflection.[63] The hard questions about the roots of this violence, including the theological roots, are seldom raised. As such, she notes, a "false dichotomy and ideologically based division of faith and ethics" stands in the way of a substantial and unified response to gendercide.[64]

It is here, I argue, that a rhetorical approach to theology becomes appropriate. In such an approach, doctrine is not primarily examined for its internal purity or coherence with other doctrines, but for its messy practical landscape. Rhetorical theology asks the question: How do doctrines function in

---

60. Elisabeth Schüssler Fiorenza, "Introduction," in Schüssler Fiorenza and Copeland, *Violence against Women*, xviii.

61. Marie Marshall Fortune is a leading activist and academic in the area of violence against women in the United States. For more on Marie Fortune's work, her blog, http://www.faithtrustinstitute.org/blog, contains links to many resources and articles.

62. Marie Fortune, "The Church and Domestic Violence," *TSF Bulletin* 8, no. 2 (1984): 17.

63. Elizabeth Gerhardt, *The Cross and Gendercide: A Theological Response to Global Violence against Women and Girls* (Downers Grove, IL: IVP Academic, 2014), 17.

64. Ibid., 18.

the lives of churches, families, and individuals, and for that matter—even today in our increasingly secular age—of societies? What kind of social spaces do doctrines create? What do the symbols of the faith actually do? How do they function?[65]

The focus of this book is on the ways in which one doctrine—the doctrine of sin—functions in the lives of women, specifically as it pertains to the issue of gender violence. Gender violence is the central crisis, the exigence that in part constitutes the *kairos* that calls forth feminist engagement in the rhetorical situation. This *kairos* calls us to be critical of the rhetoric that contributes to this crisis, and to launch a counter-rhetoric. It calls us to reflect on the question: what kind of rhetorical space is created when sin-talk denigrates women or encourages them to accept abuse? And it calls us to reflect on the possibilities of a counter-rhetoric, the creation of an alternative rhetorical space that addresses real sin instead of being destructive. In short, how *does* this doctrine function in the lives of women, and how *should* it function? In the next two chapters, we focus on the first half of this double-sided question, before moving to the second half in the two final chapters. In other words, we first look at how feminist theology responds to the exigence of gender violence by engaging in critical rhetorical inquiry into the harmful rhetoric present in classical sin-talk, and after that we inquire into ways in which feminist theology can be constructive in its own sin-talk.

---

65. My language here is influenced by Elizabeth A. Johnson's recurring question in her landmark publication *She Who Is: The Mystery of God in Feminist Theological Discourse* (New York: Crossroad, 1995), where she examines the ways in which patriarchal God-language functions in the lives of women.

3

Mary

> In humility regard others as better than yourselves.
> —*Philippians 2:3 NRSV*

In the two introductory chapters we examined rhetorical theory and its implications for rhetorical theology, introduced the rhetorical tools for use in tracing feminist discourses on sin, and then discussed the rhetorical situation within which these feminist discourses occur, with specific reference to gender violence. In the next two chapters, we turn to the two main criticisms lodged against classical sin-talk by feminist theologians.

The question, "what do feminist theologians say about the doctrine of sin?" is most often answered by a focus on the now almost-classical criticism of the traditional focus on pride as the root of sin, and the related advice to "in humility regard others as better than yourselves." This critique has its origins in Valerie Saiving's 1960 essay "The Human Situation: A Feminine View," in which she argued against the tendency to depict pride or self-elevation as the root of human pathology, and to see self-sacrificial love as the remedy for this sin.[1] Building on her work, albeit with somewhat different theoretical frameworks, other feminist theologians, such as Judith Plaskow and Susan Nelson Dunfee, have argued that the emphasis on sin-as-pride tends to encourage women to "lose" themselves in harmful ways. Saiving's critique was premised upon a feminist rhetoric of difference, which asked for the inclusion of women's experiences in sin-talk. However, in Plaskow, Dunfee, and others, one can trace a gradual shift toward

---

1. Valerie Saiving, "The Human Situation: A Feminine View," in *Womanspirit Rising: A Feminist Reader in Religion*, ed. Carol Christ and Judith Plaskow (San Francisco: Harper & Row, 1979), 25–42. Although I am using the later publication of this essay for references, it was originally published in *Journal of Religion* 40, no. 2 (April 1960): 100–112.

a feminist rhetoric of oppression, which points to harmful effects in the lives of women as a result of the overemphasis on pride. Therefore, the "pride critique" in fact consists of two distinct (albeit overlapping) feminist critical discourses.

Moreover, the critique of the pride paradigm is only one of two broad themes in feminist criticism of classical sin-talk. The other feminist critique centers around the theme of the blaming of women for sin, as symbolized in the figure of Eve. In chapter 4 I discuss this theme and argue that the symbol of Eve is at the heart of a patriarchal rhetoric of death, in which women are depicted as agents of evil deserving of violence. In this chapter, however, our focus is on Mary, that other quintessential female symbol in classical Christianity. I argue that in the "pride paradigm" of classical sin-talk, the patriarchal ideal of the humble and self-sacrificial Mary is implicitly evoked: the emphasis on pride as the root of sin calls for the virtues of humility and self-sacrifice, which, in a situation of oppression and gender violence, become not virtues but indeed pathologies. As such, an emphasis on pride as the root of sin, without attention to the rhetorical risk in addressing an oppressed audience with the more typical pathology of the oppressor, ends up constituting a patriarchal rhetoric of life-denial.

In short, in this chapter, after a brief historical overview of the emphasis on pride in classical sin-talk, I trace the rhetorical shift in the feminist critique of the pride paradigm, from a rhetoric of difference to a rhetoric of oppression. In combination, these two feminist rhetorical strategies expose a patriarchal rhetoric of life-denial in classical sin-talk, which emphasizes self-sacrifice and humility as cardinal virtues, and which plays a role in the normalization of gender violence.

HISTORICAL OVERVIEW

The emphasis on pride is part of the legacy of St. Augustine of Hippo. Augustine's view of sin is complex, so this chapter merely aims to point to problems in the broader Augustinian trajectory of sin-talk as picked up by feminist scholarship, and not to provide more than a basic analysis of Augustine's doctrine of sin. Augustine's view of sin is rooted in an understanding that humans are defined by what they primarily love: God or themselves. He expressed this in his vision of the two cities, the heavenly formed by love of God, and the earthly by love of self and the things of this world.[2] Within this perspective he

---

2. Augustine, *The City of God*, trans. Henry Bettenson (New York: Penguin, 1984), 14.28, 593–94. This trajectory of sin-talk stands in the "Two Ways" tradition, which we encounter, for example, in the *Didache*, where the "Way of Life," that which is oriented to God, and the "Way of Death," that which is oriented to "this world," are set in stark contrast. See *Didache* 1.1–6.3, http://www.ccel.org/ccel/richardson/fathers.viii.i.iii.html.

developed an understanding of sin as characterized by three moves: the move toward the self (self-elevation or *hubris*, also expressed in love of self or *amor sui*, and pride or *superbia*); the move away from the eternal or heavenly (rebellion against God, also expressed in unbelief); and the corresponding move to the temporal or earthly (concupiscence, that is, inordinate desire). The move to the self is usually seen as the primary one for Augustine. For example, in *The City of God* he writes, "This then is the original evil: man regards himself as his own light, and turns away from that light which would make man himself a light if he would set his heart on it."[3] In other words, there he argues that humans turn away from God as a result of their turn to the self. Pride in the Augustinian sense is not simply a matter of thinking too much of oneself but rather of centering one's life on the self instead of on God. The move to the self therefore logically precedes the move away from God. This furthermore leads to concupiscence, that is, a distorted desire for the things of this world. Pride is therefore fundamentally an antidivine disposition that distorts one's relationship with self, others, and the world. As such, it might best be seen as the root of original sin.

Augustine's perspective on sin includes the view that we lose the happiness we have in God when we turn toward ourselves, and thus we seek to find happiness in the things of this world (concupiscence)—a futile effort, in his view, since time destroys all earthly happiness. That is why, as he so famously says in the first paragraph of the *Confessions*, "our heart is unquiet until it rests in you."[4] The relationship between pride and concupiscence is a complex one, and at times he seems to suggest that concupiscence is actually the root of sin. These words from *The Trinity* are illustrative (although not exhaustive) of Augustine's view: "by the apostasy of pride which is called the beginning of sin, [the soul] strives to grab something more than the whole . . . and because there is nothing more than the whole it is thrust back into anxiety over a part. . . . That is why greed [that is, concupiscence] is called the root of all evils."[5] In other words, whereas pride can be seen as the root of original sin, concupiscence, while itself rooted in pride, is the practical root of actual sins (and both exhibit an antidivine disposition, which is the third interrelated move in his view of sin). As a result, the medieval Scholastics saw concupiscence as the material element in sin, whereas the Reformers often identified concupiscence itself as the essence of sin.[6]

---

3. Augustine, *City of God* 14.13.
4. Augustine, *The Confessions*, in *The Works of Saint Augustine: A Translation for the 21st Century* 1, book 1, trans. Maria Boulding (New York: New City Press, 2001), 1.1.
5. Augustine, *The Trinity*, trans. Edmund Hill (Brooklyn: New City Press, 1991), 12.3.14.
6. Wolfhart Pannenberg, *Anthropology in Theological Perspective*, trans. Matthew J. O'Connell (Edinburgh: T&T Clark, 1985), 87.

This analysis of the roots of sinful actions is compelling in many ways. Augustine suggests that sin is the cause of our unhappiness, because it is at heart a distorted relationship with God, self, and others, thereby offering a concept of sin that centers on the idea of sin as broken relationality or even brokenness of the self. Moreover, in his doctrine of original sin, Augustine teaches that sin is more than individual transgressions, thereby sidestepping the naked moralism of the Pelagian perspective on sin. These emphases on sin as something systemic and not just individualistic, on sin as the cause of unhappiness, and on sin as broken relationality, all resonate with feminist sensibilities. I say more about this in the final two chapters, where I retrieve elements of Augustine's sin-talk in conjunction with John Calvin's prophetic mode of sin-talk.

Despite these and other positive elements, the Augustinian trajectory of sin-talk also often has an androcentric blindness. Augustine's analysis of sin in terms of pride, rebellion, and concupiscence, when placed within a traditional gender framework, becomes harmful to women in two respects. In the first place, although the concept of concupiscence is not limited to the idea of distorted sexual desire in either Augustine's thought or in that of later theologians, they often primarily spoke of concupiscence in terms of sexuality. This is particularly problematic in a context of ascetic animosity toward sexuality, when coupled with an association of women with the body and sexuality. This cluster of associations contributes to the blaming of women for sin, a topic we examine in more detail in the next chapter. Our focus here is on the second problem: the classical tradition usually roots all actual sin in pride. As we already noted above, in Augustine's analysis, the primary sin of pride leads to a loss of our relationship with God, thus causing concupiscence, that is, the distorted desire for the things of this world as replacement for God, which then leads to all kinds of actual sins. Strictly speaking, then, in Augustine's thought concupiscence implies egoism. Interestingly enough, this might be a faint echo of Augustine's past as a rhetorician, as it evokes Cicero: "It would be impossible for them to desire anything unless they had an awareness of themselves and therefore loved themselves and what is theirs."[7] But it also reflects the quintessential moral struggle of a man who had lived a life of ambition and pride: although, as is clear from his *Confessions*, much of his personal struggle was with concupiscence, he clearly saw the latter as rooted in his prideful resistance to God. The result of this way of describing the relationship between pride and concupiscence is that it ultimately defines all sin as an active grasping beyond what is one's God-given position in life.

---

7. Cicero, *De finibus bonorum et malorum*, trans. Harris Rackham, Loeb Classical Library 40, ed. G. P. Goold (New York: Macmillan, 1914), 3.5.

Augustine scholar Ellen Charry remarks that Augustine was likely generalizing from his own sinful proclivities and that his universalization of pride as sin par excellence may be unwarranted, and in fact, since some "suffer from undue timidity, fear, meekness, and excessive anxiety in facing life's normal exigencies . . . touted virtues collapse into faults."[8]

The problem is that, despite the rich and nuanced understanding of sin in Augustine, his emphasis on pride as the root of original sin gave rise to a tradition in Western thought of rhetorically presenting pride as the paradigmatic actual sin. And, as Alistair McFadyen points out, "to view sin as having a paradigmatic form is implicitly to invoke a normative standard of reference for the good, over against which pathological deviations may be discerned."[9] If the fundamental human pathology is the elevation of the self, then the humbling or even the shattering of the self is seen as the prerequisite of becoming "good."

The essence of the feminist critique here is that, by and large, female pathology is typically not rooted in the elevation of the self but in the negation of the self—hence, calling for the shattering of the self or the humility that "regards others as better than ourselves" will end up aggravating, rather than addressing, women's sin. However, the focus of feminist critiques is not so much on Augustine's analysis of sin as an error of love per se, but on the trajectory of sin-talk established by this analysis, in particular the way it functions rhetorically in the pulpit and how it finds its way into the thought of influential modern theologians. Ruth Duck notes that the typical prayer of confession in many churches runs along the lines of, "O God, we confess that we think of ourselves more highly than we ought. Forgive us our pride and teach us humility."[10] She wonders how women, amid their struggles with lack of power, issues of self-esteem, and violence, are going to hear such prayers. In other words, how will the emphasis on sin-as-pride function rhetorically in the lives of women? What kind of "goodness paradigm" is born from such a paradigm of sin, and how does that type of expected "virtue" play into the lives of the oppressed, in this case, women in various patriarchal contexts?

The problem is therefore a rhetorical one. While the Augustinian trajectory of sin-talk has much to recommend it, in particular an underlying recognition

---

8. Ellen T. Charry, "Augustine of Hippo: Father of Christian Psychology," *Anglican Theological Review* 88, no. 4 (Fall 2006): 588.
9. Alistair McFadyen, *Bound to Sin: Abuse, Holocaust and the Christian Doctrine of Sin* (Cambridge: Cambridge University Press, 2000), 136.
10. Ruth Duck, "Sin, Grace, and Gender in Free-Church Protestant Worship," in *Women at Worship: Interpretations of North American Diversity*, ed. Marjorie Proctor-Smith and Janet R. Walton (Louisville, KY: Westminster/John Knox Press, 1993), 55.

that sin is essentially about brokenness in need of healing, it does not always function in the lives of women in a way that is healing. Instead, it adds to the very brokenness it ought to address. Indeed, depending on the context and the audience, the Augustinian trajectory can be very destructive. Feminist critics have not in fact focused sufficiently on Augustine's analysis itself, but have instead looked primarily at the modern Protestant heirs of the Augustinian paradigm, such as Reinhold Niebuhr and Paul Tillich, in part because both of them represent efforts to modernize Augustine's perspective on sin.

Although Niebuhr's and Tillich's existentialist reinterpretations of the Augustinian paradigm attempted to overcome the androcentric assumptions built into it, feminist theologians have pointed out that they ultimately fall back on the rhetorically problematic rooting of human pathology in the turn to the self. Since I look at Niebuhr in more detail when analyzing Plaskow's and Dunfee's critiques of him, a brief summary will suffice here. For Niebuhr, sin takes two basic forms: pride, that is, a negation of one's finitude; and sensuality, that is, the negation of one's freedom, the losing of the self in the world's vitalities.[11] Yet pride remains the real problem for Niebuhr: while his initial analysis seems to point to two opposite forms of sin, he eventually subsumes sensuality under pride, thereby reiterating the traditional framework and its problematic androcentrism.

Something similar happens in Tillich, although he does slightly better than Niebuhr in recognizing "sins of weakness" instead of just hubris.[12] Tillich associates the fall with a universal human estrangement from the Ground of Being, other beings, and the self.[13] In this, Tillich partially echoes Augustine's three sinful moves (away from God, to the self, and to the things of this world in an unhealthy way), as well as Augustine's insights into our existential experience of "restlessness" without God, but the three moves are reinterpreted more explicitly in existentialist and relational terms; it also seems to place the estrangement from God first, rather than the turn to the self (thus reversing Augustine's order). The problematic turn to the self is also seen in terms of estrangement from the true self, rather than self-elevation—a tragic, more than a moral, perspective on hubris.

When it comes to the critique of the pride paradigm, Tillich's ontology, rather than his comments on sin itself, is useful, and here one might note a tension in Tillich's theology. In his ontology, in the first volume of the *Systematic Theology*, Tillich describes humans' essential nature in terms of three

---

11. Reinhold Niebuhr, *The Nature and Destiny of Man: A Christian Interpretation* (New York: Charles Scribner's Sons, 1948), esp. chs. 7–9.
12. Paul Tillich, *The Interpretation of History* (New York: Charles Scribner's Sons, 1936), 93.
13. Paul Tillich, *Systematic Theology*, vol. 2 (Chicago: University of Chicago Press, 1957), 44–59.

sets of polar ontological elements, of which the polar elements of individualization and participation are of particular relevance for our purposes. In the aforementioned existential estrangement these two polar elements risk breaking down into either loneliness, "in which world and communion are lost," or collectivization, "a loss of individuality and subjectivity whereby the self loses its self-relatedness and is transformed into a mere part of an embracing whole." Both of these are moves toward "not being what we essentially are."[14] Within the logic of this ontology, estrangement can include either the extreme individualization that is called pride, or a loss of self in collectivization that feminists point to as the more typical female sin.

However, Tillich's discussion of various forms of sin in volume 2 of his *Systematic Theology* focuses on the traditional categories of hubris, concupiscence, and rebellion, in such a way as to privilege hubris as the real problem.[15] His privileging of hubris here is a disappointing return to a more traditional mode of sin-talk and seems to contradict the potentially helpful insights in his ontology. Therefore, while promising from a feminist perspective, Tillich's view on sin ultimately reflects a reliance on the traditional concept of pride as the root of sin. As such, his sin-talk remains somewhat androcentric.

Although the most prominent feminist critiques of the pride paradigm have focused on the work of Niebuhr and Tillich, in the work of Karl Barth we see most clearly how problematic this paradigm can be even when modern theologians try to be more balanced in their perspective. Like Niebuhr and Tillich, Barth originally focuses not just on pride but includes sloth (similar to Niebuhr's sensuality and Tillich's sin of weakness), as well as falsehood, as other basic forms of sin.[16] However, Barth illustrates the use of the pride theme as a weapon against women when he argues that the notion of gender equality is an attempt to overcome a limit that God thought proper to the creature, and thus a reflection of pride.[17] Moreover, in Barth's argument that a "rebellious" woman will aggravate male tyranny, and that male tyranny should be countered by the "mature and therefore self-restricting woman" who is "in her whole existence an appeal to the kindness of man," the paradigmatic "virtues" of the pride paradigm (humility and self-sacrifice) are clearly directed at women.[18] Indeed, Barth seems to advise women to meet male tyranny with passive nonresistance. So, even though Barth does not, in his basic

14. See Paul Tillich, *Systematic Theology*, vol. 1 (Chicago: University of Chicago Press, 1951), 174–86, 199.
15. Tillich, *Systematic Theology*, 2:47–55.
16. Karl Barth, *Church Dogmatics*, IV/2, ed. G. W. Bromiley and T. F. Torrance, trans. G. W. Bromiley (Edinburgh: T&T Clark, 1958), 403–5.
17. Karl Barth, *Church Dogmatics*, III/4, ed. G. W. Bromiley and T. F. Torrance, trans. A. T. MacKay, T. H. L. Parker, Harold Knight, et al. (Edinburgh: T&T Clark, 1961), 154–59.
18. Ibid., 180–81.

analysis, view pride as the paradigmatic sin, he nevertheless uses the notion of pride to offer potentially detrimental advice to women—in particular, women who find themselves in a violent domestic situation.[19] Here we see how the emphasis on pride is particularly aimed at women because of the traditional Christian belief in the submission of women: if women are expected to be humble because of an ideology of female submission, then the charge of pride is easily directed at women when they make even the slightest move toward self-assertion. As we see in more detail below, although the feminist critique of the pride paradigm starts with merely observing that pride is not always the root sin in people's lives, the critique develops further to respond to this use of the pride paradigm as weapon against women.

Let us now turn to a more in-depth analysis of the feminist critique of the classical emphasis on pride as the root of sin and examine the particular rhetorical strategies that feminist theologians employ in this critique. Initially making use of a rhetoric of difference, feminist theologians have pointed to the fact that the pride paradigm of Christian sin-talk reflects the situation of elite ruling males more than that of women. To this has gradually been added a rhetoric of oppression that exposes some dangerous dynamics inherent in the emphasis on pride. By making use of these distinct rhetorical strategies, feminist theologians expose a patriarchal rhetoric of life-denial in classical sin-talk, aimed particularly at women. This rhetoric of life-denial is closely associated with the patriarchal symbol of Mary, who represents the quintessential humble and self-sacrificial "good woman."

THE FEMINIST RHETORIC OF DIFFERENCE

As mentioned above, the feminist conversation on the pride paradigm originated in 1960 with Valerie Saiving's argument that the "widespread tendency in contemporary theology to describe man's predicament as rising from his separateness and the anxiety occasioned by it and to identify sin with self-assertion and love with selflessness" excludes women's experience, since women tend more to the negation of the self than to pride.[20] This critique therefore clearly starts with a feminist rhetoric of difference.

One should note that Saiving's essay reflects an essentialist understanding of gender. Although allowing for some "plasticity of human nature," she argues

---

19. For a thoughtful defense of Barth, see Daniel Migliore, "Sin and Self-Loss: Karl Barth and the Feminist Critique of Traditional Doctrines of Sin," in *Many Voices, One God: Being Faithful in a Pluralistic World*, ed. Walter Brueggemann and George W. Stroup (Louisville, KY: Westminster John Knox Press, 1998), 147–49.
20. Saiving, "Human Situation," 25–26.

for an essential "substratum or core of masculine and feminine orientations."[21] Based on her reading of the basic structures of male and female sexuality, she posits an essential femininity characterized by passivity, closeness to nature, and lack of ambition due to the fulfillment of motherhood. Conversely, in her understanding, masculinity is constructed from the basis of a greater sense of insecurity, partly because Saiving believes that the male individual has to disassociate himself more from his mother (the primary caregiver) and has to compensate for the inability to bear children by external achievement. So, in Saiving's view, masculinity is characterized by an endless process of becoming, while in femininity the emphasis is on being, which leads to a greater degree of natural security and a lesser degree of anxiety in women than in men, which lead to a difference in the way men and women sin. From this perspective, she launches her critique of the classical emphasis on pride as the root of sin:

> For the temptations of woman *as woman* are not the same as the temptations of man *as man*, and the specifically feminine forms of sin—"feminine" not because they are confined to women or because women are incapable of sinning in other ways but because they are outgrowths of the basic feminine character structure—have a quality which can never be encompassed by such terms as "pride" and "will-to-power." They are better suggested by such items as triviality, distractibility, and diffuseness; lack of an organizing center or focus; dependence on others for one's own self-definition; tolerance at the expense of standards of excellence; inability to respect the boundaries of privacy; sentimentality, gossipy sociability, and mistrust of reason—in short, underdevelopment or negation of the self.[22]

Saiving's contribution is simultaneously brilliant in its originality and problematic in some ways. In her reliance on essentialism, her essay reflects Western patriarchy's association of women with nature and men with culture, which leads her to conclude that women, being "closer to nature," lack a creative drive, which enables women to perform routine tasks "cheerfully," but which also leads to diffuseness of purpose, distractibility, a lack of discrimination, and an inability to focus.[23] Her language here reminds one of the dangers of a feminist rhetoric of difference: it often sounds quite similar to patriarchal rhetoric and risks being coopted by it. Furthermore, Saiving identifies emerging Western cultural trends in terms of greater "feminizing," which she associates with "indiscriminate tolerance which suspects or rejects all objective criteria of excellence."[24] Hence, her primary focus in the essay is

21. Ibid., 29.
22. Ibid., 37.
23. Ibid., 38.
24. Ibid., 10, 38.

not the impact that the emphasis on pride might have on women, although she does include that in her reflection. Instead, what she seems to be most concerned with is what she perceives as a cultural shift toward "feminization," in which the "typical sin" will not be pride but underdevelopment of the self. Saiving argues that, in view of what she sees as the increasing "feminizing" of society—that is, a growing tendency to merge individual identity into the identities of others—theology ought to reconsider its estimate of the human condition, for "a feminine society will have its own special potentialities for good and evil, to which a theology based solely on masculine experience may well be irrelevant."[25] This view of the prevailing culture in the West does not seem to be based on any particular sociological analysis.

Despite these flaws, Saiving's contribution is very important, both in itself and because of the conversation it birthed. Her primary contribution lies in the suggestion that the "feminine" needs to be part of scholarly analysis of the human situation. Her essay thereby represents the birth of modern feminist theology, which starts with a rhetoric of difference, that is, an emphasis on the ways in which women's experiences differ from those of men (in general). Secondarily, her essay also foreshadows the rhetoric of oppression, that is, the feminist approach that emphasizes the ways in which the rhetoric of sin-as-pride is harmful to women, which more clearly emerges in later contributions to this conversation. This foreshadowing of the rhetoric of oppression can be discerned in her comments on how Christianity's "doctrine of love" is bad for women. Saiving is, of course, writing at the end of the 1950s, a decade when, as she notes, women were being pressured to return to the traditional role of nurturing just when they had started to develop a greater sense of self. Theology, however, responds inadequately to the desire of women to develop a greater sense of self: "Yet theology, to the extent that it has defined the human condition on the basis of masculine experience, continues to speak of such desires as sin or the temptation to sin."[26] Her premise is that the notion of sin is a concept that is mutually dependent on the ethics of love, and that, therefore, to the extent that contemporary theology has described the human condition inaccurately, its love ethic is also in question. That means that if pride is not typically "women's sin," then the concomitant virtue of self-sacrificial love is to be questioned as a central norm for women. Although she primarily operates with a rhetoric of difference, Saiving's essay therefore opens the door for a more in-depth critique of the pride paradigm premised on a rhetoric of oppression.

In terms of rhetorical theory, one can say that Saiving is among the first theologians to recognize and rhetorically create awareness of the feminist

25. Ibid., 41.
26. Ibid., 39.

rhetorical situation. Her discerning of the *kairos* of the feminist rhetorical situation is flawed, particularly in her identification of a Western cultural shift toward greater feminization and her essentialist assumptions about gender. But in other ways she names the crisis element of the *kairos* well in noticing that the full human experience is not included in Christian theology's language of sin, and in perceiving that this in fact has harmful effects on women.

Judith Plaskow, writing nearly two decades later, accepts and expands Saiving's understanding of women's more typical sin, naming women's sin "sensuality."[27] Plaskow both borrows from and criticizes Reinhold Niebuhr in her argument. She points to an ambiguity in Niebuhr's view of sensuality: his initial, broader definition understands sensuality as the abdication of troublesome freedom and thus as the opposite of pride, but later he defines sensuality as a secondary form of pride, which leads to a narrower understanding of sensuality in terms of undue identification with particular impulses and desires, that is, concupiscence.[28] In subordinating sensuality to pride, Niebuhr ends up focusing only on those aspects of sensuality that do seem to follow from pride, thus neglecting important dimensions of the sin of flight-from-freedom. In arguing that sensuality is "women's sin," Plaskow has the broader of Niebuhr's definitions in mind, that is, abdication of freedom, and not classical concupiscence—in other words, sin that is the opposite, and not the result, of pride. Her argument is therefore that, "given society's expectations concerning them, [women] are more liable to 'become lost in the detailed processes, activities, and interests of existence.'"[29]

According to Plaskow's analysis, then, "women's sin" is sensuality, although not a sensuality that derives from pride, but something that is the opposite of pride. However, as Susan Nelson Dunfee points out, the term "sensuality" for this sin leads to problems because of its association with traditional concupiscence. She recognizes the fact that Niebuhr uses the terms in two distinct ways but is critical of Niebuhr's choice of the term in the first place.[30] She believes that the use of the term "sensuality" reveals a lack of development in Niebuhr's thought, in that the full meaning of sensuality as a state of escapism is not developed, and that the narrowness of his terminology leads him away from his initial insight. Hence she opts to call "women's sin" the "sin of hiding" rather than "sensuality."

27. Judith Plaskow, *Sex, Sin, and Grace: Women's Experience and the Theologies of Reinhold Niebuhr and Paul Tillich* (New York: University Press of America, 1980), 63. She does note in a footnote (188n45) that this might not be the best term to use, but uses it due to Niebuhr's use of the term.
28. Reinhold Niebuhr, *The Nature and Destiny of Man*, 185, 228.
29. Plaskow, *Sex, Sin, and Grace*, 63.
30. Susan Nelson Dunfee, "The Sin of Hiding: A Feminist Critique of Reinhold Niebuhr's Account of the Sin of Pride," *Soundings* 65 (Fall 1982): 316–27.

This distinction between a broader understanding of sensuality as flight from freedom, and a narrower understanding of sensuality as concupiscence (especially if understood largely in sexual terms), is an important one to make. Christian tradition has indeed tended to say that "women's sin" is sensuality, but then in the narrow sense of carnality due to an association of women with the body. In making a distinction between two definitions of sensuality in Niebuhr's thought, Plaskow and Dunfee are clearly arguing that the typical sin of which women are the agents is not rooted in a deficiency of women's bodies (something that is suggested by Aristotelian/Thomistic biology), but in the cultural captivity of their minds. It is, in other words, a cultural construct of patriarchy, not an essential weakness attributable to women being the "weaker sex." In short, feminist theologians, in speaking of "sensuality" as women's sin, do not have in mind concupiscence in the classical sense (i.e., the carnal result of the sin of pride, or the material element of sin), but rather a sin that is the opposite of pride, where the self is not hubristically set in the place of God, but rather lost. However, Susan Nelson Dunfee is correct in noting that describing this sin with the term "sensuality" is ultimately problematic, given its associations with concupiscence, especially in light of women/body/sexuality/concupiscence associations in classical sin-talk. The language of "loss of self" is a more accurate description of the typical female pathology identified in this feminist critique.

To conclude this section, in the earlier layers of the feminist critique of the pride paradigm in sin-talk, in the writings of Saiving, Plaskow, and Dunfee, the emphasis is primarily on the difference that gender makes. The basic argument is that gender needs to be accounted for when analyzing sin and its roots. If women are prone to sins of self-loss, then rhetorically presenting pride as the paradigmatic sin fails to address women, thus not reaching women with the word of grace that is implicit in sin-talk. The recognition that notions of sin and grace are intertwined (a recognition already present in Saiving's essay, although it is not her primary focus) gives rise to a new kind of rhetoric in feminist theology's discussion of the pride paradigm. Although building on Saiving's original critique, feminist theologians have gradually moved away from the idea that theology should merely recognize that "women sin differently," and toward the idea that an inordinate focus on sin as pride may be physically and psychologically harmful to women. So, the implicit rhetoric of oppression already present in Saiving's essay becomes more pronounced as other feminist theologians continue the conversation. In other words, as the feminist conversation on the pride paradigm develops, the *kairos* of the feminist rhetorical situation is increasingly named not only in terms of androcentrism but also of sexist patterns and more broadly of patriarchal oppression.

THE FEMINIST RHETORIC OF OPPRESSION

I have suggested that there is a shift in rhetorical strategy from Saiving, on the one hand, to Plaskow and Dunfee, on the other hand: from a strong rhetoric of difference accompanied by a subtle hint at the rhetoric of oppression to a more subdued rhetoric of difference increasingly accompanied by a rhetoric of oppression. This eventually connects with the strong rhetoric of oppression one sees in the other main feminist conversation on sin, on the symbol of Eve. Here it is not Eve, however, but the symbol of Mary that is evoked by sin-talk, and here, too, feminist rhetoric gradually shifts to a strong and explicit rhetoric of oppression.

The shift toward a rhetoric of oppression is rooted in a less essentialist perspective on "women's experience." In contrast to Saiving, Judith Plaskow takes a more constructivist route in her understanding of "women's experience," rejecting both an understanding of women's experience in terms of some kind of "true" feminine nature rooted in biology, and speculation of what women's experience would be in abstraction from male culture and education. She therefore defines "women's experience" as "the experience of women in the course of a history never free from cultural role definitions."[31] Making use of anthropologist Sherry Ortner's insight that "the whole scheme is a construct of culture rather than a fact of nature," Plaskow argues that women are not in reality any closer to or further from nature than men.[32] In Western culture, says Plaskow, the woman/nature association is linked to a woman/passivity association and subsequent relegation of women to the domestic sphere, including an understanding of women's sexuality in terms of passivity. Plaskow sees naturalness and passivity as the two main cultural gender inscriptions that form Western women's subjectivity and agency. This leads her to conclude that feminine psychology, including the traits of naturalness and passivity, is a portrait of the "total feminine situation," which includes cultural expectations as to role and psychology.[33] She therefore agrees with Saiving's premise that women's experiences are generally different from those of men and that this needs to be kept in mind in theology, but she sees this as based on the different socialization of women from that of men, and not on biological grounds.[34]

Because anthropological studies have exposed a variance in sex roles in different cultures, Plaskow concludes that there is little logical coherence between gender inscriptions and women's bodies—a conclusion that is

---

31. Plaskow, *Sex, Sin, and Grace*, 11.
32. Ibid., 13.
33. Ibid., 33.
34. Ibid., 48.

typical of constructivism. It also shows that there is no single female experience, because women's experience is tied up with the specific cultural expectations within which they live.[35] Relatedly, one can point out that race, class, or other variants will lead some women to have a great deal more pride than others, and some men to have a great deal less. But this complexity does not negate the basic point of this critique, namely that it is problematic for Christianity to present pride as the paradigmatic sin without taking into consideration how this might rhetorically function in the lives of oppressed groups, and especially the billions of women who live with various forms of male domination.

Due to her emphasis on the cultural construction of women's experience, Plaskow's question for traditional theologies is somewhat different from that of Valerie Saiving: not only whether they exclude "women's experience" but also whether they have appropriated and are perpetuating traditional patriarchal gender constructs. Therefore Plaskow's shift in theoretical presuppositions leads to a shift in the feminist rhetorical strategy that she employs: from a rhetoric of difference to a rhetoric of oppression. A strong rhetoric of difference is still possible on constructivist grounds and is present in Plaskow's analysis, but the more explicit use of a rhetoric of oppression here is significant. No longer is the focus primarily on how sin-talk might be missing out on previously ignored aspects of sin by ignoring the particular experiences of women. Rather, the focus is on how an androcentric rhetoric of sin actually perpetuates structures that oppress women. This rhetoric of oppression grows stronger as the focus shifts to the view of "grace" that would follow in the wake of the androcentric sin-talk critiqued by Saiving, Plaskow, and Dunfee—a question already present in Saiving's remarks on the doctrine of love implicit in this way of talking about sin, but not fully developed there. Once more, Plaskow's and Dunfee's discussions of Niebuhr serve as illustrations.

Because Niebuhr abandons his initial insights to ultimately depict pride as the primary sin, says Plaskow, grace is depicted as a shattering of the self. This view of grace, she says, "does not take into account the fact that the structure of human freedom both poses a danger (its prideful misuse) and imposes a responsibility (its full realization)—and that therefore the other side of the shattering of the self must be its reconstitution in responsibility before God."[36] Furthermore, humility and self-sacrifice are the ideals held before a self constantly tempted to sinful self-assertion. The problem is that the language of humility and self-sacrifice becomes destructive when it

---

35. Ibid., 31.
36. Ibid., 84.

suggests that the struggle to become a centered self is sinful. This theology, as Plaskow points out, is not merely irrelevant to women's experience but serves to reinforce women's servitude.[37]

Plaskow argues that Tillich's ontology leads him into a similar mistake.[38] His ontological, rather than moral, understanding of the fall equates it with the moment of self-actualization. Thus, self-constitution is also simultaneously the realization of estrangement, while the failure to act has no clear ontological claim to be considered sin. Although he does recognize a "sin of weakness," Plaskow argues that "it remains the case that Tillich's identification of the choice for self-actualization with the fall provides no way of explaining how or why uncreative weakness is not, so to speak, a 'fall back' toward essence or reunion with the divine ground."[39] In fact, Plaskow argues that Tillich seems to be running the risk of reinforcing the stereotype that lack of self-assertion is good and holy. Thus she concludes that Tillich's theology, like Niebuhr's, "protects and reinforces the status quo."[40]

My earlier analysis of Tillich in this chapter shows that my reading of Tillich differs somewhat from Plaskow's. Plaskow's critique of Tillich does not consistently keep in mind that Tillich's notion of estrangement is not understood wholly in moral terms, which means that blame is not necessarily attached to self-actualization. Since self-actualization is an ontological concept in Tillich, it is not the personal self-actualization that feminist discourse aims at. Tillich sees self-actualization as necessary, not blameworthy, since the state of innocence prior to self-actualization is not a state of perfection. Even if, as Plaskow seems to believe, self-actualization could be attached to some form of blame, this would still not make non-self-actualization (i.e., remaining in the "state of innocence") a virtue for Tillich. Plaskow might be running the risk of reading traditional moral categories into Tillich's theology at a point where he is not operating with moral categories. Her critique of this type of problem is more applicable to Niebuhr, who does work with moral categories. However, to the extent that Tillich's ontological concept of estrangement is rhetorically associated with the fall, his theology can be seen as succumbing to the same problem as the one found in Niebuhr: when "sensuality" is rooted in a primary sin of pride instead of being seen as its opposite, the loss of self is transformed into a "virtue" that is harmful to women. More importantly, as I mentioned earlier, Tillich does eventually fall back onto traditional moral categories that privilege pride as the primary sin.

37. Ibid., 87.
38. Ibid., 110, 117–20.
39. Ibid., 118.
40. Ibid., 120.

In a similar vein, Susan Nelson Dunfee argues that, by subsuming the sin of hiding under the sin of pride, Niebuhr lost sight of his original insight and ended up positing that which he initially calls "sin" as virtue.[41] The result of positing this "sin of hiding," as she calls it, as a virtue is that one becomes glorified for not asserting oneself. However, Dunfee argues that the problem with the emphasis on pride does not remain on the level of either excluding women's experience in our understanding of sin (Saiving's emphasis), or of preserving a status quo that acculturates women into passivity (Plaskow's emphasis), but extends to the creation of patterns of bondage and repression of women, and of encouraging self-hatred (including self-hatred taken to violent extremes). The result is that gender violence is not limited to the traditional categories of rape, gynecological mutilation, and so on, but "is also being etched into the secret lives of women who turn against themselves in self-hatred; who lose themselves in alcohol, drugs, starvation diets—or in the frenetic activity of trying to please everyone else."[42]

Dunfee argues that the emphasis on pride and its subsequent narrow understanding of sensuality leave women in a threefold bondage of guilt.[43] In the first place, if the root of sin is pride, then a woman is guilty if she desires to become a self, that is, if she is not willing to fit the patriarchal model of female humility and self-sacrifice. Second, as we have seen, if sensuality is seen as secondary to pride, the aspect of "sensuality" as self-loss is lost, and only an understanding of sensuality as carnality remains, which, in connection with Western gender binaries that identify women with the body and sexuality, declares her guilty of being the Temptress, symbolized by Eve. Third, since this scheme of things ignores her real sin, that of "flight from freedom," and actually rewards it and declares it virtuous, she is left in the state of alienation from her true self and from what God wants for her. Dunfee argues that, until women repent of their "real sin," that is, the sin of self-sacrifice to the point of near-annihilation, they will know no end to the cycle of guilt and violence turned inward. The problem is that the traditional emphasis on pride as sin leads to a soteriology that prohibits women from "repenting" of the "sin of self-loss" by describing it as a virtue, and thereby keeping women locked in a logic of self-hatred and the acceptance of violence.

To summarize, while the feminist critique of the pride paradigm is rooted in an initial rhetoric of difference, it also includes, and eventually almost completely shifts to, a feminist rhetoric of oppression that exposes a patriarchal rhetoric of life-denial. We now turn our attention to the patriarchal rhetoric of life-denial, captured in the symbol of Mary, in more detail.

41. Dunfee, "Sin of Hiding," 320–24.
42. Ibid., 316.
43. Ibid., 323.

THE PATRIARCHAL RHETORIC OF LIFE-DENIAL

As we have seen, in shifting from an essentialist to a more constructivist approach in her understanding of women, Judith Plaskow changes the *kairos* question at the heart of the pride critique: not merely whether the tradition excludes women's experience in formulating its doctrine of sin, but whether it perpetuates the dominant culture in which women are oppressed. This move constitutes a shift from a rhetoric of difference that names "women's sin" to a rhetoric of oppression that names the way in which sin-talk sins against women. Susan Nelson Dunfee makes the move to an even stronger rhetoric of oppression, by arguing that the overemphasis on pride results in the active repression of women to the point of self-hatred. This feminist analysis shows that the later Augustinian trajectory of sin-talk, by rhetorically suggesting that pride (understood simply as thinking too highly of oneself) is the paradigmatic *actual* sin, loses some of the nuances in Augustine's thought. In emphasizing pride in this manner, classical sin-talk therefore ignores women's sin of hiding, and it also encourages a destructive "virtue" of denying an already barely existing self to the point of denying life itself. A situation is created in which women (as subordinate members of traditional society) are either to be "good" in terms of being humble and self-sacrificial, or they are branded as "evil" and thus are to be sacrificed. In the process, as Mary Daly points out in her strong rhetoric of oppression, women are sketched as quintessential victims:

> It is significant that it is not only the *negative* qualities of a victim that have been projected upon women: the propensity for being temptresses, the evil and matter-bound "nature" of the female, the alleged shallowness of mind, weakness of will, and hyper-emotionality. The qualities Christianity *idealizes*, especially for women, are also those of a victim: sacrificial love, passive acceptance of suffering, humility, meekness, etc.[44]

This quote neatly captures the two themes in classical Christian sin-talk criticized by feminist theologians, and the two corresponding female symbols that dominate the Christian tradition, those of Eve and Mary. From both sides, it would appear, women are set up as victims: scapegoats for the problem of sin and therefore "punishable," women in particular are exhorted to humility, thus creating a "goodness paradigm" that sets forth ideals that support victim status for women. If the sin to which grace responds is rooted in pride, then justification (the restoration of the divine-human relationship)

---

44. Mary Daly, *Beyond God the Father: Toward a Philosophy of Women's Liberation* (Boston: Beacon, 1973), 76–77.

has to start with the shattering of the self, and sanctification (the day-to-day overcoming of sin and the living of a "good" life) is understood in terms of humility and self-sacrifice. Instead of grace clearly presented in terms of healing, it then all too easily becomes "destructive grace."[45]

As I suggested earlier, there is a strong healing metaphor in Augustine's understanding of sin if it is interpreted in terms of brokenness in the self and its relationships. But the classical Augustinian trajectory of sin-talk, in its emphasis on pride, loses this healing emphasis and instead becomes destructive, for three reasons, the first of which is that pride is often rhetorically presented simply as an individual moral failure rather than a statement about a systemic distortion of human relationality to self, others, and the divine. This rhetorical emphasis on individual sin is more Pelagian than Augustinian, of course, even though it is superimposed upon an Augustinian framework. Second, and related, rhetorically presenting pride as an individual actual sin separates it from the existential and relational insights in Augustine's analysis of the human condition, which is classically named "original sin," where pride is intimately related to the loss of the divine-human relationship and the breaking of the authentic self. Pride therefore comes to stand alone as the "ultimate sin," with little reference to the fact that what is really at the heart of Augustine's insights is a loss of integrity in the self and in relationality. Here Augustine is partially at fault for prioritizing pride as the first among the three relationality-breaking "moves" at the heart of original sin, but the later Augustinian trajectory aggravates the problem by emphasizing pride in such an aggressive, moralistic way. Third, as is emphasized in the above-mentioned feminist critiques, the most important reason why the emphasis on pride is destructive is that it functions within an overall rhetorical situation characterized by a blaming of women for sin, cultural beliefs about women's secondary status, religious prescriptions of female submission, and female socialization into inferiority, self-sacrificial relationality, passivity, and so forth.

Here Augustine and indeed almost the entire Christian tradition, by emphasizing female inferiority and submission, are deeply guilty of contributing to the patriarchal oppression that makes up the crisis at the heart of the feminist rhetorical situation. Given the "total feminine situation" in a world characterized by pervasive male domination and gender violence, it becomes clear that a soteriological paradigm suggesting that the essence of sin is the overstepping of God-given boundaries by the affirmation of the self, and

---

45. For a lengthier discussion of this concept, see Rachel Sophia Baard, "Original Grace, Not Destructive Grace: A Feminist Appropriation of Paul Tillich's Notion of Acceptance," *Journal of Religion* 87 (July 2007): 411–34.

which suggests that the essence of virtue is self-sacrificial and humble giving of the self, is dangerous to those who are already oppressed.

A telling example of the ominous undertones in a seemingly pious text can be found in St. Benedict's ladder to humility, which includes reverence for God, rejection of desires, obedience, patience, confession, contentment, self-reproach, silence, seriousness, simple speech, and humility in appearance and demeanor. In this schema, writes feminist author Carol Lakey Hess, anger is discouraged and patience in suffering is encouraged as expressions of humility. How do women and girls, scripted by the oppressions of the patriarchal system and its sexism and androcentrism, hear this? Hess writes,

> Girls, already raised to reject their own needs, are further instructed to reject their own will as inherently opposed to God's will; girls, already expected to obey men, are told to submit themselves to others in all obedience; girls, already assumed to endure subordination, are told to endure patiently everything that comes their way and to be content in all things; girls, already self-doubting, are encouraged to reproach themselves fully; girls, already hesitant to express their voices, are trained to cultivate quietness and silence as spiritual virtues. In a culture where discrimination and violence against women are prevalent, we are training women to be accomplices in the sins against them.[46]

In short, the emphasis on humility, given the overall rhetorical situation that women typically inhabit, encourages the acceptance of gender violence. Simply said, in the words of Christine Gudorf, "To a battered wife the message of self-sacrifice is easily interpreted in terms of accepting her abuse."[47] Similarly, Mary John Mananzan points to the "interiorization of women about their inferiority and all the other stereotyped ideas about femininity which have contributed to their susceptibility for victimization."[48] After all, hegemony is not simply top-down force, but it is the "discursive face of power," the power to establish the "common sense" of a society, thereby manufacturing the "consent" of the oppressed in their own oppression. Does Christian theology, inadvertently or not, manufacture the consent of the oppressed to

---

46. Carol Lakey Hess, "Reclaiming Ourselves: A Spirituality for Women's Empowerment," in *Women, Gender, and Christian Community*, ed. Jane Dempsey Douglass and James F. Kay (Louisville, KY: Westminster John Knox Press, 1997), 147.
47. Christine E. Gudorf, *Victimization: Examining Christian Complicity* (Philadelphia: Trinity Press International, 1992), 91. See also Joanne Carlson Brown and Rebecca Parker, "For God So Loved the World?" in *Christianity, Patriarchy, and Abuse*, ed. Joanne Carlson Brown and Carole R. Bohn (Cleveland, OH: Pilgrim Press, 1989), 1.
48. Mary John Mananzan, "Feminine Socialization: Women as Victims and Collaborators," in *Violence against Women*, Concilium 1994/1, ed. Elisabeth Schüssler Fiorenza and Mary Shawn Copeland (Maryknoll, NY: Orbis Books, 1994), 44–52.

their own oppression by positing humility as the heart of Christian spirituality? Sexist hegemony in the church not only consists of male hierarchies but also of various theological theories about the inferior status of women, the particular "role" women are to play, ideas like "gender complementarity," and so on, all of which explicitly or implicitly seek the "consent" of women to their own oppression. The emphasis on sin-as-pride, and the corresponding positing of humility and self-sacrifice as virtues, is part of this: although this rhetoric is ostensibly aimed at both genders, it functions differently in the case of those who are already expected to be subservient than in the case of those who are encouraged to be dominant.

"Consent" should not be taken here to indicate individual, overt consent to violence. The concept of consent is obviously controversial in relation especially to rape, where it is often argued by rape apologists that women "really wanted it." Instead, what I am talking about here is a general acculturation of women into submissiveness and acceptance. It is not a question of acculturating women into "really wanting it," but rather of encouraging women's "endurance" instead of resistance. Of course, as Mary Potter Engel points out, there are times when endurance, "passivity," and nonresistance are necessary for survival; my point here is a more general cultural one, which does not negate the need for strategic passivity for the sake of survival in specific situations of violence.[49] This emphasis also does not mean that women have no agency (an impression that might be given by Plaskow's use of the term "passivity," even though she does not intend to negate female agency), but rather that women's agency is often shaped to conform to a patriarchal status quo that includes routine gender violence. Alistair McFadyen notes that even when pride is seen primarily as the sin of men, the "good" woman is still expected to react with acquiescence, lest she should also "fall" into pride: "The teaching of the tradition appears to be that the sin which belongs to the male role of 'heroic' (Promethean) agency is to be met by the patient virtue of female passivity: don't resist when he beats you, for that would add your pride to his."[50]

With this sin-and-grace pairing, female anger and resistance to oppression are easily construed as the sort of self-concern that counts as sinful pride. As a matter of fact, Susan Brooks Thistlethwaite points out that resistance to violence is often met with reproach that such resistance is unbiblical and wrong—a reproach that is especially devastating to women of more traditional

---

49. Mary Potter Engel, "Evil, Sin, and the Violation of the Vulnerable," in *Lift Every Voice: Constructing Theologies from the Underside*, ed. Susan Brooks Thistlethwaite and Mary Potter Engel (San Francisco: Harper & Row, 1998), 160.

50. McFadyen, *Bound to Sin*, 138.

Christian persuasions.[51] Thistlethwaite notes that some women, when met by this kind of reproach, cease to struggle further, while others abandon the church for the sake of their very survival. Her focus is particularly on those women who find themselves in an enduring situation of violence, such as women living with an abusive partner, but it would be an oversimplification to assume that her point is only valid in such extreme situations. In fact, while some women obviously live in situations of more immediate danger, no woman lives outside of the context of pervasive gender violence.[52] By suggesting that standing up for yourself is sinful, the church suppresses female anger at this situation of violence. Indeed, female resistance against systemic violence is often met with derision, rooted in both a denial of the extent of gender violence and disapproval of female anger.

Shaped by cultural discourses that frown upon female anger, women often react to violence with self-blame instead of anger. Mary Potter Engel notes that self-blame is both a major cause and reinforcer of "surplus powerlessness, for it deflects attention away from the real problems."[53] Instead of putting the blame where it belongs, namely on the aggressor, women who are raped, battered, or harassed often blame themselves, thereby echoing society's blaming of women. Referring to Harriet Lerner's notion that anger is the crucial first step in developing self-awareness, feminist theologian Rita Nakashima Brock argues that anger that frees us to claim ourselves must be recognized and embraced as an aspect of ourselves.[54] In teaching that anger is sinful, and in suggesting through its teachings on female submission that women in particular should not be angry, Christianity contributes to a culture that leads women to turn their anger inward and discourages women from developing a spirit of rebellion against gender violence. Therefore, traditional understandings of sin as rooted in pride have robbed women of the power and impact of righteous indignation and healthy anger, because anger and resistance have been portrayed as expressions of pride.[55] The emphasis on pride as sin therefore ironically paralyzes the sin-talk that would call gender violence to account. As a result, even as the churches now speak out against

---

51. Susan Brooks Thistlethwaite, "Battered Women and the Bible: From Subjection to Liberation," *Christianity and Crisis* 41:18 (1981): 311; and "Every Two Minutes: Battered Women and Feminist Interpretation," in *Feminist Interpretation of the Bible*, ed. Letty M. Russell (Philadelphia: Westminster Press, 1985), 99.
52. Thistlethwaite, "Every Two Minutes," 96.
53. Engel, "Evil, Sin, and the Violation of the Vulnerable," 159.
54. Rita Nakashima Brock, *Journeys by Heart: A Christology of Erotic Power* (New York: Crossroad, 2000), 20–21.
55. Christine M. Smith, "Sin and Evil in Feminist Thought," *Theology Today* 50, no. 2 (1993): 214.

gender violence, many of their underlying theological premises—including the idea of female submission, theories of complementarity of the sexes, and an androcentric approach to sin-talk—undermine these prophetic utterances. In short, the church does very little to address the rhetoric of life-denial that is constructed as a result of this cluster of theological themes.

That patriarchal rhetoric of life-denial finds its symbol in one of the quintessential symbols of "woman" in Christian and Western imagination, namely Mary, the Virgin-Mother. The symbol of Mary, which transcends both the historical Mary and official Christian Mariology, is highly ambivalent. Not only can she be either an oppressive or a liberating presence in women's lives, but at times the oppressive and liberating elements are intertwined. One example of this ambivalence can be found in Virgilio Elizondo's appropriation of that complex manifestation of Mary, the Lady of Guadalupe. Elizondo argues that the veneration of Mary in the figure of the Lady of Guadalupe is a liberating response to the violent oppression suffered by the people of Mexico at the hands of Western colonizers.[56] He asserts that Guadalupe's virginity is in opposition to the scandal of violated womanhood (seen in *La Malinche*, who symbolizes the colonial "rape" of the people of Mexico). Feminist theologians, however, take exception to the notion that Mary's virginity is salvific in some way, for, as Catharina Halkes argues, it "legitimizes the gap that has been allowed by the Church to persist between female sexuality and the mediation of holiness."[57] My suggestion is obviously not to equate rape, with which Guadalupe's virginity is here contrasted, to female sexual expression, nor to deny the empowering message of Guadalupe, but merely to point to the way Elizondo expresses the classical elevation of Mary's virginity as salvific. This overemphasis on Mary's virginity plays a role in undermining the liberating message in even the most powerful images of Mary by suggesting that a woman who has had sexual relations, or even a woman whose physical "virginity" was forcibly taken from her in rape, is somehow damaged goods. As such, even though many manifestations of Mary give hope to the hopeless, she also encourages cultural patterns that may be harmful to women, thereby illustrating the ambiguity of the symbol of Mary.

Feminist theologians from various cultural and ecclesial contexts do find in Mary a symbol of resistance and hope, especially when attention is shifted from Mary as symbol to the historical Miriam of Nazareth, as Elizabeth A.

---

56. Virgilio Elizondo, "Mary and the Poor: A Model of Evangelizing Ecumenism," in *Mary in the Churches*, ed. Hans Küng and Jürgen Moltmann (New York: Seabury Press, 1983), 60–61.

57. Catharina Halkes, "Mary and Women," in Küng and Moltmann, *Mary in the Churches*, 66–73.

Johnson proposes.[58] By examining the historical Mary's virtues, Johnson points out that Mary was not obedient to patriarchal expectations, but to God. Mary, argues Johnson, submitted to that which is truly good, not to that which is damaging, and she exhibited courage and leadership skills.

Nonetheless, the dominant way in which Mary has functioned in Christian theology is as a symbol of female sexual purity, humility, and self-sacrifice. One therefore needs to distinguish between Mary as retrieved by feminists and the "patriarchal Mary" with whom I take issue here. The latter, writes Ann Carr, is that of "an idealizing Mariology that sought to venerate her at the expense of real women and that projected onto her the passive virtues of submission, humility, and docility that women, in a misogynist and patriarchal Christian culture, were expected to imitate."[59]

In the classical patriarchal symbol of Mary, female goodness is defined in terms of humility and sexual purity. Her motherhood is defined in terms of obedience and passivity, resignation and suffering, and as part of her humble dedication to domestic tasks in accordance with the role that is "naturally" hers in the private sphere.[60] She therefore typifies precisely that which Saiving and her successors have pointed to as the more typical female sin. In the patriarchal symbol of Mary the loss of self is depicted as the ultimate virtue to be emulated. In line with the effect of the rhetoric of life-denial that she embodies, this symbol runs the risk of fostering an acceptance of abuse. Note, for example, psychologists Rosa Maria Gil and Carmen Inoa Vasquez's description of the Latinx cultural concept of "marianismo," which discourages independence in women, reminds women not to criticize their husbands for infidelity or verbal or psychological abuse, and tells women not to challenge things that make them unhappy.[61]

Leonardo Boff's summary of the Second Vatican Council's statements on Mary is illustrative of the patriarchal Mary: "Mary never lived in or for herself. Mary was a woman ever at the service of others—of God, of Christ, of redemption, of the Church, of the ultimate meaning of history."[62] Ann Carr notes that the Second Vatican Council statement is uncritical in its use of

---

58. Elizabeth A. Johnson, *Truly Our Sister: A Theology of Mary in the Communion of Saints* (New York: Continuum, 2006). See also María Pilar Aquino, *Our Cry for Life: Feminist Theology from Latin America* (Maryknoll, NY: Orbis Books, 1993), 174–77, for a brief overview of the liberating use of the symbol of Mary in Latin American women's theologies. For Protestant appreciations of Mary, see Beverly Roberts Gaventa and Cynthia L. Rigby, eds., *Blessed One: Protestant Perspectives on Mary* (Louisville, KY: Westminster John Knox Press, 2002).

59. Ann Carr, *Transforming Grace: Christian Tradition and Women's Experience* (New York: Continuum, 1998), 189.

60. Aquino, *Our Cry for Life*, 173.

61. Rosa Maria Gil and Carmen Inoa Vazquez, *The Maria Paradox: How Latinas Can Merge Old-World Traditions with New-World Self-Esteem* (New York: Putnam, 1996), 8.

62. Leonardo Boff, *The Maternal Face of God* (San Francisco: Harper & Row, 1987), 10.

the traditional Eve/Mary symbolism, which attributes sin and evil to Eve's disobedience in contrast to Mary's perfect obedience, and still serves to cast all real women with the sinful Eve while rendering Mary as the ideal of perfection.[63] This ideal of perfection is stripped of its overtly Mariological garb in Protestantism, yet the ideal lives on in various ways. Some of the examples that come to mind include the Goodwife of Puritanism, the Angel in the House of Victorian Protestantism, and the gendered "family values" ideology of the contemporary Religious Right in the United States. The patriarchal-Mariological ideal takes on different forms, yet the essentials remain: an emphasis on women's submissiveness, humility, and self-sacrifice, and relegation to the private sphere.

As signified by the apt subtitle of Joan Arnold Romero's article, "Karl Barth's Theology of the Word of God: or, How to Keep Women Silent and in Their Place," Protestantism, despite its general silence about Mary, occasionally even calls upon Mary herself in upholding this ideal.[64] In being "non-willing, non-achieving, non-creative, non-sovereign,"[65] Mary is depicted as the true hearer of the Word in Barth's theological thought. In this way, it is woman, the "ideal woman," Mary, that represents the creature. The Word to which this creature-symbolized-by-Mary must bow is the masculine Christ (against whose feminization Barth elsewhere rages).[66] For Barth the qualitative difference between God and humanity seems to have been extended to man and woman. In his thought the "good" woman is symbolized by Mary, but the Word confronting her, which she is to hear passively, is the male Christ. In this, Barth stands in a long line of Christian theologians who have insisted that women cannot represent Christ, even though he does not express this explicitly. Earlier I pointed out how Barth advises women to meet male tyranny with the passive and long-suffering nonresistance that I now explicitly identify as symbolized in Mary. Within this framework, the "ideal" Christian woman is to serve and obey male power, submitting to the male/divine economy, and bear children for the purposes of the patriarchal system.

Patriarchy's Mary is particularly problematic because she acts as a foil for Eve. Virtually no one can live up to the ideal of patriarchy's Mary—and if a

---

63. Carr, *Transforming Grace*, 191.
64. Joan Arnold Romero, "Karl Barth's Theology of the Word of God: Or, How to Keep Women Silent and in Their Place," in *Women and Religion*, ed. Judith Plaskow and Joan Arnold Romero, rev. ed. (Missoula, MT: Scholars Press, 1974), 65; Karl Barth, *Church Dogmatics*, I/2, ed. G. W. Bromiley and T. F. Torrance, trans. G. T. Thomson and Harold Knight (Edinburgh: T&T Clark, 1956), 188ff.
65. Barth, *CD* I/2: 191.
66. Barth, *CD* III/4: 161: "Christian art ... has had a fatal tendency brazenly to represent the figure of Christ, when it lays its violent hands upon it, with that well-known and frightful mixture of masculine and feminine traits ... instead of honorably at least in the form of a man."

woman does not, she is often seen as Eve. In her study of women in social movements in Latin America, anthropologist Lynn Stephens notes the following enactment of this dynamic:

> In El Salvador, Argentina, Chile, and other Latin American countries where women organized as mothers confronting military regimes in search of the disappeared, women were uniformly raped in the process of their torture and detention.... If women were not living up to the traditional Catholic image of the Virgin Mary as an obedient, pure, and self-sacrificing mother, then they could be interpreted as the opposite—as a whore, an aggressive, impure, sexual object. Rape becomes a justified treatment of women who are behaving incorrectly.[67]

It seems that it is all too easy for women who do not conform to the image of the self-sacrificial and humble Mary to be depicted as rebellious and impure Eve, thus deserving of male violence. It would therefore seem that the rhetoric of life-denial, with its emphasis on humility and self-sacrifice, contains an ominous undercurrent of violence, as it is linked to the violent rhetoric of death that is captured in the symbol of Eve. More about this in the next chapter.

In conclusion, in this chapter we have seen how Valerie Saiving's original rhetoric of difference, with which she rejected classical sin-talk's androcentric emphasis on sin-as-pride, is supplemented by an increasingly strong feminist rhetoric of oppression at which she herself only hints. In Judith Plaskow, we start to see a more explicit shift in emphasis, from whether typical female pathologies have been considered to the question of whether the androcentric emphasis on sin-as-pride has appropriated, and is perpetuating, the mythology of a patriarchal culture. Thus we see Plaskow asking the rhetorical questions of power relations that lie behind certain theological symbols, and of how these symbols reinforce those power structures. In other words, we notice a shift toward a feminist rhetoric of oppression, which asks not only whether the rhetoric of pride as paradigmatic sin has excluded women, but also whether it oppresses women. In the work of Susan Nelson Dunfee this question is asked with greater urgency, as she focuses on the self-destructive tendencies that this emphasis encourages in women. In the contributions of feminist scholars such as Carol Lakey Hess, Mary Potter Engel, and Susan Brooks Thistlethwaite, we encounter an explicit rhetoric of oppression built upon an implicit rhetoric of difference, as they point out how the emphasis on sin-as-pride, given women's patriarchally constructed "difference" in terms

---

67. Lynn Stephen, *Women and Social Movements in Latin America: Power from Below* (Austin: University of Texas Press, 1997), 283.

of subjugation, is destructive in the lives of women, especially in the face of gender violence.

In other words, feminist critiques of the pride paradigm do not merely point to the exclusion of "women's experience," but also to the way the overemphasis on pride helps to set up an extremely dangerous situation for women, by attributing the qualities of a victim to the ideal woman. In light of the "total feminine situation," which includes expectations as to role and psychology, as pointed out by Plaskow, women are both encouraged to and will be more prone to construct an ideal self-image in terms of these victim qualities. Carol Lakey Hess, Joanne Carlson Brown, and Rebecca Parker furthermore argue that this acculturates women to accept abuse. Hess also points out that this imaging of women leads to a religious and cultural taboo on female anger, which leads to female self-blame and a lack of resistance to the culture of violence. This is compounded by the problem pointed out by Susan Nelson Dunfee, which is that traditional Christian praise of typical female pathologies, such as losing the self in others, leaves women bound to their real sin and hence to violence turned inward. These authors, in their various ways, have therefore explored in greater detail the suggestion by Valerie Saiving that, insofar as theology has described the human situation inaccurately, its doctrine of love is in question. The "doctrine of love" that follows upon the Promethean sin is a destructive grace, and it is especially destructive to women. I have added to this analysis the link to the classical symbol of Mary, who far too often captures these harmful traits of humble self-sacrifice. We next turn our attention to the other classical female symbol in Christianity, that of Eve.

4

Eve

> From a woman sin had its beginning, and because of her we all die.
> —*Sirach 25:24 NRSV*

In the previous chapter we examined the critique of classical sin-talk that launched modern feminist theological scholarship: utilizing a rhetoric of difference, and then increasingly a rhetoric of oppression, feminist theologians criticize the classical focus on pride as androcentric and ultimately harmful to women. In this chapter we turn to another critical theme in feminist conversations on sin—namely, the classical patriarchal blaming of women for sin, which relates to the concept of concupiscence. The latter is classically seen as the material element in sin, is often sexualized, and is often associated with women, thereby contributing to the blaming of women for sin. The feminist critique of the classic woman-sin association primarily makes use of two intertwined rhetorical strategies: a rhetoric of oppression, which brings forward the atrocities committed against women, and a rhetoric of reason, which aims at exposing the philosophical assumptions that lead to the association of women with sin.

The pride critique discussed in the previous chapter clearly follows a logical pattern, moving from a central critique about androcentrism in classical sin-talk to a deeper realization of the gender oppression created by that androcentrism. In comparison, the feminist critique of the classical blaming of women for sin is somewhat scattered. It centers around several interlocking themes, each of which has its own complexities: a particular interpretation of the story of Adam and Eve; the association of women with the body as a result of classical dualism; the frequent rhetorical association of the body with sin; and the corresponding association of women with sin, which leads back to the symbol of Eve. In this chapter, I attempt to gather the scattered pieces of this conversation into a somewhat coherent whole by providing a brief overview of these interlocking themes, giving a few illustrative examples of classical theologians blaming women for sin, and discussing the two rhetorical strategies that feminist theologians use in their response to the classical women-sin association, namely a rhetoric of oppression and a rhetoric of reason. The chapter concludes with some reflections on Eve, and the way she relates to the symbol of Mary mentioned in the previous chapter.

HISTORICAL OVERVIEW

At the heart of Christian sin-talk is the story of Adam and Eve found in Genesis 2–3, which is usually interpreted as the story of the first sin and the origins of a fallen state for all humanity. This story has spelled trouble for women for centuries. Eve's handing of the forbidden fruit to Adam was seen as her tempting the man to sin, which made her the primary culprit, the one who was really to blame for the onset of sin in the world. This blame has been transferred to all women in much of Christian history. The story has alternatively been used to point to a supposed inferior nature in women that makes women more gullible and prone to sin, and to argue that female submission to men is God's punishment to women for Eve's sin. These arguments were strengthened by pointing to the suggestion in Genesis 2:18 that Eve was made as "helper" to Adam, which has traditionally been interpreted as placing her in a subservient position in the order of creation, and by citing Genesis 3:16, where Eve's punishment includes the idea that her husband shall be her master.

The blaming of women for sin as a result of the Genesis narrative was exacerbated by an erotic hermeneutic. This hermeneutical angle originated in the centuries before Christ, but it increased in the postapostolic period, at the same time that the story was increasingly read as a history of human sin.[1] One of the factors in this sexualizing and indeed demonizing of Eve was the use of the Greek Pandora myth as an interpretative lens. According to this myth, Pandora released evil into the world when she opened a jar (*pithos*), which has often been taken to be a crude reference to female genitalia.[2] This

---

1. Helen Schüngel-Straumann, "'From a Woman Sin Had Its Beginning, and Because of Her We All Die.' (Sir 25:24)," *Theology Digest* 45, no. 3 (1998): 203.
2. Theodore Reik (*Myth and Guilt* [New York: G. Brazilier, 1970], 64) writes that "the student of the symbolic language that pervades all primitive myths will easily guess that the vessel in which all evils are contained represents the female genital" (cf. the vulgar English term "box" for female genitalia). Artist Paul Klee painted "Pandora's Box" as a kind of goblet containing some flowers, but emitting evil vapors from an opening clearly representing female genitalia (Dora Panofsky and Irwin Panofsky, *Pandora's Box* [New York: Pantheon, 1962], 113).

sexualization of the story of Adam and Eve, and particularly of Eve's role in it, in turn connected with problematic ideas in Christian thought about women, the body, and sexuality. There is a profound ambivalence in the Christian tradition with regard to sexuality, which is often traced back to St. Augustine and his personal struggles. This is not always a fair accusation, since Augustine was in fact far more balanced and nuanced than some, but he did exhibit and contribute to this ambivalence, which is unfortunate given his importance in the Christian canon and especially his centrality in classical Christian sin-talk. Let me explain in a bit more detail.

Despite some remarks that seem to point to body-rejecting dualism, the church fathers did not in fact condemn the body. In fact, as Margaret Miles notes, the church fathers "instinctively realized that the Incarnation 'settles' the question of the value of the body."[3] More generally, among both pagans and Christians in antiquity there was general agreement that the body was not evil and that the metaphysical was an "inadequate foundation for thought." (One of the exceptions would be the Manicheans, who associated the material world with evil.) Yet Miles notes that an "existential dualism," and therefore the problem of how to describe the body as valuable, remained.[4] It was Augustine who took up the task of "reuniting soul and body," which makes it particularly ironic that in our time Augustine is often associated with sexual repression and the denigration of the body. Miles attributes this to the fact that Augustine never really completed his task.

Nevertheless, in contrast to the Manichean idea that the body is composed of evil matter, Augustine insisted on the good of the body, at least in principle. One can trace this back to three factors: his emphasis on the goodness of all creation (which was part of his rejection of Manichean dualism); the influence of the Bible, which tends to be far more body-affirming than the dualistic traditions of the classical world; and, as mentioned, the doctrine of the incarnation. In line with these influences, Augustine locates the origin of sin in the will, not in the body. He writes in *The City of God*,

> And so we are weighed down by the corruptible body; and yet we know that the cause of our being weighed down is not the true nature and substance of our body but its corruption; and therefore we do not wish to be stripped of it, but to be clothed with the immortality of the body.... Those who imagine that all the ills of the soul derive from the body are mistaken.... For the corruption of the body, which weighs down the soul, is not the cause of the first sin, but its punishment; *it was the sinful soul that made the flesh corruptible.*[5]

---

3. Margaret R. Miles, *Augustine on the Body* (Eugene, OR: Wipf and Stock, 1979), 127.
4. Ibid., 131.
5. Augustine, *The City of God*, trans. Henry Bettenson (New York: Penguin Books, 1984), 14.3.

Remarkable words from a theologian who is often associated with body-negativity. Augustine, therefore, reverses the Platonic notion that the body imprisons the soul by suggesting that the soul in a certain sense imprisons the body by subjecting it to corruption and death. Within this framework, the body is only secondarily a source of sin as a result of the corruption of the flesh by the soul. Augustine backs up this argument by referring to the devil, who "has no flesh," but is ruled by the "fountainhead of all these evils," pride.[6] This observation raises an interesting point: it would seem that there is a parallel between his insistence that sin originates in the soul and then corrupts the body (corruption both in the sense of death and in the sense of sin), on the one hand, and his insistence that the fundamental nature of sin is pride, and its material element is concupiscence. What makes this parallel interesting for the purpose of feminist analysis is that Augustine's emphasis on pride as the root sin therefore seems to go hand in hand with his rejection of the idea that the body is evil and the original source of sin. Herein lies a certain irony for feminist criticism of classical sin-talk, since both the emphasis on pride (associated with rooting sin in the soul) and the association of sin and the body (which in turn is classically associated with women) are troublesome from a feminist rhetorical perspective. It is also clear that the rooting of concupiscence in pride, which we saw as problematic in the previous chapter, goes hand in hand with Augustine's insistence that the body is not itself evil.

However, Augustine himself, despite his firm rejection of the idea that the body is the source of original sin, still uses language that implicitly associates the body and sinfulness. In the *Confessions*, for example, when speaking of sinful ways of thinking, he would refer to them as the result of a "carnal imagination."[7] And in *The City of God*, in the section just following his insistence that sin originates in the soul, he goes on to explain his use of the language of carnality to refer to ungodly behavior: "some men live by the standard of the flesh, others by the standard of the spirit."[8] While the language is metaphorical here, and biblically rooted, it is nevertheless an unfortunate association, given the already-existing ambivalence about the body in the world of both Greek philosophy and early Christian theology. As such, Augustine contributes to a rhetoric of body-negativity, despite his doctrinal insistence that sin originates in the soul, and his emphasis on the original goodness of bodily existence. Augustine's perspective is an improvement on much of the thought of the day, but does not quite avoid negative associations with the body. In short, both because of the paradox present in his thought

6. Ibid.
7. Augustine, *The Confessions*, in *The Works of Saint Augustine: A Translation for the 21st Century* 1, Book 1, trans. Maria Boulding (New York: New City Press, 2001), 6.3.4.
8. Augustine, *City of God* 14.4.

and his own use of body-negative metaphors, he contributes to the gender problems present in classical sin-talk in spite of his better inclinations.

The problem is further aggravated when classical sin-talk turns to the question of how original sin is transmitted from generation to generation, and when the sin of concupiscence is discussed largely with reference to sexuality. Augustine and others could never quite get away from the concept, inherited from predecessors such as Cyprian, that Adam's sin is physically transmitted through sexual intercourse.[9] Let us look briefly at this issue before turning more directly to the problem of blaming women for sin. First, the doctrine of original sin, which teaches that all humans inherit Adam's sin and are subject to its corruption, begs the question: How is original sin transferred from generation to generation? If sin does not originate in the body, but in the soul, how does it enter each individual soul? This raises the question of the origins of the soul. Augustine initially seemed to lean toward the Platonic idea of the preexistence of the soul (an idea coupled with disdain for the body), but later dismissed this as a remnant of Manichean thought, instead opting for some version of the idea that the soul is created with the body at the time of conception.

There are, broadly speaking, two versions of the latter view: creationism, which holds that God creates each individual soul at or around the time of conception; and traducianism, which holds that the soul is created with the body by the parents at conception. Of these two perspectives, only traducianism would fit the doctrine of original sin. Augustine did not adopt this perspective and never seemed to resolve the question of how original sin is transmitted (nor has it ever been given doctrinal status), but for our purposes it is sufficient to note that the traducian view of the transmission of original sin continued to circulate throughout Christian history and as such forms part of the rhetoric of classical sin-talk. Paradoxically (again!), although traducianism is coupled with a more positive view of the body in principle, since it is premised upon the insistence that sin has its origins in the soul and not the body, it also suggests that original sin is associated with sexuality. Therefore, in spite of a formal emphasis on the goodness of physical existence in God's original creation, and on the origins of original sin in the soul, the doctrine of original sin nevertheless rhetorically associated sin with the body.

Moreover, concupiscence—that is, distorted desire as a result of humanity's loss of God-directedness—while not necessarily a sexual concept, was often understood primarily in sexual terms. This added to the negative associations attached to the body and sexuality, which had negative consequences

---

9. Tatha Wiley, *Original Sin: Origins, Developments, Contemporary Meanings* (New York: Paulist Press, 2002), 49.

for women, due to the classical Western dualistic framework that associated women with the body. We look at this issue more later in this chapter when we discuss the feminist rhetoric of reason. For now, suffice it to say that given this dualistic association of women with sexuality and the body, and the rhetorical association of the body with sin—in particular since concupiscence was primarily described in terms of sexual desire—it is not surprising that there is a theme of blaming women for sin in classical sin-talk. This theme is strengthened by the story of Adam and Eve, read as a source narrative for sin in which Eve is the first sinner, and read through a sexualized lens. A few examples of comments by theologians through the centuries serve to illustrate this theme.

Perhaps the most infamous expression of the misogynist association of women with sin comes from the church father Tertullian:

> And do you not know that you are (each) an Eve? The sentence of God on this sex of yours lives in this age: the guilt must of necessity live too. *You* are the devil's gateway: *you* are the unsealer of that (forbidden) tree: *you* are the first deserter of the divine law: *you* are she who persuaded him whom the devil was not valiant enough to attack. *You* destroyed so easily God's image, man. On account of *your* dessert—that is, death—even the Son of God had to die.[10]

Although his language is particularly extreme, Tertullian was not alone in his sentiments. In *The City of God*, Augustine opined that the serpent "no doubt" started with "the inferior of the human pair" because the "man would not be so easily gullible, and could not be trapped by a false move on his own part, but only if he yielded to another's mistake."[11] The suggestion there is one of ontological inferiority that makes women more prone to submit to temptation. Thomas Aquinas offered a more complex version of the belief in female ontological inferiority when he adopted Aristotelian biology to declare women "misbegotten" as to their individual nature (although he deemed women a necessary part of creation due to their role in reproduction, and due to God's refusal to remove all occasion for sin!).[12]

The Protestant Reformers did not engage in much speculation about a supposed female ontological inferiority, but they nevertheless continued the association of women with sin in other ways. Luther argued that female subjugation to male authority is punishment for sin—an indirect reference to the

---

10. Tertullian, *De Cultu Feminarum*, in *The Ante-Nicene Fathers* 4, ed. Alexander Roberts and James Donaldson, trans. S. Thelwall (Grand Rapids: Eerdmans, 1986), 1.1.14 (italics in original).
11. Augustine, *City of God* 14.11.
12. Thomas Aquinas, *Summa Theologica*, trans. Fathers of the English Dominican Province (New York: Benziger Brothers, 1946), I, q.92, a.1, ad 3.

story of Eve.[13] Luther did argue that marriage to women is a good "antidote" against (sexual) sin, but added that one's wife is "hardly" spoken of without a feeling of shame.[14] Thus, sin, shame, and women remained intertwined. Calvin, on the other hand, saw women's subjugation as a matter of order and decorum rather than a punishment for sin, and at times seemed quite contemptuous of the blaming of women for sin, insisting that all human beings are responsible for sin and evil.[15] Yet he also at times blamed women for tempting men with their "lawless desires."[16] His Puritan heirs challenged earlier images of the carnal, lustful woman, but often paradoxically believed that the devil could more easily assault the "weaker bodies" of women, thus making them more prone to fall into temptation.[17] Therefore, although Protestantism generally abandoned the idea of an ontological basis for women's supposed sinful tendencies (in part because of the Protestant rejection of an Aristotelian basis for theology), it nevertheless ended up in the same place as earlier theologians, namely that of blaming women for sin.

These examples briefly illustrate the multiple ways in which themes of women's supposed inferiority (whether of mind or body) resurfaced time and again in the writings of prominent classical Christian theologians. Within this rhetoric, women were often portrayed as temptresses who lure men into sin. Furthermore, within a dualistic framework that implicitly associated women with the body and sexuality, combined with discomfort with sexuality, women were all too easily viewed as symbols of temptation, sin, and even outright evil. In short, although Christian theology took great care through the centuries to emphasize the sin of men as well, there was also a strong undercurrent that depicted women as the primary agents of sin, and men as victims of women's sinful tendencies.

The patriarchal woman-sin association—which included the ideas of women's weakness for sin, partnership with evil forces, and wily seduction of men—is traditionally captured in the symbol of Eve; as such, the

---

13. Martin Luther, "Lectures on Genesis," in *Luther's Works*, vol. 1, ed. Jaroslav Pelikan (St. Louis, MO: Concordia Publishing House, 1958), 115, 202–3.

14. Ibid., 118.

15. Mary Potter, "Gender Equality and Gender Hierarchy in Calvin's Theology," *Signs* 11, no. 4 (1986): 725–39; Claude-Marie Baldwin, "John Calvin and the Ethics of Gender Relations," *Calvin Theological Journal* 26 (1991): 133–43; André Bieler, *L'homme et la femme dans la morale calviniste* (Geneva: Labor et Fides, 1963), 8.

16. See his commentaries on Isaiah 3:17 (*Commentary on the Book of the Prophet Isaiah*, vol. 1, ed. William Pringle [Grand Rapids: Eerdmans, 1948], 145) and Jeremiah 2:33 (*Commentaries on the Book of the Prophet Jeremiah and the Lamentations*, vol. 1, ed. John Owen [Grand Rapids: Eerdmans, 1950], 139), his Sermon No. 19 on 2 Samuel, and Sermon No. 32 on 2 Samuel, or his Letter to Nicholas Parent, December 14, 1540 (*Ioannis Calvini opera quae supersunt omnia* [Braunschweig, Germany: C. A. Schwetschke, 1863–1900], 11.131).

17. Elizabeth Reis, *Damned Women: Sinners and Witches in Puritan New England* (Ithaca, NY: Cornell University Press, 1997), 109.

symbol of Eve transcends the narrative of Genesis 2–3. Feminist theologians of various stripes have lodged critical rhetorical inquiries into the practical consequences of this symbol and the rhetoric that surrounds her. The main rhetorical question driving this inquiry is: what happens to women when they become symbols of sin and are blamed for men's weaknesses? The evidence suggests that the patriarchal woman-sin association becomes a rhetoric of death: when women are associated with sin, evil, or moral weakness, and blamed not only for their own but also for men's failures, they all too easily become objects of hate and fear against whom retaliation is justified. Feminist theologians have understandably been very critical of this theme in classical sin-talk. In the process of launching a feminist critical rhetorical inquiry into the patriarchal rhetoric of death, feminist theologians make use of two primary feminist rhetorical strategies: an often–strongly worded rhetoric of oppression that points to the atrocities that the Eve symbol leads to, and a rhetoric of reason that aims at examining the problematic arguments that lie beneath the patriarchal rhetoric of death. Below I examine each feminist rhetorical response in turn, although they overlap significantly. I not only report on other feminist theologians using these rhetorical strategies but participate in them by adding further analysis.

THE FEMINIST RHETORIC OF OPPRESSION

The traditional threefold distinction of radical, reconstructionist, and reformist feminisms indicates which position feminists might take toward the church and its traditions: seeing it as irredeemable (the radical position), attempting critical retrieval of classical traditions (the reconstructionist position), or accepting most of the church's tradition and trying to provide a stronger feminine presence in it (the reformist position). In chapter 1, I suggested that Hawkesworth's distinction of feminist rhetorical strategies is a more helpful classification for understanding the differences among feminists, but in general, one could associate radical feminism with a strong rhetoric of oppression, revisionist feminism with a strong rhetoric of reason, and reformist feminism with a strong rhetoric of difference, although these categories frequently overlap.

Mary Daly is the most famous example of a feminist theologian in the radical feminism mode, and her work is indeed characterized by a strong and uncompromising rhetoric of oppression in which atrocities against women are placed under intense scrutiny. In her first book, *Beyond God the Father* (1973), Daly argues that the misnaming of women as inherently sinful leads to an experience of non-being for women. She locates the root of the problem in the myth of the fall, which reflects and perpetuates a destructive image of women that turns women into Christianity's primordial scapegoats.[18] In her 1978 publication *Gyn/Ecology*, Daly broadens the scope of her rhetoric of oppression by identifying patriarchy itself as the prevailing "religion" of the entire planet, and calls all religions "parts of the male's shelter against anomie," that is, women as the projected personifications of "The Enemy."[19] Continuing to use the ontological categories that characterize her earlier work, Daly now talks about patriarchy's real "fall" as "the murder/dismemberment of the Goddess—that is, the Self-affirming be-ing of women."[20] The sin of patriarchy is therefore the destruction of the very being of women as participation in Being. Deepening this critique, Daly also refers to violence against women as "the various manifestations of Goddess-Murder on this patriarchal planet," the "deep and universal intent to destroy the divine spark in women."[21]

Although her perspective on patriarchy lacks nuance, Daly certainly points to a real problem at the heart of Christian sin-talk. Her uncompromising tone has the merit of offering a powerful rhetoric of oppression, providing what feminist rhetorical theorist Mary Hawkesworth calls a "pitiless description" that aims at shocking readers into rethinking the apparent goodness of religion.[22] For Daly, the rhetorical remembering of the atrocities committed against women by the church, coupled with her own experiences of sexism in the church, led her to an eventual post-Christian, radical feminist position. But those feminist theologians, such as Rosemary Radford Ruether, who might be better described as activist-reconstructionist theologians within the Christian tradition rather than post-Christian, also engage in a rhetoric of oppression on this issue.

Ruether notes that the blaming of women for sin was used to deprive women of legal rights and to exclude them from higher education and leadership roles in church and society, and to justify physical violence against women.[23] Church history is especially infamous for the justification of "wife

---

18. Mary Daly, *Beyond God the Father: Toward a Philosophy of Women's Liberation* (Boston: Beacon Press, 1973), ch. 2 ("Exorcising Evil from Eve: The Fall into Freedom").

19. Mary Daly, *Gyn/Ecology: The Metaethics of Radical Feminism* (Boston: Beacon Press, 1978), 39.

20. Ibid., 111.

21. Ibid., 315.

22. M. E. Hawkesworth, *Beyond Oppression: Feminist Theory and Political Strategy* (New York: Continuum, 1990), 113.

23. Rosemary Radford Ruether, "Home and Work: Women's Roles and the Transformation of Values," *Theological Studies* 36 (December 1975): 647–59; Ruether, "Male Clericalism and the Dread of Women," in *Women and Orders*, ed. Robert J. Heyers (New York: Paulist Press, 1974), 1–13; Ruether, *Sexism and God-Talk: Toward a Feminist Theology* (Boston: Beacon Press, 1993), 195ff.

beating" and the persecution of "witches," mostly women. Medieval canon law justified domestic violence by presenting it as a matter of family discipline (a man's right to chastise his wife if she is insubordinate). Ruether speculates that Christianity's historic hostility to marriage may have contributed to this justification of violence against wives, since the celibate legislators of canon law held married women in contempt as the epitome of the carnal Eve.[24] But, as we saw earlier, the Protestant Reformers, despite approving of marriage and being less inclined to suggest the idea of ontological female inferiority, did not do much better and still often associated women with sin. In Protestant teachings on the family, domestic violence was not prophetically addressed: Luther, as we saw in chapter 2, suggested hitting his wife when she got "saucy," and Calvin's admonition that women should patiently bear their cross (of gender violence) results from the emphasis on patriarchal order that took the place of an ontological argument for women's secondary social status. As such, from classical sin-talk as a whole emerges a patriarchal rhetoric of death: while theologians would not advocate that men should kill their wives, the rhetoric of family discipline, chastisement, or women's patient submission contributed to the suffering of women, and, all too often, to their death.

The most extreme expression of the patriarchal rhetoric of death occurred in relation to the witch hunts, which were largely directed at women. Rosemary Radford Ruether notes that the majority of those executed during the Massachusetts witch trials were women, and the ones particularly at risk were women who fell outside the normative role of the "goodwife." (Once again we see how easily women are associated with Eve if they do not fit the image of patriarchy's Mary, here represented by the "goodwife.") She therefore interprets the witchcraft persecution as a central tool for terrorizing "insufficiently subservient" women.[25] Similarly, the European witch hunts resulted in the deaths of anywhere from one hundred thousand to several million victims, an estimated 80 to 90 percent of them female.[26] Indeed, Ruether remarks that "the official image of the witch was female," noting that historically witch hunting tended to cease when this image was violated and men of some social standing came to be accused.[27]

---

24. Rosemary Radford Ruether, "The Western Religious Tradition and Violence against Women," in *Christianity, Patriarchy, and Abuse*, ed. Joanne Carlson Brown and Carole R. Bohn (Cleveland, OH: Pilgrim Press, 1989), 34.
25. Ruether, *Sexism and God-Talk*, 170.
26. Elizabeth Clark and Herbert Richardson, eds., *Women and Religion: A Feminist Sourcebook of Christian Thought* (New York: Harper & Row, 1977), 116; Hedwig Meyer-Wilmes, "Persecuting Witches in the Name of Reason: An Analysis of Western Rationality," in *The Fascination of Evil*, Concilium 1998/1, ed. Herman Häring and David Tracy (Maryknoll, NY: Orbis Books), 11–17; Nel Noddings, *Women and Evil* (Berkeley: University of California Press, 1989), 44.
27. Ruether, "Western Religious Tradition and Violence against Women," 36.

The very title of the witch hunters' handbook, the infamous *Malleus Maleficarum* (Hammer of Witches), was a self-fulfilling prophecy, notes Mary Daly, since "maleficarum" is the feminine form of the term for witch/evildoer.[28] The *Malleus Maleficarum* contains the themes in classical sin-talk that we noted earlier: women are both ontologically inferior to men and more prone to sin, which is linked to female sexuality, and women are therefore dangerous agents of evil. In a section subtitled "Why Superstition Is Chiefly Found in Women," we encounter the idea that "women are feebler both in mind and body" and therefore they tend to "come under the spell of witchcraft." Women are depicted as "of a different nature from men . . . intellectually like children . . . more carnal than a man . . . an imperfect animal" who "always deceives." And for good measure the authors add that "nearly all the kingdoms of the world have been overthrown by women," and "the world now suffers through the malice of women." The authors conclude that all witchcraft comes from carnal lust, which they believe "is in women insatiable." They also identify three general vices that "appear to have special dominion over wicked women," namely infidelity, ambition, and lust.[29] This appears to be a bizarre twist on Augustine's three primary categories of sin (rebellion against God, pride, and concupiscence), now narrowed and specifically identified as female sins against men.

It is easy to dismiss the witch hunts as merely the product of medieval superstition, but it was in fact much more of a Renaissance phenomenon: although they started in the thirteenth century, the witch hunts were waged with special ferocity between 1500 and 1700. A systematic "demonology" did not exist in the so-called Dark Ages, although beliefs about witches and magic were widespread among the laity. Indeed, in the eighth century St. Boniface declared the belief in witches "unchristian," and in the same century Charlemagne decreed the death penalty for anyone who burned supposed witches, calling it a "pagan custom." Up until the twelfth century, the church denied the very existence of witches. But a reversal of ecclesiastical opinion started to take place in the late Middle Ages, so that, by the time of the Renaissance, in the sixteenth and seventeenth centuries especially, the witch craze exploded.[30] The question is why it happened at this time.

Perhaps the answer lies in the fact that this was a lengthy period of socioeconomic upheaval and change. Social upheavals create scapegoats, argues British historian Hugh Trevor-Roper: "Like the Jew, the witch became the stereotype

---

28. Daly, *Gyn/Ecology*, 188.
29. J. Sprenger and H. Kramer, *Malleus Maleficarum*, trans. Montague Summers (New York: Dover Publications, 1971), part 1, q.6.
30. Hugh Trevor-Roper, *Religion, the Reformation, and Social Change* (London: Macmillan, 1967), 91–93.

of the incurable nonconformist; and in the declining Middle Ages, the two were joined as scapegoats for the ills of society."[31] Elizabeth Clark and Herbert Richardson argue that the witch hunts expressed a "repressed resentment against women that broke forth in this difficult period."[32] Moreover, so-called witches were believed to have secret knowledge that enabled them to abolish the laws of nature, thus contradicting the new scientific rationality and science of the era. As scientific progress enabled greater control over nature, the desire to control women may also have increased, since, as Hedwig Meyer-Wilmes notes, "woman always represented nature," and as such, their suppression was symbolically associated with increased control over nature.[33] Other feminist scholars have made similar observations: for example, anthropologist Shirley Ardener shows how women, in being marginal to public life and in having reproductive "powers," are associated with the wild; ecofeminist Karen J. Warren argues that the relationship of men over both nature and women is characterized by a "logic of domination" that accompanies the valuing of the traditionally masculine virtue of rationality; and feminist theologian Rosemary Radford Ruether sees the domination of nature as part of the same dualism that she identifies as the central problem in gender relations.[34] In short, it would appear that the witch hunts went hand in hand with the development of an increasing *ethos* of control (over nature and those associated with it, whether women or people of color) in early modernity. Control over nature was extended to control over those associated with nature: women and, increasingly, people of color in the rest of the world as a result of colonial expansion.

Some feminist scholars trace this *ethos* of control and its gendered subtext back to the Genesis 1 creation account with its theme of the conquest of chaos. It is well known that the story of the six-day creation is based on the Babylonian *Enuma Elish*, in which the god Marduk kills the goddess Tiamat, mother of the gods, who is associated with the chaotic primordial waters that surround the habitable world in the Babylonian worldview. Tiamat is present only as vague cultural and linguistic memory in Genesis in the abstract deep (Tehom), but that does not mean that the basic *ethos* of male control of a (vaguely) female

---

31. Ibid., 186.
32. Clark and Richardson, *Women and Religion*, 119–20.
33. Meyer-Wilmes, "Persecuting Witches in the Name of Reason," 16. Meyer-Wilmes refers in this regard to Max Horkheimer and F. W. Adorno, *Dialektik der Auflkärung* (Frankfurt, Germany: S. Fischer, 1969), 298.
34. Shirley Ardener, *Perceiving Women* (London: J. M. Dent & Sons, 1975), 23; Karen J. Warren, "The Power and the Promise of Ecological Feminism," in *Environmental Ethics: Readings in Theory and Application*, ed. Louis P. Pojman (Belmont, CA: Wadsworth, 1998), 173–83; and Rosemary Radford Ruether, "Ecofeminism: Symbolic and Social Connections of the Oppression of Women and the Domination of Nature," in *Ecofeminism and the Sacred*, ed. Carol J. Adams (New York: Continuum, 1993), 13–23.

nature/chaos does not still lurk. Rosemary Radford Ruether identifies the sublimation of the Mother as the step following the slaying of the Mother in the historical progress of misogyny. She argues that, whereas the old religions celebrated life as coming from the living body of the goddess, within this shift, life is seen as springing forth from the hands of the male god who has killed the goddess. Eventually, says Ruether, her carcass is not even needed for that anymore; it has decomposed into nothing, and only the Word is necessary for world creation. Modernity—that ultimate victory of mind over matter—and matricide—the victory of male over female—seem inseparable.[35] Catherine Keller similarly concludes that the Tehom eventually becomes "the theological Nothing out of which is posited the alienated world."[36]

Without belaboring the point, I would slightly disagree with the fluid movement in these analyses from the narrative of creation out of chaos to the idea of creation out of nothing; given that the doctrine of creatio ex nihilo goes hand in hand with an affirmation of the goodness of the material world, I suspect it is potentially valuable in its own right for feminist sin-talk. This is, however, a topic for another time. What is relevant for this discussion is the way in which feminist scholars rightly point to the violent subtext of the first creation account, in which a male god kills the Mother of the Living. In a certain sense, therefore, the issue is not so much the text as it exists now as the cultural world that the text implicitly evokes.

In the second (but older) creation account, Eve, a figure who is also associated with the Mother of the Living, becomes the one who goes against the created order by disobeying God (at least in the classical Christian interpretation of the text).[37] In the Adam and Eve story, as interpreted in the Christian tradition, Eve's desire for wisdom becomes a transgression of the divine order. The ancient symbol of immortality, the serpent, now becomes the symbol of evil and is eventually associated with the devil, the one to be crushed by Eve's opposite, Mary. In terms of the language of sin and redemption, Eve becomes associated with pride, and Mary with humility, as shown in the previous chapter.[38] Eve, the Mother of the Living, becomes the Mother of Death, the one

---

35. Rosemary Radford Ruether, *New Woman, New Earth: Sexist Ideologies and Human Liberation* (New York: Seabury Press, 1975), ch. 1.

36. Catherine Keller, "Of Swallowed, Walled, and Wordless Women," *Soundings* 65 (Fall 1982): 335.

37. The text lends itself to multiple plausible interpretations: the classical Christian reading of it as the story of humanity's fall into sin, an opposite reading of it as an allegory of growing up and leaving the nest, an allegory for Israel's relationship with God and a warning that disobedience to God will lead to the loss of the promised land / garden of Eden, among other possibilities.

38. Jaroslav Pelikan, *The Growth of Medieval Theology (600–1300)*, vol. 3 of *The Christian Tradition: A History of the Development of Doctrine* (Chicago: University of Chicago Press, 1978), 167: "The curse of Eve had been a consequence of her pride and disobedience, the blessing of Mary a consequence of her humility and obedience."

who brings death and disorder into the world through her disobedience. She becomes, indeed, the very symbol of sin.

Although the Adam and Eve story is originally separate from the chaos/order myth found in Genesis 1, and although in Genesis 1, in contrast to the Tiamat myth, the chaos is technically ungendered, the traditional placing of the two stories within one large creation narrative, as well as the contextual background of the ancient chaos/order myth, work together to shape Eve into "woman as such," the embodiment of a feminine chaos / male order dualism. Charles Ess writes that the "near Middle-Eastern context of Genesis 2–3 may suggest that we understand the story of Eve as a chaos/order myth which directly justifies male violence against women." It does so, he argues, by defining "primordial woman" (and hence all women) as "agents of chaos who threaten the male order of hierarchy and patriarchy." Thus the story serves to "excuse the batterer's use of violence to maintain control and order—understood precisely as male control over a subordinate female."[39] He furthermore notes that the image of the female as the chaos agent who threatens male control (and the gender violence justified by this image) continues to thrive in contemporary Western culture. Like Pandora (whose story, we noted earlier, has been used as an interpretative lens for Genesis 2–3), Eve therefore becomes an agent of chaos, and as such, her story, especially since it is read in connection with the Genesis 1 account with its theme of divine control of the chaos, implicitly becomes one of chaos that must be brought under control. This finds resonance in the control of nature that increases especially during the scientific revolution, and which likely contributed to the *ethos* of control that gave rise to the witch hunts.

To conclude this section, feminist scholars such as Mary Daly, Rosemary Radford Ruether, Catherine Keller, et al. suggest that a deep misogyny lurks beneath the surface of some foundational Christian texts, and that this misogyny historically contributed to extensive patterns of killing women. By rereading (church) history as a history of atrocities, the rhetoric of oppression of feminist theologians aims at breaking through denial by "providing a pitiless description that forces its own acceptance," as Hawkesworth put it.[40] Mixing their rhetoric of oppression with analytical elements of the rhetoric of reason, feminist theologians—alongside other scholars—suggest that the foundational texts employed in classical sin-talk contain underlying mythical themes of matricide, the defiling of women "as such" through the symbol of Eve, and an *ethos* of control of women and nature.

---

39. Charles Ess, "Reading Adam and Eve: Re-Visions of the Myth of Woman's Subordination to Man," in *Violence against Women: A Christian Theological Sourcebook*, ed. Carol J. Adam and Marie M. Fortune (New York: Continuum, 1995), 97.

40. Hawkesworth, *Beyond Oppression*, 113.

In the following section, we examine a clearer rhetoric of reason, especially that of Rosemary Radford Ruether, which probes the philosophical assumptions underlying the theme of blaming women in classical sin-talk.

THE FEMINIST RHETORIC OF REASON

As we have seen, Rosemary Radford Ruether is a strong articulator of a rhetoric of oppression. Yet, in contrast to Mary Daly, she does not operate with the concept of a monolithic patriarchy, nor is she as skeptical of the possibility of retrieving elements of the classical Christian traditions. She argues that women must reject the concept of the fall that scapegoats women, but also argues that "women cannot neglect the basic theological insight that humanity has become radically alienated from its true relationship to itself, to nature, and to God," thereby echoing the central insight contained in the doctrine of original sin.[41] Her work, while extensively utilizing a rhetoric of oppression, is primarily characterized by a strong rhetoric of reason, that is, an analysis that aims at exposing the misinformation about women contained in the classic texts of Christianity. This can be seen most particularly in her focus on dualism as the underlying *logos* problem in classical Christian sin-talk.

Ruether sees sin as rooted in the distortion of the self-other relationship. Among the primary distortions of this self-other relationship, she says, is the distortion of humanity as male and female into a dualism of superiority and inferiority, which has served the double purpose of supporting male identity as normative humanity and justifying servile roles for women. On one side of this dualism stands Pure Spirit, goodness, truth, and even God, all gendered as male; on the other side, "brute" matter, evil, and duplicity, gendered as female (and even though "the Devil" was gendered as male, he was seen as particularly attractive to women and therefore associated with female evil).[42] As a result, the theological dualism of *imago Dei* / fallen humanity connects with a sexual duality, or humanity as male and female, so that we end up with a tendency in classical Christian theology to see men as more *imago Dei* than fallen being, while seeing women more as fallen being than *imago Dei*.[43] Women come to represent the qualities of materiality, irrationality, carnality,

---

41. Ruether, *Sexism and God-Talk*, 37.
42. Men of subordinated groups are also often gendered female. See, for example, James McBride, *War, Battering, and Other Sports: The Gulf between American Men and Women* (Atlantic Highlands, NJ: Humanities Press, 1995), for an analysis of the construction of masculinity in terms of dominance over the submissive female Other, which is not limited to male/female relations: he shows how, in war and male sports such as football, the opponent is depicted in terms of submissive "femininity."
43. Ruether, *Sexism and God-Talk*, 93.

finitude, and so on, which debase the "manly" spirit and drag it down into sin and death.

This distortion is supported by myths of female evil. In the two primary examples in Christian-Western history of such myths, those of Pandora and Eve, the female is seen as the enemy of harmony, good order, and felicity in human affairs. This mythology, says Ruether, not only holds women responsible for the advent of evil in the world (Pandora opens the box; Eve eats from the tree—hence evil is born), but it translates female evil into an ontological principle. Ruether suggests that this "original paradise" is likely the mythologizing of early infancy, when the mother provided comfort and nourishment from her body, in which case "such male myths actually scapegoat women as mothers for the loss of the paradise which *she* had once provided but which is lost to the male, wrenched from childhood into the adult (male) world of harsh struggle."[44] According to Ruether's analysis, then, myths of female evil and a dualizing pattern of thought are combined to form a heady mixture in which women come to be seen as the primary agents of sin.[45] Both the self/other dualism and the is/ought dualism are then confused with the subject/object differentiation. In other words, her analysis points to a fusion of moral, ontological, and sociological categories into a coherent worldview, in which the distinction between consciousness and objects of sight is reified as the primary ontological dualism of "spirit and matter," which, in turn, "is identified with an absolutized moral distinction between good and evil."[46]

She notes that the ontological dualism of mind and body (and good and evil) in Western thought becomes a dualism of gender, race, and class in Western thought. Thus, "males come to be seen as closer to mind and reason," whereas women are seen as "more 'carnal,' both in the sense of irrational, prone to sensual impulses, and in the sense of more prone to evil."[47] Within this worldview, elite ruling males identify their capacity to think (or rather, to define who thinks and what counts as rational thought) with an abstract spiritual realm of thought, which, in turn, is associated with "the good." These elites then project upon others the qualities of the devalued "body."[48]

Since, for Ruether, the category of the Other on whom sin and evil are projected is not limited to women, her view of the patriarchy, in contrast to Daly's view of patriarchy as the universal false religion that scapegoats women,

---

44. Ibid., 168.
45. Ibid., 161.
46. Rosemary Radford Ruether, "Dualism and the Nature of Evil in Feminist Theology," *Studies in Christian Ethics* 5, no. 1 (1992): 31. In his multivolume study on dualism, Petrus Fontaine argues that the good/evil dualism is fundamental. See Fontaine, *The Light and the Dark: A Cultural History of Dualism* (Amsterdam: J. C. Gieben, 1986).
47. Ruether, "Dualism and the Nature of Evil in Feminist Theology," 26.
48. Ibid., 32.

is more multilayered and complex.[49] But within the multilayered phenomenon of patriarchy, the woman/body association decrees a "natural" subordination of female to male, "*as flesh must be subject to spirit in the right ordering of nature.*"[50] The association of women with the body that has to be controlled (and even punished) by the ruling spirit (men) justifies measures taken, however violent, to ensure the subjugation of women. In other words, projection makes the (female) Other the cultural "carrier" of rejected qualities, and thus serves as rationale for the exploitation, and even the killing of the Other. Furthermore, one of the results of this dualizing pattern of thought is the depiction of women as simple-minded and fit only for menial tasks, thus justifying an ideology of exploitation, argues Ruether.[51] Hiding within this ideology of exploitation is an insecure fear of the dominated as plotting against their "betters." This fear of the Other leads to the scapegoating of the Other. Within this cultural script, women are easily scapegoated as witches in league with the devil to subvert male power, people of color as rapists and murderers, or Jews as diabolical agents subverting the Christian order. The demonized Other, writes Ruether, becomes "demonic matter," "dirt" that pollutes and contaminates, "vermin" that spreads disease. They are, in short, depicted as agents of chaos. This, she says, is the "rhetoric of extermination," which splits up into various genocidal rhetorics that justify violence against the Other, including the gendered rhetoric of death that is part of the feminist rhetorical situation.[52]

At the same, paradoxically, the dualistic thought pattern that demonizes the Other also idealizes the Other. Then the Other is seen as representing unfallen or innocent "goodness," in harmony with "nature," and uncomplicated by alienated reason and power. This "ideal" can be seen in cultural creations such as the "virgin-mother" who combines sexual innocence and devotion to the well-being of the fathers and their sons, the "kindly darky" who sings and dances in spontaneous happiness, and the "good Jew" personified by Old Testament heroes and the saintly Jesus. This paradoxical idealization is not a

---

49. Nicholas John Ansell notes that, in contrast to Daly, who is best described as a radical feminist, Ruether can be "more accurately described as a liberation theologian for whom women's liberation is one of a large number of concerns" (*"The Woman Will Overcome the Warrior": A Dialogue with the Christian/Feminist Theology of Rosemary Radford Ruether* [New York: University Press of America, 1994], 3). Thus, although feminist concerns are clearly prominent in her thought, she connects them with analyses of anti-Semitism, heterosexism, racism, capitalism, and ecological concerns.

50. Rosemary Radford Ruether, "Virginal Feminism in the Fathers of the Church," in *Religion and Sexism: Images of Woman in the Jewish and Christian Traditions*, ed. Rosemary Radford Ruether (Eugene, OR: Wipf and Stock, 1998), 157. The text in italics refers to Augustine, *On Continence* 1.23, in which Augustine parallels the supra- and subordinations of Christ and the church, man and woman, and the soul and the body. See Augustine, *On Continence*, in *The Nicene and Post-Nicene Fathers* 3, ed. Philip Schaff (Grand Rapids: Eerdmans, 1988), 1.23, 388–89.

51. Ruether, "Dualism and the Nature of Evil in Feminist Theology," 32–33.

52. Ibid., 33.

recognition of the humanity of the gendered, racial, or religious Other, and it does not change any of the existing power relationships, but in fact reinforces victim status for the Other, as I already suggested in the previous chapter's focus on Mary. Ruether's response is to call for the transformation of social relations toward shared power and the recognition of all people's complex humanity.[53]

Making use of Jungian analysis, feminist philosopher Nel Noddings sheds further light on this seemingly paradoxical demonization and idealization of the Other, particularly that of women.[54] Noddings's analysis of dualism differs slightly from that of Ruether, focusing more on a consciousness/unconsciousness dualism in which men are associated with consciousness and women with unconsciousness.[55] Noddings argues that the idea of both female goodness and female evil as largely unconscious played a central role in the arguments of the Christian witch hunters, since they argued that women were more sensitive to the supernatural, which made them more "likely" to become the unconscious vehicles of demonic power.[56] But the notion of women being driven by their unconscious also stands at the root of a particular understanding of female goodness. Noddings points to some interesting elements in Western fairy tales and legends, where we often find the themes of unconscious female victory over evil and of conscious male heroism.[57] Within these stories, those not associated with reason are often favored with miraculous interventions as long as they are innocent, stupid, and friendly. When these characters do get power, they become "evil." Noddings writes, "Act unconsciously, goes the message to women, and all will be well; begin to think, lay your own plans, conquer your own realms, and evil has taken possession of you. The wolf-woman, then, 'wants really to eat the whole world.'"[58]

In Jungian analysis, the "feminine principle," *Eros*, defines woman and commands submission and obedience, whereas the "masculine principle," *Logos*, sets man free to define himself through rational thought and action.[59] This, says Noddings, is no improvement on the Aristotelian associations of men/active and women/passive. The only difference is that, in the Jungian framework, feminine powers are not ineffective but rather unconscious. In other words, in this framework, for good or evil, the feminine principle that we encounter in myth, legend, ancient religions, and even in modern Goddess movements is essentially unconscious. In the words of another Jungian, Erich

53. Ibid.
54. Noddings, *Women and Evil*, 44, 48–89.
55. Ibid., 36.
56. Ibid., 44–45.
57. Ibid., 48–49.
58. Ibid., 49.
59. Ibid., 64.

Neumann, "consciousness is identified with the figure of the male hero, while the devouring unconscious is identified with the image of the female monster.... In both sexes the active ego consciousness is characterized by male symbolism, the unconscious as a whole by a female symbolism."[60] If *Logos* is male and *Eros* female, then women are trapped by the classical dilemma: to think like a woman is not to think at all, and to think like a man is to become unnatural and therefore dangerous. This analysis suggests that the same dualistic symbolism undergirds (Western) notions of both female goodness and female evil. The idealization of the Other is no solution to the denigration of the Other, for it still functions within the same dualistic framework.

The rhetoric of reason, that is, the feminist rhetorical strategy aimed at exposing and correcting misconceptions in views on women, which Ruether and Noddings use, therefore focuses on analyzing the *logos* of sin-talk. It asks about the explanations for sin offered by classical sin-talk, the stories found at the root of Christian understandings of sin, and the philosophical presuppositions inherent in classical sin-talk. The value of Ruether's work lies in the way she exposes the dualistic *logos* lurking in patriarchal rhetoric, which has contributed to the extermination of millions of Jews, enslavement of people of color, and systemic gender violence. The work of Nel Noddings further highlights some of the same dynamics, and shows even more clearly how idealization is not a solution to denigration, but simply part of a dualistic framework in which women are dehumanized and eventually associated with evil. In short, the feminist rhetoric of reason exposes the *logos* of classical sin-talk as for the most part deeply sexist, indeed misogynist—rooted in myths of female evil and the violent overthrow of female power—and as intertwined with dualistic thought patterns that associate women with nature and the body that are to be "controlled" by the ruling masculine mind.

Here Christian sin-talk, which by definition is theocentric speech, interacts with patriarchal constructs of God in a destructive way. In patriarchal Christian culture, manhood is implicitly intertwined with the "rhetorical masculinity of God" (I use this phrase to refer to the fact that while Christian theology teaches that God has no gender, it nevertheless mostly uses and even insists on male terminology for God). Insofar as God is understood as powerful but benign, ideal manhood will be constructed in terms of supposedly "benevolent" patriarchy, as defended by conservative Christians. However, there is nothing benevolent about patriarchy, no matter how "mildly" defined. In fact, the feminist rhetoric of oppression we encountered earlier in this chapter suggests that there is an ominous undertone to the classically

---

60. Erich Neumann, *The Great Mother* (Princeton, NJ: Princeton University Press, 1955), 27–28.

male-symbolized Christian God that belies this superficially benign patriarchy, a violence that is present in the most ancient myths in which Christianity is rooted. This feminist rhetoric suggests that the mythology of the male warrior-god (associated with reason, order, and the mind) overcoming the female goddess (associated with the earth, the body, and chaos) forms part of the collective unconscious of Christianity. Eve, all-woman, is the final Christian symbol of the chaos-monster, to be conquered and ruled. In the words of Mircea Eliade, "One becomes truly a man only . . . by imitating the gods. . . . In *illo tempore* the god has slain the marine monster. . . . Man repeats this blood sacrifice, sometimes even with human victims."[61] Add to this the dualistic patterns that identify women with evil and men with the divine order, and we see the creation of a patriarchal logic in which men rule and women submit, men govern and women are controlled, men represent order and women chaos, men "chastise" and women submit to violence.

So far this chapter has shown that feminist theologians point out that the association of women with sin and evil has historically led to a rhetoric of death that explicitly or implicitly justified gender violence. In chapter 3 we saw that feminist theologians also point out that the emphasis on pride as sin contributes to a rhetoric of life-denial that sometimes plays a role in women accepting gender violence. These patriarchal rhetorical practices in combination look eerily familiar from a feminist perspective: on the one hand, the woman who is evil incarnate (Eve); on the other hand, the woman who is too good for her own good (Mary). Both of these female symbols are unrelated to real women and are expressions of what I call the "patriarchal feminine," and both play a role in cultural patterns that normalize gender violence. In short, at the heart of classical sin-talk are two damaging patriarchal rhetorical practices that find expression in the patriarchal feminine, the so-called Mary/Eve dichotomy. This dichotomy plays a central role in patriarchal politics of the control of women. It is the patriarchal divide-and-conquer strategy at its most classic. Let us look more closely at this dichotomy and its relation to classical sin-talk.

THE PATRIARCHAL FEMININE AND THE RHETORIC OF DEATH

The Mary/Eve dichotomy (also known as the Madonna/Whore dichotomy) constitutes a patriarchal way of classifying and organizing women. It is also, of course, deeply dehumanizing. Rosemary Radford Ruether argues that, while

---

61. Mircea Eliade, *The Sacred and the Profane: The Nature of Religion*, trans. Willard R. Trask (New York: Harcourt, Brace & World, 1959), 100.

on the surface Mary is an expression of the *idealization* of women, in reality she arises not as a solution to, but as a corollary of, the denigration of fleshly maternity and sexuality.[62] Similarly, Mary Daly notes that this dichotomizing of women into "good" and "bad" women was "spawned" by the depiction of women as Other in the first place.[63] Mary Potter Engel makes a similar observation, albeit from a different historical context, where this dichotomy was used more explicitly to justify gender violence. She says that one of the conditions for "allowing" violence against wives found in popular late medieval and Renaissance European literature was the condition of "just cause." This was based on the assumption of female subordination, an assumption that was associated with the use of female stereotypes:

> Five stereotypes, Gateway to Ruin, Temptress, Adulteress, Deceiver, and Shrew, together form the antitype to the Good Wife. . . . The type of the Good Wife and the antitype of the Bad Wife contribute to a theory of just battery by providing specific material for the just cause rule. If a wife does not adequately fill the role expected of her, to be a good wife wisely administering the household and her body . . . she deserves to be disciplined. . . . Thus, the use of stereotypes undergirds the condition of just cause by specifying just causes for violence against women in particular circumstances. The use of these stereotypes also undergirds the condition of just cause in another, equally powerful and more insidious way: by implying that all women eventually behave in these ways. Therefore, even when one's wife is not acting wrongly, she is perceived as being on the verge of revealing her true nature as Gateway to Ruin, Temptress, Adulteress, Deceiver, or Shrew. In other words, the use of these stereotypes implies that all women inevitably act out their evil nature and therefore are always deserving of whatever chastisement they receive.[64]

The patriarchal symbols of Eve and Mary are often co-mingled with other scripts and symbols of patriarchy, most notably those of class and race. For example, Rosemary Radford Ruether notes that the nineteenth-century Cult of True Womanhood, a form of secular Mariology, was a class myth.[65] It

---

62. Ruether, *New Woman*, 18: "Actual sexuality is analyzed as 'dirt,' while the repressed libidinal feelings are sublimated in mystical eroticism, expressed by the spiritual sacred marriage of the virgin soul with Christ. The love of the Virgin Mary does not correct but presupposes the hatred of real women."
63. Daly, *Beyond God the Father*, 60.
64. Mary Potter Engel, "Historical Theology and Violence against Women: Unearthing a Popular Tradition of Just Battery," in *Revisioning the Past: Prospects in Historical Theology*, ed. Mary Potter Engel and Walter E. Wyman Jr. (Minneapolis: Fortress Press, 1992), 64.
65. Rosemary Radford Ruether, "The Cult of True Womanhood," *Commonweal* 99, November 9, 1973, 130; and Ruether, "'Home and Work': Women's Roles and the Transformation of Values," *Theological Studies* 36 (December 1975): 654.

was also, in fact, a race myth, as Sojourner Truth so poignantly expressed in her famous speech, "Ain't I a Woman?" On the surface, the "True Woman" seemed to be a positive symbol, especially in contrast to the earlier tendency in Western culture to depict women as the "Gateway to Hell." "True" women (in reality, white middle- and upper-class virgins and wives) were now depicted as icons of purity to whom hard-working men of the industrial age could return as to a haven. But the asexual "purity" of the "good woman" in the nineteenth-century Cult of True Womanhood had its underside in the proliferation of houses of prostitution, and in the exploitation of black and working-class women. These groups of women were still associated with conquered nature (a central part of the designation of women as defiled Other), while white ruling-class women were portrayed as the epitome of culture.[66] In other words, "Eve" was now visited upon women who were already "marked" by their race or class, while the secular Mariology of the Cult of True Womanhood was reserved for white upper-class women. This new ideological dualism served the economic order well, for while it removed "idealized" women from public life, it made a group of "defiled" women available for sexual and labor exploitation.[67]

The link between gender violence, on the one hand, and the two symbols of the patriarchal feminine, on the other hand, is starkly illustrated here. In the case of those women deemed defiled and exploitable ("Eve"), violence took severe and sometimes public forms: the rape of black women was deemed a nonoffense, and the bodies of poor women were seen as expendable commodities for the purposes of labor exploitation and prostitution. In other words, violence was especially visited upon those women depicted in

---

66. Delores Williams notes that an often-felt sense of unworthiness in African American women has its source in both the elevation of white women and its corresponding devaluation of black women, and the indifference of the US legal system to the defilement of black women's bodies through overwork, lynching, and rape by white men (Delores Williams, "A Womanist Perspective on Sin," in *A Troubling in MY Soul: Womanist Perspectives on Evil and Suffering*, ed. Emilie M. Townes [Maryknoll, NY: Orbis Books, 1993], 143–44). There is an interesting discussion among feminist and womanist scholars regarding the women/nature association, which should be noted. See Angela West, *Deadly Innocence: Feminist Theology and the Mythology of Sin* (London: Cassel, 1995), 44, and Susan Brooks Thistlethwaite, *Sex, Race, and God: Christian Feminism in Black and White* (New York: Crossroad, 1989), 42. West remarks that white feminism often falls into the trap of wanting to "reconnect with nature," while "for black women, who were cast in the role of the exploited body, there is not the same passion to return to the body." See also Delores Williams, "Sin, Nature, and Black Women's Bodies," in Adams, *Ecofeminism and the Sacred*, 24–29, who links the rape of the earth and the rape of black women. She argues that the negative value given to the color black makes black women particularly vulnerable to violence. I agree with the cautionary tone struck here by womanist scholars. I believe that Christianity's own history, the awareness of the plight of prostitutes in the history of the West, and the stories of working-class women should likewise caution feminists against a too-easy embrace of "nature" as the antidote against the politics of abstraction.
67. On the latter point, see Ruether, "'Home and Work,'" 652.

the image of a defiled "Eve," associated with the earth and material reality. But the supposedly idealized women did not escape gender violence either. It was precisely the passivity of the secularized "Mary" (the "Angel of the House")—that is, her obedience, submissiveness, and being-for-the-other—that was used to justify sexual violence within marriage. For example, Harry Campbell, a prominent nineteenth-century London pathologist, said that women need not be a willing agent in sexual relations (indeed, how could they be willing sexual partners if they are too "pure" to even have sexual desires?), thereby encouraging domestic rape. Indeed, other "authorities" of the time, such as Auguste Forel, declared confidently that women *like* to be raped and beaten—the same women who were supposedly idealized as the epitome of purity and innocence.[68]

It would seem that a deep misogyny underlies *both* categorical female symbols of Western culture (and Christian theology). Eleanor McLaughlin notes that the witch hunts arose at a time when evil was increasingly symbolized as female, and where the cult of the Virgin Mary started to grow stronger—that is, a period where the good woman / bad woman polarity was intensified.[69] The Eve/Mary dichotomy, then, is not merely a matter of these two symbols reflecting the dualism of earth and sky, the "Two Ways" tradition of classical Christianity, as Erin White and Marie Tulip suggest.[70] No, it rather seems to be the case that both symbols—sublimated spiritual femininity and the carnal, disruptive woman—are rooted in a dualistic thought pattern that depicts women as the Other. One could argue that dualism functions on two levels: a primary dualism of self and Other, where the male mind is the subject and associated with "good," and the female body the object, associated with "bad"; and a second dualism of the earthly and the heavenly woman, of absolute female "sin" and absolute female "purity," symbolized in Eve and Mary.[71] But if this dichotomized female symbolism is the result of the primary self/other dualism that depicts women as Other, it would mean that *both* Eve and Mary stand on the inferior (negative) side of the primary dualism. Mary is not to Eve as Self/subject/good is to Other/object/bad. Rather, *both* Eve and Mary are the Other/object to the male Self/subject. Patriarchy's "Mary" is not the "solution" to patriarchy's "Eve," for both are androcentrically defined as other than truly human. Both symbols are dehumanizing.

68. Bram Dijkstra, *Idols of Perversity* (New York: Oxford University Press, 1986), 112, 119–20.
69. Eleanor Commo McLaughlin, "Equality of Souls, Inequality of Sexes: Woman in Medieval Theology," in Ruether, *Religion and Sexism*, 254.
70. Erin White and Marie Tulip, *Knowing Otherwise: Feminism, Women, and Religion* (Melbourne, Australia: David Lovell Publishing, 1991), 41.
71. See Ruether's argument that three different distinctions are confused in this dualizing pattern of thought: the is/ought distinction, the self/other distinction, and the subject/object distinction ("Dualism and the Nature of Evil in Feminist Theology," 30–31).

It has long been argued that dehumanization of groups of people is the starting point of genocidal practices.[72] Some of history's most infamous examples of this include the depiction of Jews as vermin in the era leading up to the Holocaust or Tutsis as cockroaches before the Rwanda genocide. How this scapegoating mechanism plays itself out in the case of gender violence is starkly illustrated in the following confession of a would-be rapist:

> I grabbed her from behind, and turned her around and pushed her against the wall. . . . I pulled her back and hit her several times in the face quite hard, and she stopped resisting and said, "All right, just don't hurt me." And I think when she said that . . . all of a sudden a thought came into my head. My God, this is a human being. . . . *It was difficult for me at that time even to admit that when I was talking to a woman, I was dealing with a human being*, because, if you read men's magazines, you hear about your stereo, your car, your chick.[73]

To summarize, our interrogation of classical sin-talk in this chapter has pointed to its complicity in creating dehumanizing stereotypes of women. In this manner classical Christian sin-talk becomes oppressive: in its androcentrism and sexism, it helps to create a hegemonic script that reinforces a patriarchal culture in which women are exploited, marginalized, disempowered, dehumanized, and ultimately physically attacked. Not only does the depiction of women as "Eve" in the rhetoric of death serve to justify violence against women in various ways. Not only does the rhetoric of life-denial, which I have argued is associated with the Mary symbol, hijack a spirit of rebellion in women, which keeps them in positions of vulnerability. But in helping to create the dehumanizing Mary/Eve dichotomy by which women are divided and conquered, and ultimately dehumanized, classical sin-talk has traditionally helped to constitute character, community, and culture in such a way that women become the "appropriate victims" of society. The latter is a concept developed by R. Emerson Dobash and Russell P. Dobash, who argue that "the seeds of wife beating lie in the subordination of females and in their subjection to male authority and control. This relationship between women and men has been institutionalized . . . and is supported by a belief system,

---

72. See, e.g., Maurice Bloch, *Prey into Hunter: The Politics of Religious Experience*, Lewis Henry Morgan Lecture Series 1984 (Cambridge: Cambridge University Press, 1992), 8–23; Avraham Barkai, "*Volksgemeinschaft*, 'Aryanization,' and the Holocaust," in *The Final Solution: Origins and Implementation*, ed. David Cesarani (London: Routledge, 1994), 34–43; and René Girard, *Things Kept Secret from the Foundation of the World*, trans. Stephen Bann and Michael Metteer (Stanford, CA: Stanford University Press, 1987).

73. Cited by Mary John Mananzan, "Feminine Socialization: Women as Victims and Collaborators," in *Violence against Women*, Concilium 1994/1, ed. Elisabeth Schüssler Fiorenza and Mary Shawn Copeland (Maryknoll, NY: Orbis Books, 1994), 50 (italics added).

including a religious one, that makes such relationships seem natural, morally just, sacred."[74] Sin-talk does not accomplish this by itself, of course. But in reflecting and, above all, strengthening these patriarchal and dehumanizing symbols, classical sin-talk shows itself to be characterized by life-negating rhetorical practices in the lives of women in particular, and ultimately in the life of the whole community.

In other words, insofar as Christian sin-talk participates in creating women in the dual image of the patriarchal feminine, it also participates in the dehumanization of women. It does this as it encourages women to emulate an obedient, self-sacrificial Mariological ideal by emphasizing the virtue of humility in response to the sin of pride. And it does so insofar as it depicts women as Eve, conquered nature to be controlled by violent means if necessary. Christian sin-talk is not the only problem: Christianity is deeply patriarchal, even to this day, as reflected in all its doctrines. But Christian sin-talk needs to address human pathology, not contribute to it. As long as it remains rooted in a patriarchal *ethos*, linked to sexist and indeed misogynist *logos* patterns, and ignores the *pathos* of its gendered audiences, it risks contributing to a rhetoric of death and life-denial. Sin-talk is theocentric talk. It is supposed to speak with the voice of God, to name that which is not as it should be. But insofar as sin-talk speaks with the voice of the patriarchy instead, and contributes to a culture of gender violence, whether directly or indirectly, Christian sin-talk is itself sinful. This recognition marks an important turning point in our analysis, as we pivot in the final two chapters from the critical mode to the constructive mode. In the next chapter we examine how feminist theologians are in fact already speaking the language of sin in criticizing classical sin-talk, and in the final chapter I provide an outline for an explicitly constructive feminist rhetoric of sin.

---

74. R. Emerson Dobash and Russell P. Dobash, *Violence against Wives: A Case against the Patriarchy* (New York: Free Press, 1979), 33–34.

5

Grammar

Of the tree of the knowledge of good and evil you shall not eat, for in the day that you eat of it you shall die.
—*Genesis 2:17 NRSV*

As the two previous chapters have made clear, feminist theologians are highly critical of classical modes of sin-talk, and the ways in which it can be life-denying and death-dealing in women's lives. Utilizing feminist rhetorical strategies of oppression, difference, and reason, feminist theologians expose the patriarchal *ethos* present in classical sin-talk, its androcentric lack of awareness of the *pathos* of its audiences, and the sexist *logos* inherent in it. Most importantly, they point to ways in which the patriarchal rhetoric of classical sin-talk participates in the crisis element (exigence) of the *kairos* at the root of the rhetorical situation: the oppression of women, especially expressed in gender violence. It is the discerning of this *kairos* that calls forth a constructive rhetorical response. However, this constructive response is neither the antithesis of the critical response nor just something that follows it, but is already implied in it.

It might seem as if feminist theologians are suggesting that the very notion of sin is so deeply flawed that it should be jettisoned altogether. Indeed, there is deep distrust of sin-talk in feminist circles, and deservedly so. But at the same time, the denunciation of death suggested in feminist critical interrogation of classical sin-talk operates with the same theological grammar as classical sin-talk itself, by denouncing that which is against the divine will and by pointing to broken relationality at the heart of sin-talk.

In fact, I argue that some feminist theologians, when they point to the structural-systemic nature of oppression, explicitly employ the language of "fall" or "original sin" to do so. Rosemary Radford Ruether recognizes that "[f]eminism's own claim to stand in judgment on patriarchy as evil means it cannot avoid the question of the capacity of humanity for sin."[1] Similarly, Serene Jones, although aware that the patriarchal history of Christian sin-talk makes it difficult to contemplate the relevance of sin-talk for women, notes that feminist antipathy to classical sin-talk is "balanced by the fact that no single topic in Christian theology has more resonance with feminist theory." In fact, she argues that the "recognition of the pervasive, insidious, and historically persistent forces of destruction at work in the world sits at the heart of the feminist movement."[2] In other words, as we have seen in the preceding chapters, much of classical sin-talk is so destructive in the lives of women that it becomes sinful itself. Therefore, responding to it requires a concept of sin.

My point, in short, is that a strong hermeneutic of retrieval is at work within the hermeneutic of suspicion that drives feminist critical rhetorical inquiry into classical sin-talk. This chapter looks at this hermeneutic of retrieval by pointing to the ways in which feminist criticisms of the patriarchy, and of the ways in which classical sin-talk supports and participates in it, in fact structurally resemble classical sin-talk, and in particular the doctrine of original sin. This discussion lays the groundwork for our final chapter, where I shall outline a constructive feminist rhetoric on sin.

TOWARD CRITICAL RETRIEVAL

My approach to the retrieval of sin-talk is shaped by the awareness that sin-talk is about rejecting the forces of death and embracing that which is life-giving. Rhetorical theologian Don Compier expresses this awareness well when he argues that, if we identify the core of the gospel as the "ethics of reverence for life," then any charge suggesting that the doctrine of sin has "collaborated with the forces of death" deserves the serious attention of Christian theologians. The analysis in the previous two chapters shows how classical sin-talk has indeed collaborated with the forces of death by (both accidentally and deliberately) participating in patriarchal rhetorics of death and life-denial. On the other hand, as Compier also notes, the fact that the doctrine of sin has been distorted argues in favor of its reformulation, not its abandonment. As a matter of fact, as I remarked earlier, the very recognition of that distortion already constitutes a form of sin-talk. Therefore, I agree with Compier

---

1. Rosemary Radford Ruether, *Sexism and God-Talk: Toward a Feminist Theology* (Boston: Beacon Press, 1993), 161.
2. Serene Jones, *Feminist Theory and Christian Theology: Cartographies of Grace*, Guides to Theological Inquiry (Minneapolis: Fortress Press, 2000), 96.

that it is neither feasible to jettison sin-talk altogether nor to ignore critiques of Christian sin-talk as misguided and inconsequential.³ Within the feminist hermeneutic of suspicion leveled against distortions in classical sin-talk, we can trace the beginnings of a feminist rhetorical doctrine of sin, a theo-ethical judgment of some sin-talk as sinful. If one were to suggest that we should abandon sin-talk because of its negative effects, it would be tantamount to saying that we should stop talking about sin because it is too sinful to talk about, which would obviously be theological nonsense. Our task therefore becomes one of critical retrieval—particularly in our case for the purpose of developing a constructive feminist way of talking about sin.

I therefore also agree with Mary McClintock Fulkerson, who, in a discussion of the critiques of sin-talk encountered in Saiving, Daly, and Ruether, argues that Christian feminist discourse about sin is indeed critically constructive.⁴ Feminist theologians, she says, "speak" a traditional language but say something new with it because they speak from a different place. In chapter 2, I introduced that "different place" as the feminist rhetorical situation characterized by the exigence of gender violence, which gives rise to feminist rhetorical engagement. From the poststructuralist perspective on language as functioning through relationships of difference, Fulkerson concludes that the similarities between "classical" sin-talk and feminist sin-talk should not be sought in correspondence of entities or terms, but rather in the discovery of similar relational patterns. Feminist sin-talk is not simply a different speaking of the same language, nor is it a completely alternative way of speaking. Instead, like "classical" sin-talk, it is theological, because it speaks within the constraints of theocentric discourse. Yet it also moves beyond that, into what Fulkerson calls *theacentric* discourse, because it is produced from the social position of women, that is, in what I have called the feminist rhetorical situation. As such, Fulkerson says, it *contests* and even *modifies* the dominant discourse.⁵

In the previous two chapters, our focus was particularly on the feminist contestation of patriarchal sin-talk. In order to further trace this contestation and, increasingly, also the modification of sin-talk, I introduce in this chapter some salient points of the classical doctrine of original sin. These salient points are then correlated with the ways feminists talk about both women's victimization and oppression, and how women's agency is to be understood. The focus on the systemic not only shows us more clearly the nature of the patriarchal *ethos* behind classical sin-talk, but also helps us understand the

---

3. Don H. Compier, *What Is Rhetorical Theology? Textual Practice and Public Discourse* (Harrisburg, PA: Trinity Press, 1999), 53.
4. Mary McClintock Fulkerson, "Sexism as Original Sin: Developing a Theacentric Discourse," *Journal of the American Academy of Religion* 59, no. 4 (1991): 653.
5. Ibid., 656.

ways in which women suffer from the sins of others and engage in sinful action themselves. Therefore, my argument here is that, when some feminist theologians implicitly or explicitly evoke the language of "original sin," what we see is not merely a rhetorical similarity, but both a contestation and a modification of the classical doctrine of original sin.

THE DOCTRINE OF ORIGINAL SIN

In the previous chapters I noted that the doctrine of original sin, which originates primarily, although not exclusively, with Augustine, operates with the idea of a threefold movement: the move toward the self (pride), the move away from God (rebellion), and the move toward the world (concupiscence). This doctrine offers a profound perspective on human moral agency but is also marked by several internal tensions and contradictions. First, although Augustine emphasized the free choice of the will at the root of original sin, there is nevertheless a tragic element in this understanding of sin, in two senses. Sin is tragic, first, in the sense of it being partially beyond our control: original sin having occurred, it is now the inheritance of all humans, something that exists prior to individual choices. Augustine tried to steer clear of two alternatives: the gnostic identification of sin with finitude, and Pelagian moralism that located sin in purely willed acts. Practically speaking, then, individual sinful agency is here understood as something that never happens in a vacuum; the moment of choice for evil is recognized, indeed, but that choice is rooted in a more fundamental distortion of human nature that has radically effected the formation of personhood on a universal scale. One could furthermore argue that there is a tragic tone in the doctrine not only in the sense of something that is beyond our control to some extent, but also in the sense of something painful: it names not just human pathology, but human *pathos*. The depth structure of sin is that of broken relationality and inner brokenness. This latter element, I have already suggested, should resonate well with feminist theology as a whole, in which the concept of brokenness is a central one. Humans are perpetrators of sin while simultaneously being its victims.

Second, we have seen, in the two major feminist critiques of classical sin-talk, how both the emphasis on pride as the primary move in sin, and the rhetorical association of sin with the body, have been harmful to women, and in fact contributed to the systemic dehumanization of women by helping to cast them in the image of the patriarchal feminine expressed in Mary and Eve. I suggested in the previous chapter that, somewhat ironically, Augustine's insistence on pride as the root sin can be seen as part of his efforts to not locate the origins of sin in the body. However, as we saw in chapter 3, this leads to another rhetorical problem in suggesting that the Promethean sin of pride is the paradigmatic sin, which leads to the problematic universalization of the prescription of self-sacrifice and humility. In other words, a bit of tension seems to exist between the two feminist critiques, at least as it relates to classical thought: association of sin with the body, which happens in spite of Augustine's original insistence on the goodness of physical existence, is obviously problematic in light of the traditional association of women with the body, but at the same time the focus on pride as the root sin, which is part of a rejection of the idea that sin originates in the body, is also problematic.

Third, apart from the above-mentioned tensions in the classical doctrine of original sin, which are particularly problematic for feminist theologians, the doctrine also suffers from the fact that as a doctrine operating with a premodern worldview, it has not fared well in the modern era. There are two aspects to this: original sin as event, and original sin as condition. As a historical event, the doctrine leans heavily on the narrative of Adam and Eve, which is no longer accepted as historical reality except in fundamentalist circles. In the twentieth century, theologians such as Reinhold Niebuhr and Paul Tillich tried to replace the historical account of Adam and Eve and their "fall" with existentialist categories. From a feminist perspective this has the laudable effect of abandoning the mythology of Eve as the mother of all evil, but as we saw in chapter 3, the efforts of these theologians remain androcentric in tone when they privilege the "male" sin of pride as the primordial sin. They are, however, correct in abandoning the idea of original sin as a historical event. Tatha Wiley notes that the reduction of the doctrine to the story of Adam and Eve has overshadowed the fundamental Christian teaching that evil "is a feature of our existence prior to our personal choices and decisions," that we "are born into a world shaped—distorted—by such evils as violence and abuse in families, apartheid, genocide, and discrimination," and that the "doctrine of original sin was one means by which early Christians named this dimension of human existence and its threat to human well-being."[6] Wiley therefore points to the importance of the concept of original sin as condition, which is where we can see some compatibility with feminist concerns.

To be sure, the idea of original sin as condition also sometimes clashes with modern sensibilities, since it seems to suggest that we should be held accountable for sins we have not committed, instead of only our own freely chosen acts.[7] However, this critique of the doctrine of original sin rests on the idea

---

6. Tatha Wiley, *Original Sin: Origins, Developments, Contemporary Meanings* (New York: Paulist Press, 2002), 9.

7. Alistair McFadyen, *Bound to Sin: Abuse, Holocaust and the Christian Doctrine of Sin* (Cambridge: Cambridge University Press, 2000), 21–22.

of the autonomous agent, which is a highly questionable concept. Views on agency developed by feminist theorists generally operate with a more nuanced understanding of the acting or willing subject. Likewise, several significant strands of modern theology operate with a more situated understanding of agency, including sinful agency, thereby echoing some of Augustine's existential insights. These theologians, in various ways, while rejecting the historicist premises of the classical doctrine of original sin, and while affirming the reality of individual complicity in evil, nevertheless affirm the corporate nature of sin—the very embeddedness of human beings in structures of sin. With Friedrich Schleiermacher, they understand sin as "common to all; not something that pertains severally to each individual and exists in relation to him by himself, but in each the work of all, and in all the work of each; and only in this corporate character indeed, can it be properly and fully understood."[8] In short, the idea of original sin as condition remains relevant, in part because it constitutes an effort to think about human pathology in a less individualistic and therefore less harshly moralistic manner, and in part because its emphasis on the corporate nature of sin is similar to the rhetoric of social, structural sin.

Liberation and feminist theologians especially tend to emphasize the corporate nature of sin, or more particularly, the reality of structural-systemic sin, what Gustavo Gutiérrez (following José María González) calls the "hamartiosphere," that is, the sphere of sin.[9] The notion of structural sin, writes José Ignacio González Faus, "enables us to explain *how personal evil is both active and masked at the same time.*"[10] If it is theologically legitimate to speak of original sin, he says, it is also legitimate to speak of structural sin. In this, Faus echoes the insights of the Puebla Final Document no. 281, which states that "sin is not just something done by each individual but is also committed in these sinful structures, which are created by human beings."[11] I would even reverse that a bit and suggest that the language of structural sin invites us to rethink the doctrine of original sin, since the view of human moral agency is similar in both, but also because modern perspectives on the doctrine of original sin, divorced as they are from a historicist premise, overlap significantly with the concept of structural sin.

In contrast to the faint echoes of Pelagianism found in modernist notions of autonomy and individuality, the thinking of liberation theologians and many

---

8. Friedrich Schleiermacher, *The Christian Faith*, ed. H. R. Mackintosh and J. S. Stewart (Edinburgh: T&T Clark, 1989), 288.

9. Gustavo Gutiérrez, *A Theology of Liberation: History, Politics and Salvation*, trans. Sister Caridad Inda and John Eagleson, rev. ed. (Maryknoll, NY: Orbis Books, 2001), 103.

10. José Ignacio González Faus, "Sin," in *Systematic Theology: Perspectives from Liberation Theology*, ed. Jon Sobrino and Ignacio Ellacuriá (Maryknoll, NY: Orbis Books, 1996), 197 (italics added).

11. Cited in ibid., 198–99.

other modern theologians focuses on the embeddedness of sinful choices, and of human agency in general, in social structures. As in the Augustinian tradition, these theologians nevertheless want to hold on to the notion of individual responsibility, even while recognizing the complexities of the situation. This is very clear in their prophetic judgment that, within these social structures, there are definite victims and perpetrators. Liberation theologians insist that sinful conditions do not simply exist (as if by fate, which would be a modern version of Manicheism), but they are the result of sinful choices. The structures are personal. But within those structures, there is definite human responsibility to be exercised. We encounter a similar rhetoric in feminist theologians, who point out that women's oppression is a systemic phenomenon. As we have seen, feminist theologians suggest that the moral agency of men and women is formed by these structures of oppression, and as such cannot be simply understood with an individualistic model. In this, feminist sin-talk echoes the internal logic of the doctrine of original sin.

PATRIARCHY AS ORIGINAL SIN

Earlier we noted that Mary Daly argues that the "cosmic false blaming" of women in the Christian myth of the fall is itself patriarchal religion's fall. She charges that the myth of the fall, "together with its offspring—the theology of 'original sin,'" by its built-in bias and its blind reinforcement of prejudice, constitutes the real "original sin" of patriarchal religion.[12] Similarly, Rosemary Radford Ruether speaks of sexism in terms of original sin. She writes that the recognition of sexism as wrong, evil, and sinful brings about the collapse of the myths of female evil, and that this recognition calls for a fundamental *metanoia*, a repentance from the perception of woman as negative Other. In other words, the entire ideological and social superstructure of the patriarchy (including its androcentric and misogynist sin-talk) is now "open to question," and indeed, is now seen as sin.[13] Calling sexism "sin" does not point merely to an understanding of individuals acting wrongly within neutral structures, but to the sinful nature of structures of marginalization, including its ideological elements (particularly the myths of female evil). For Ruether sexist oppression is primarily expressed as distorted relationality. In particular, she calls attention to the idea of masculine-feminine complementarity, which in fact destroys an authentic I-Thou relationship between men and

---

12. Mary Daly, *Beyond God the Father: Toward a Philosophy of Women's Liberation* (Boston: Beacon Press, 1973), 47.
13. Ruether, *Sexism and God-Talk*, 173–83.

women. This distorted relationship is characterized by a power inequality and male control of women's bodies. Violence is not merely incidental to it, but is rather integral to it, as Ruether notes:

> The reduction of woman to the body-object of male use is enforced by a vast network of control, ranging from the most subtle to the most brutal. Direct physical assault is certainly the ultimate weapon that males assume they hold in reserve over women.... There are few women, even today, who have not experienced at least one or two beatings from husbands or boyfriends. Historically, this weapon of control over women has been taken for granted as a male prerogative, defended in civil and ecclesiastical law. Male power over women means a denial of women's right to control their own bodies.... The male who "owns" a woman is assumed to have total sexual access to her.... The woman not under a particular male's control and protection, in turn, is regarded as available for rape. The rape of women is fundamentally an expression of hostility and contempt for women, rather than an expression of "uncontrollable sexual desire."... Gang-rape of conquered women also is a way in which males send messages to other males.[14]

She then continues to make the assertion that this systemic distorted relationality, in which women are abused and oppressed, is akin to what was classically called original sin. The classical distinction between actual and original sin features strongly in her description of sexism. She writes that recognizing sexism as sin has nothing to do with any notion that males are "by nature" evil or that women are incapable of any sin other than the sin of cooperating in their own victimization. Women sin indeed, she says, by cooperating in their own subjugation, by lateral violence to other women who seek emancipation, or by oppressing groups of people such as children or domestic servants. Ruether's point is that the actual sins of individuals are, to a great extent, shaped by the particular space they occupy within the larger system of oppression. This, of course, resonates with the way feminist theorists tend to understand agency. Like the Augustinian tradition, Ruether rejects a "false individualization of responsibility for sin" as a major way of trying to evade the reality of, and responsibility for, the history of distorted humanity. Likewise, she points to both the difference and the interconnection between individual and social-systemic evil.[15] Ruether points out that "the ancient religious writers of late Judaism and early Christianity were not wrong in suggesting that there is a pervasive 'atmosphere' of malevolent influences that dispose the self to choose evil more often than good." Where they went wrong, obviously,

---

14. Ibid., 175.
15. Ibid., 181.

was in scapegoating women for the advent of these forces. In fact, somewhat paradoxically, such scapegoating of women is, as an expression of sexism, one of the "powers and principalities" that conditions the personal choices of both men and women before any actual choices are made. As such, she writes, "We are all the products of the original sin of sexism."[16]

Like the classical doctrine of original sin, the feminist recognition of the embeddedness of men and women in a system of sexist-patriarchal oppression seeks to strike a balance between recognizing both the inevitability of, and the responsibility for, sin—in other words, between the social and individual nature of sin. Thus, Ruether notes, no male as an individual can or is expected to carry the total burden of guilt for sexism. In other words, this is not about a Pelagian blaming of men. Yet at the same time sexism is a human product, and we perpetuate it by cooperating with it. Thus, she concludes, "in spite of the reality of systemic evil which we inherit, which has already biased us before we can choose, we have not lost our ability to choose good rather than evil, and hence our capacity for responsibility."[17] Compared to Daly, Ruether opts for a more constructive route when talking of sexism (and patriarchy) as original sin, but they both make a similar observation: much of the rhetoric inherent in classical sin-talk is sinful. In the process they both, in different ways (and Ruether more than Daly), appropriate the language of original sin to voice their critique.

Serene Jones also points to similarities between feminist perspectives on oppression and the doctrine of original sin, specifically with regard to the question of agency. With respect to oppression's collective character, she notes, feminists point out that relations of domination are embedded in large social forces that constrain groups of women.[18] Her argument again shows the general feminist refusal to resort to a Pelagian individualistic blame game: recognizing oppression's collective character, she argues, allows us to see that injustice is not solely the product of the individual's malevolent intent to "oppress," but is instead the product of larger institutional and social forces. Jones here emphasizes the very important point that it is not helpful to associate oppression solely with intent, because injustice is often a partly unintended effect of institutional forces. She suggests that recognizing these impersonal dimensions of oppression may be important in stopping women from trying to figure out what we as individuals may have done to "deserve injustice," that is, self-blame. I would add that this would also allow men to face the realities of patriarchal oppression and their own role in it without necessarily feeling

16. Ibid., 182.
17. Ibid.
18. Jones, *Feminist Theory and Christian Theology*, 73.

blamed as individuals: what feminist discourse should aim at is not instilling feelings of guilt in men (which is a useless response that just leads to defensiveness), but rather to encourage men to take up responsibility, alongside women, to fight oppressive cultural concepts and structures.

Despite her emphasis on the impersonal dimensions of oppression, however, Jones points out that the personal does "play a role in dynamics of domination."[19] She relates this personal dimension to both the victims and architects of social oppression: social forces harm women in personal ways that can only be articulated in the intimate stories of individual lives and not in grand narratives; and although large cultural forces are involved, the oppression of women is also the result of individuals' intentions and actions. Therefore, individuals and not just large institutions or systems must be held responsible in those cases where clear personal responsibility can be discerned. Feminists also argue for the importance of affirming the agency and personal responsibility of the victims of oppression. The idea is not that of blaming the victim, which happens all too often (e.g., when women are told they are responsible for being raped because of the way they dress), but rather of emphasizing that the victim is more than the recipient of victimization, and that she can be an active agent in her own recovery. In this way she contributes not only to her own healing, but may help to prevent specific forms of oppression from happening to other women.[20]

What needs to be added to this analysis, in my view, is the insistence that this understanding of sin also calls those of us (especially those of us who are relatively privileged in any way) to greater realization of our responsibility. Somewhat paradoxically, the emphasis on the collective nature of sin implies both a reduction and an increase in individual responsibility. What I mean is that the emphasis on collective sin lifts the burden from the individual by moving beyond the blame game and recognizing root causes. At the same it also calls us to be responsible for more than our individual choices: it calls us to be responsible for the kind of society we help to shape. It calls us to resist oppression, because insofar as we do not resist it, we implicitly condone it. Hence, there is a shift away from trying to make individuals feel guilty as individuals and toward recognizing individuals' responsibility as members of the community to transform systems of power and oppression. This simultaneously lifts the moral burden from the individual by avoiding a simplistic individual blame game, but it also increases the individual's moral responsibility, by suggesting that we are all responsible for the kind of societies we create.

19. Ibid.
20. Ibid., 74.

Refusal to take up that responsibility would be what makes the individual guilty even when he or she did not actively choose to transgress morally.

Of course, this does not take away the moral responsibility of those individuals who do transgress as individuals. Let me explain by way of an example: if Johnny beats Suzie, he is guilty of sin as an individual. But as a community we are all guilty insofar as we participate in, and do not contest, cultural and religious narratives that dehumanize Suzie, or that shape Johnny's masculinity in terms of violence, and so on. Within the inner grammar of both original and structural sin, moral responsibility becomes a complex matter that goes well beyond a simplistic Pelagian-style blame game that merely points fingers at the individual who is marked as a sinner, moving to call us to responsibility for the world in which we live.

Daly, Ruether, and Jones, despite methodological, rhetorical, and generational differences, all paradoxically evoke the language of fall or original sin in critiquing the classical doctrine of original sin. One feminist theologian who very explicitly rejects not only the classical doctrine of original sin, but also the rhetorical use of the concept in arguing against it, is Rita Nakashima Brock. Brock talks about sin in terms of brokenheartedness in need of healing, and wants to replace the category of "original sin" with that of "original grace."[21] It is not that Brock does not recognize that sin exists. But, she writes, "While feminists are not naïve about human evil and suffering, we understand sin as historically and socially produced, which requires us to take responsibility for understanding and stopping oppression and suffering."[22] Like other feminist theologians, Brock therefore rejects the notion of biological inheritance of sin and instead emphasizes the ways in which the conditions of our sociality damage us and lead us to damage others.

Despite her rejection of the concept of original sin, there is not that great a difference between what Brock suggests and the kind of emphases we find in Daly, Ruether, or Jones. Her language of brokenheartedness is a poignant restating of the tragic theme in the concept of sin, which resonates well with ideas of broken relationality at the heart of other feminist conversations on sin. However, as stated before, I do not believe that those kind of emphases diverge that much from the classical doctrine of original sin, since the latter in fact operates with ideas of an inner brokenness and broken relationality. As such, it seems to me that while Brock wants to abandon the language of the doctrine of original sin, she is in fact restating much of its inner relational

---

21. Rita Nakashima Brock, *Journeys by Heart: A Christology of Erotic Power* (New York: Crossroad, 2000), 6–9.
22. Ibid., 7.

grammar, and doing so by brilliantly capturing the *pathos* inherent in the concept of sin.

Brock is furthermore absolutely correct in emphasizing grace as an original state. However, I do not find it helpful as a replacement for the concept of original sin. In fact, the classical doctrine of original sin is premised upon the idea of original grace and does not, as Brock describes it, classically function as "a description of our original human state."[23] To state it differently, the classical doctrine of original sin does not argue that sin is an expression of human nature, but rather that it is a distortion of it. To be sure, among the laity sin is all too often thought of as an expression of our true humanity. But classical sin-talk, flawed as it is in many ways, in fact insists that the brokenness we witness in ourselves, our relationships with each other and the world, and our relationship with divine reality, need not be accepted as normal, but is something unnatural that calls us to responsibility and protest. This aspect of classical sin-talk is quite obviously valuable for feminist sin-talk. In order to create a feminist rhetoric of sin, feminist theologians need to be able to insist, firmly, that there is nothing natural about sin, that sin is not an expression of our "original human state." When it comes to gender violence, for example, we need to be able to go beyond the idea that "boys will be boys," that violence defines masculinity, and that gender violence is not a natural phenomenon that should be accepted as the way things are. We need to be able to say that this is not what defines us, that this is that-which-is-not-what-it-should-be, that this is therefore something that calls us to protest and action.

In short, Brock is right in critiquing the biological inheritance concept with which the doctrine of original sin was often implicitly tied, especially since this contributed to the blaming of women for sin. She is also right in emphasizing "original grace" as a foundational Christian concept. She is right to speak of sin in terms of relationality, and her emphasis on "brokenheartedness" adds a further depth dimension to the talk of relationality. At the same time I think original grace is not a replacement for the idea of original sin, and the brokenheartedness and broken relationality of which she speaks in fact constitutes a reiteration of the grammar of the doctrine of original sin. I therefore embrace her language of original grace, but, instead of replacing the concept of original sin with that of original grace, I argue that feminist sin-talk, while retaining the language of original sin, should insist that all talk of brokenness, that is, of original sin, should be premised upon the concept of original grace. In line with the best insights of the classical tradition, feminist sin-talk ought to keep at its center the insistence that sin does not define

23. Ibid., 9.

our humanity, since the recognition of humanity's fundamental value grounds prophetic protest.

The explicit and implicit recognition of the central insights of the doctrine of original sin in depicting the feminist rhetorical situation by Daly, Ruether, Jones, and yes, even Brock, does not stand in direct continuation with the classical doctrine of original sin. It is rather, as Mary McClintock Fulkerson notes, a contestation and modification of the doctrine of original sin. The doctrine has been too problematic for women to be simply cleaned up and presented once more as a previously misunderstood doctrine. Feminist critical rhetorical inquiry has shown that the doctrine has been seriously ethically flawed in that it participated in an *ethos* of patriarchal control, often operated with a woman-blaming (and woman-defiling) *logos*, and tapped into the respective *pathos* (and indeed, since we are speaking of sin here, the pathologies) of men and women instead of addressing them—hence suffering from a lack of *decorum*, that is, from a lack of attention to the *pathos* of its audience.

Yet there are elements in the classical doctrine of original sin that provide useful categories for talking about the sin of oppression, and the nature of human agency within systems of oppression. We turn to that next as we note seven similarities between feminist sin-talk and the classical doctrine of original sin.

FEMINIST SIN-TALK AND THE GRAMMAR OF ORIGINAL SIN

In this concluding section, I want to summarize my findings with regard to the ways in which feminist sin-talk already, explicitly or implicitly, retrieved the classical doctrine of original sin. I do so by noting seven similarities: four of these I derive from the creative analysis of British theologian Alistair McFadyen, now applied to feminist concerns, and three are additions of my own, based on my analysis.

McFadyen lists four interrelated characteristics of the doctrine's perspective on sin which are helpful in showing the strong similarities between classical and feminist sin-talk: contingency, radicality, communicability, and universality.[24] In the first place, as I have already pointed out, the doctrine of original sin does not say that human beings were created sinful: in contrast, it suggests that sin is a distortion, not an expression, of human nature. Therefore it is not an inevitable concomitant or consequence of our creaturely

---

24. McFadyen, *Bound to Sin*, 16.

finitude, but instead something that is contingent.[25] The doctrine, second, holds that sin's reality and grip on people are radical. As such, sin is primarily a serious situation in which we find ourselves, and only secondarily an individual act. Third, the doctrine of original sin presents sin as something that effects a fundamental distortion of the conditions of sociality through which we are "called into personhood." Thus, before we are capable of performing morally culpable acts, sin constructs our very personhood. This distorted reality may be expressed in terms of alienation from the divine. And, in the fourth place, this distorted reality is universally extensive, both as a condition and as an actualizing possibility. McFadyen writes that this universality of sinning represents more than the claim that no one so far has avoided actually committing sin (which would be a Pelagian perspective on the universality of sin). Instead, the doctrine of original sin implies "a universal solidarity in sin which is certainly exhibited in, but is neither simply the product of nor reducible to, the fact that all do, in fact, perform sinful acts."[26] In other words, the solidarity that is claimed here is not merely axiological, accidental, or empirical. McFadyen's handy summary is helpful in tracing the similarities between feminist sin-talk and classical sin-talk in more detail. Let us revisit each of McFadyen's characteristics in connection with feminist sin-talk, to which I will add three further similarities between feminist sin-talk and the classical doctrine of original sin.

1. McFadyen points out that the doctrine of original sin depicts sin as contingent, that is, as a distortion of human nature, and not an expression of it. Similarly, feminist theologians generally point to the artificiality of the "hamartiosphere" of oppressive gender constructions. All feminists, whether leaning more toward constructivism or essentialism, would reject the hierarchical gender patterns that characterize patriarchy. The idea that the use and abuse of women's bodies in exploitation and violence are outflows of natural masculinity, for example, is rejected. So is the idea that female submission in marriage is an expression of women's nature. The central point of feminism as a whole is that cultural patterns that dehumanize women are a distortion of

---

25. The tension between a tragic and a moral worldview is felt the most at this point. The tragic worldview sees sin as more the consequence of finitude than a moral act. Yet thinkers from Irenaeus through Tillich have combined the tragic and the moral view of the "fallenness" of human life. For a modern version of such an attempt, see Patricia A. Williams, *Doing without Adam and Eve: Sociobiology and Original Sin* (Minneapolis: Fortress Press, 2001). Williams argues for an understanding of "original sin" in terms of the human struggle to survive: the same drives that we need to flourish as sociobiological beings also often lead us into individual and systemic sins. Rita Nakashima Brock's view of sin is also close to this perspective, as illustrated by her statement that sin is "a symptom of the unavoidably relational nature of human existence though which we come to be damaged and damage others" (Brock, *Journeys by Heart*, 7).

26. McFadyen, *Bound to Sin*, 16–17.

human nature, not an expression of it. Like the classical doctrine of original sin, feminist sin-talk indicates that the individual and cultural pathologies we see around us do not express who we are as human beings. They do not define us, but are instead expressions of how we act against our fundamental humanity, even when these patterns of oppression appear natural.

2. Although the doctrine of original sin teaches that sin is not an expression of our created nature, it simultaneously teaches that sin has a radical hold on people that would make it appear natural. Likewise, feminists recognize that patriarchy has a radical hold on people's minds and in their lives, so much so that structures of domination appear to be an expression of human nature. Recognizing this radicality does not have to mean that the patriarchy and its patterns of sexism and androcentric assumptions (not to mention its racisms, classisms, heterosexisms, etc.) are the only realities. There is much that is redemptive and healing in both secular and religious classical traditions, and in the various human cultures of the world. But the recognition of the radical insidiousness of patriarchy does mean that a strong hermeneutic of suspicion guides the interpretations of feminist theologians.

3. Feminist theologians are therefore aware that patriarchy effects a fundamental distortion of the conditions of sociality in which we are "called to personhood," a phrase that McFadyen uses regarding the classical doctrine of original sin. Similarly, feminist theorists are concerned with understanding the human subject and human agency in light of the structures of power and systems of oppression within which we live. In chapter 2, we briefly looked at these conditions of sociality by naming the *kairos* discerned within the feminist rhetorical situation in terms of various structures of oppression—and particularly in terms of gender violence. These structures, and the violence used to reinforce them, shape our persons to a large extent before we are even aware of it.

4. However, with regard to McFadyen's characteristic of universality, a note of caution in comparing it with the feminist emphasis on the near-ubiquity of the patriarchy is in order. Feminism has generally abandoned an essentialist perspective on gender and the idea of a uniform and universal patriarchy, adopting instead a more nuanced understanding of patriarchy as a constructed, not quite universal, and certainly not uniform, but nevertheless quite pervasive reality, and concomitantly, of gender as a culturally specific social construction. Nevertheless, the very pervasiveness of patriarchal gender constructions, and the way in which the multilayered nature of patriarchal oppression reaches deeply into the lives of human beings, point to a nearly universal flaw in most of human life. As such, while not quite the idea of the complete universality of sin in the classical tradition, the feminist emphasis on the nearly universal flaw of patriarchy nevertheless constitutes a further structural similarity between classical and feminist sin-talk.

Apart from McFadyen's handy summary of four characteristics of the doctrine of original sin, which has guided my comparison of feminist and classical perspectives so far, I see three further similarities between feminist sin-talk and the classical doctrine of original sin.

5. Feminist sin-talk and the classical doctrine of original sin share an emphasis on death as the outcome of sin. Augustine insisted that death is the result of original sin—and he did not mean just death in a metaphysical sense, but in fact bodily death. In a somewhat different sense, we have seen that feminist critical rhetorical inquiry points to the presence of a rhetoric of death and a rhetoric of life-denial particularly aimed at women in classical sin-talk, and indeed the ways in which these patriarchal rhetorical practices contribute to women dying at the hands of their abusers or witch hunters, for example. To be sure, Augustine was speaking in a broader, somewhat metaphysical sense, so this is perhaps more of a rhetorical similarity than a direct one. Yet it is significant: Christian sin-talk, both classical and feminist, insists that sin is so serious that it is associated with the final enemy, death itself. It is deeply ironic and sad that classical sin-talk subsequently became (literally) death-dealing in turning into a rhetoric of life-denial and a rhetoric of death, as pointed out in the two previous chapters.

6. Directly related is the value placed on bodily life. Augustine's insistence that death is the result of sin was in fact the flip side of his insistence that the life of the body is important, and that this earthly life was God's original intention.[27] Feminists also, and far more emphatically, emphasize the value of bodily existence and strongly reject dualistic thought patterns that denigrate the body. I do not wish to stretch this dual analogy too far around the themes of death and bodily existence—there are obviously fundamental differences between the classical doctrine of original sin and feminist sin-talk. At the same time, however, there is an interesting structural similarity with regard to an emphasis on the importance of the body, and shared seriousness with regard to the analysis of human pathologies as leading to death.

7. The most significant structural similarity between feminist sin-talk and the classical doctrine of sin is the idea that the essence of sin can be seen as broken relationality. This includes both the idea of a broken relationship with God and each other, and the idea of an inner brokenness—or as Rita Nakashima Brock puts it, "a sign of our brokenheartedness, of how damaged we are, not of how evil, willfully disobedient, and culpable we are ... not something to be punished, but something to be healed."[28] Although, as I mentioned before, I disagree with Brock's suggestion that "original grace"

---

27. Augustine, *The City of God*, trans. Henry Bettenson (New York: Penguin, 1984), book 13.
28. Brock, *Journeys by Heart*, 7.

should replace "original sin," I agree with her basic insights here. But I want to push it further and suggest that this emphasis on brokenheartedness, this concept of sin as something in need of healing, and this emphasis on relationality are already there in the classical doctrine of original sin. When Augustine analyzes sin as the threefold movement toward the self, away from God, and into an unhealthy relationship with all that is in the world, and when he famously remarks in *The Confessions* that our hearts are restless until we return to God, he is suggesting that there is a certain sadness about sin (earlier I referred to this as a second tragic element in the doctrine of original sin). I would even describe the tone of Augustine's doctrine of sin as melancholy in a certain sense. When he affirms the original grace of creation that says our nature is good because it comes from God, he rejects the Manichean view that this world is evil. When he also says that we are born into a "hamartiosphere" (to borrow and adapt language from liberation theology) that can be traced back to the mythical beginnings of the human story, he moves away from the harsh moralistic blame game that marked the insights of his other main interlocutor, Pelagius. The threefold movement at the heart of the classical doctrine of sin suggests a brokenness in our realities that calls for healing, far more than it suggests a moralistic crime-and-punishment schema.

At the same time, however, in its teaching that this brokenness leads to actual moral transgressions, Augustine's doctrine of original sin takes the evil that humans do more seriously than what, it seems to me, is suggested in Brock's analysis. This evil includes gender violence, among many other atrocities. One of the primary problems in the church's approach to gender violence is the silence that often surrounds it, but feminist sin-talk ought not to tolerate such silence. Much as I agree with a relational perspective on sin, and with an implicit healing metaphor, care should be taken not to take the anger—and, yes, even judgment—out of sin-talk. To speak of sin as brokenness, and to show it manifested in broken relationships, to operate therefore with a healing metaphor in responding to sin, is crucial, but so is the recognition that sometimes individuals and groups make downright evil choices and commit downright evil deeds. Evil, for Augustine, does not have ontological existence, but we do call it into existence, in a certain sense, with our choices and actions. No Christian theology ought to ever tiptoe around human moral evils such as gender violence, slavery, genocide, and other atrocities. Therefore, while I see a strong similarity between the feminist emphasis on broken relationality as the essence of sin and classical theology's threefold movement at the heart of sin, I reject a view of sin that does not sufficiently denounce death. In fact, I suggest that feminist theologians on the whole do so as well, at least implicitly, and especially when engaging in a rhetoric of oppression. More about that in the final chapter.

From the above analysis it should be clear that feminist perspectives on human moral pathology share much of the spirit and emphasis of classical sin-talk, or what I have referred to as its "grammar," especially in the way it views the complex interaction of individual and corporate moral agency. The fact is that feminist sin-talk, like classical sin-talk, speaks of a radical, nearly universal, yet unnatural distortion in human nature that shapes our agency in fundamental ways, a brokenness in our existence that even leads to death. From a rhetorical perspective, perhaps the most important similarity lies in the fact that feminist theology posits a view of human agency that is strikingly similar to that of the doctrine of original sin. Talking about women's oppression in terms of the notion of original sin is indeed helpful to indicate that sinful agency under patriarchy is both personal and structural. This appropriation is not a repetition, nor is it simply a cleaned-up version of the classical doctrine of original sin. But the striking structural similarities with the classical doctrine of original sin make this an interesting and notable twist in the broad feminist discourse about sin, representing a move from critical to constructive feminist rhetoric on sin, and in particular of a critical-constructive retrieval of classical sin-talk.

In summary, the life-denying and death-dealing patriarchal rhetorical practices examined in the two previous chapters function as ideological support for the dehumanization of women, as expressed in the dualistic patriarchal feminine symbols of Mary and Eve. This dehumanization plays a role in the exigence of gender violence that is at the heart of the feminist rhetorical situation. Feminist theologians respond to this by denouncing these death-dealing, life-denying symbols and the rhetoric that supports them. As this chapter has pointed out, such a denunciation of death is already a form of sin-talk. It also resembles the doctrine of original sin in its essential grammar. But feminist sin-talk does far more than merely criticize the problems in classical sin-talk and revisit the inner grammar of the doctrine of original sin, which have been the focus in this and the previous two chapters, respectively. In the next and final chapter, we shall see that feminist sin-talk operates with a specific rhetorical structure, as it is rooted in a prophetic *ethos*, is aware of the complexities of the *pathos* of its audiences, and affirms life and denies death in its inner *logos*. As such, I argue that it goes beyond critique and beyond similar "grammar" to constitute a unique and fresh contribution to the Christian understanding of sin.

6

Life

> A gentle tongue is a tree of life.
> —*Proverbs 15:4 NRSV*

In the previous chapter we saw that, in the depths of the hermeneutic of suspicion driving feminist criticism of classical sin-talk, there is a strong hermeneutic of retrieval at work. We also saw that, as a result of this implicit hermeneutic of retrieval, feminist sin-talk shares certain characteristics of the doctrine of original sin: while often saying things that are distinct from, and in fact critical of, classical sin-talk, feminist sin-talk nevertheless uses the same "grammar." But more needs to be said if we are to not only retrieve elements of classical sin-talk but move toward constructive feminist sin-talk. In fact, we need to move beyond both the hermeneutic of suspicion and the hermeneutic of retrieval, and toward a hermeneutic of life, in order to counter the hermeneutic of death that has accompanied so much of classical sin-talk. If we were to describe feminist emancipatory sin-talk in classical rhetorical terms, what we see is that it does (and should), first of all, operate with a prophetic *ethos* rooted in the human cry for life in the name of the God of life. Second, it should (and often already does) pay attention to the *pathos* of its varied audience, that is, to human life in its variety. Finally, I propose that the *logos* of constructive feminist sin-talk should be centered on a hermeneutic of life, resulting in an emphasis on two interrelated themes: the denunciation of death and the affirmation of life—indeed, of human flourishing in life. To the latter end, I argue that it is furthermore important for feminist sin-talk to be firmly theocentric, that is, speaking in the name of the God of life, as well as soteriocentric, that is, rooted in the transformative power of divine grace.

In other words, although feminist sin-talk is not simply a reversal of patriarchal sin-talk, it should reverse the patriarchal rhetoric of life-denial and death, by both prophetically denouncing the rhetoric of death and affirming life in its fullness. Therefore, in this final chapter we explore the contours of constructive feminist sin-talk by viewing it through the lens of classical rhetorical categories, centered on a hermeneutic of life.

ETHOS: THE CRY FOR LIFE

The *ethos* inherent in feminist critical-rhetorical interrogation of classical sin-talk is best described as a prophetic one, and I suggest that this *ethos* also drives feminist sin-talk in its more constructive mode. It is important to identify this *ethos* as an existing and necessary part of feminist sin-talk, since it avoids seeing feminist critiques as simply rooted in a reversal of the patriarchal *ethos* of classical androcentric sin-talk. As Rosemary Radford Ruether notes, some feminist theologies (specifically, some forms of Goddess feminism) tend to reverse patriarchal religion's gender dualisms by identifying goodness with women and evil with men—thereby operating with little more than a reversal of the patriarchal *ethos*. Ruether argues that a mere reversal of patriarchal dualism would mean that women do not have to take responsibility for evil, that women are only victims who have no agency to initiate social change, that ultimately the world cannot be changed for the better, and that the only available option is withdrawal into a subculture.[1] Truly constructive feminist sin-talk, while obviously premised upon recognition of the oppressive forces of patriarchy, should be more than a reaction to, or reversal of, patriarchy and patriarchal sin-talk. Indeed, what we already find in the work of feminist theologians, and should find in an authentic constructive feminist rhetoric of sin, is an underlying prophetic *ethos* grounded in the idea of divine justice, rather than a mere reversal of the patriarchal *ethos*.

---

1. Rosemary Radford Ruether, *Sexism and God-Talk: Toward a Feminist Theology* (Boston: Beacon Press, 1993), 52; Ruether, "Dualism and the Nature of Evil in Feminist Theology," *Studies in Christian Ethics* 5, no. 1 (1992): 30–31; and Ruether, "Goddesses and Witches: Liberation and Countercultural Feminism," *Christian Century*, September 10–17, 1980, 842–47. In contrast, see Carol Christ's affirmation of the Goddess symbol as a central element in the overcoming of both mind/body dualism (Ruether's central concern) and the Mary/Eve dichotomy, both of which have been central to feminist critiques of classical sin-talk (Carol P. Christ, "Why Women Need the Goddess: Phenomenological, Psychological, and Political Reflections," in *Womanspirit Rising: A Feminist Reader in Religion*, ed. Carol P. Christ and Judith Plaskow [San Francisco: Harper & Row, 1979], 280–82).

To be sure, the prophetic is not without ambiguity. In the classic prophetic texts we often find the prophetic *ethos* intertwined with a patriarchal one: the imagery of divine spousal abuse in the announcements of Hosea and some other Hebrew prophets offers a stark illustration. Yet the concept of the prophetic is that of divine judgment of oppression, and as such it can and should be divorced from patriarchy in order to call patriarchy itself to task.

My argument is not quite that the prophetic should be seen as the "norm within Biblical faith by which the Biblical texts themselves can be criticized," as Ruether argues.[2] Issues of justice are not limited to the specifically prophetic genre: the Wisdom tradition, for example, has been appropriated by several feminist scholars as a justice-oriented tradition (i.e., a tradition with a prophetic *ethos*) that may be useful in rethinking classical theological symbols. In fact, the Wisdom tradition's affirmation of daily life offers a strong complement to the death-denunciation in the name of the God of life, arising out of the cry for life, which I have posited as the essence of the prophetic traditions.[3] Moreover, as should be clear from the methodological perspectives offered in the first two chapters, I agree with theologians such as Francis Schüssler Fiorenza, David Tracy, and others, that "no external standard . . . exists independent of cultural traditions and social interpretation that can provide an independent foundation for either faith or theology," and that criteria should be found in the intersubjective, that is, in the play of diverse perspectives rather than outside them.[4] However, even if the prophetic need not be isolated as a *norm* for feminist theology, there is without a doubt a prophetic *ethos* present in feminist theologies. I find some of María Pilar Aquino's emphases helpful in formulating what constitutes a prophetic *ethos*. The prophetic, I submit, is premised upon the double awareness of the human "cry for life," and of "God's self-revelation as a God of life, in opposition to anyone or

---

2. Ruether, *Sexism and God-Talk*, 23.

3. See, for example, María Pilar Aquino and Elisabeth Schüssler Fiorenza, eds., *In the Power of Wisdom: Feminist Spiritualities of Struggle* (London: SCM Press, 2000), on the relationship between the Wisdom tradition and the struggle for justice for women. For a feminist liberation theology premised to a large extent on the justice-orientation of the Wisdom tradition, the work of Elizabeth A. Johnson is worth noting, particularly in her proposals for a feminist Christology. See Elizabeth A. Johnson, "Wisdom Was Made Flesh and Pitched Her Tent among Us," in *Reconstructing the Christ Symbol*, ed. Maryanne Stevens (New York: Paulist Press, 2004), 97, for the relationship between Wisdom and everyday life.

4. David Tracy makes it clear in his work that it is precisely in the *play of subjectivities* that something of "the whole" breaks through, that manifestation happens that brings us out of our original presuppositions (see, for example, *The Analogical Imagination: Christian Theology and the Culture of Pluralism* [New York: Crossroad, 1981], esp. 318–19, on criteria for theology, and *Plurality and Ambiguity: Hermeneutics, Religion, Hope* [Chicago: University of Chicago Press, 1987], on the relationship between "language" and experience). See also Francis Schüssler Fiorenza, *Foundational Theology: Jesus and the Church* (New York: Crossroad, 1984), 289.

any systems and institutions . . . who threaten it." The prophetic *ethos* is thus characterized by a simultaneous awareness of human suffering, and of the "God who is near, who generates hopes, shares in daily struggles."[5]

In other words, a prophetic *ethos* is premised upon a deep awareness of divine grace as concrete and present. For the prophetic, divine revelation is not seen as "from above," but as something that happens in the situation, in the awareness of crisis and opportunity. It is here, amid our daily struggles, that the God of life is near. Divine revelation constitutes the *kairos*, the awareness of the unconditioned meaning and demand present in particular contexts.[6] This means that the prophetic *ethos* is never content with religion as "opium for the people." "I hate, I despise your festivals, and I take no delight in your solemn assemblies," cries the prophet Amos, demanding instead that justice should "roll down like waters" (Amos 5:21–24 NRSV). The awareness of the living presence of God in the *kairos* constitutes an urgent call to praxis. In the *kairos* concept, which, as I have noted, gives rise to the recognition/creation of the rhetorical situation by the engaged artist-rhetor, there is both revelation and ethical demand. In *kairos* we see the unity of the sacramental and the critical, or what Paul Tillich calls the Catholic substance and the Protestant Principle: repentance is called for in the name of the transcendent-immanent divine presence *in* human need—a sense of the holy within the concrete, even within the ugly. As John Suggit notes, in *kairos* theology, "attention has turned to a view of redemption as liberation in the present. . . . For the Christian, the *kairos* is always present, demanding a response here and now if freedom is to be made real."[7] The revelatory element of the *kairos* makes clear the exigence in the context and demands justice in response: now the need for rhetorical engagement with the rhetorical situation, and a call to renewed praxis, become obvious. The prophetic is therefore never simply aimed at greater orthodoxy or personal piety, but in the first place at orthopraxis. This goal arises out of the human condition, the cry for life, but precisely in that human cry, God's revelation is encountered.

---

5. María Pilar Aquino, *Our Cry for Life: Feminist Theology from Latin America* (Maryknoll, NY: Orbis Books, 1993), 133–34. While Aquino does not explicitly discuss the notion of the prophetic here, her focus on life is a clear expression of a prophetic approach to theology.

6. Paul Tillich, "Basic Principles of Religious Socialism," in *Political Expectation*, ed. James Luther Adams (New York: Harper & Row, 1971), 60–61. Black prophetic theology in South Africa made explicit use of this concept in drafting *The Kairos Document: A Challenge to the Church*, which was one of the central theological statements against apartheid. Other documents followed in its wake, such as *The Road to Damascus: Kairos and Conversion*, and *El Kairos en Centroamerica*. See Robert McAfee Brown, ed., *Kairos: Three Prophetic Challenges to the Church* (Grand Rapids: Eerdmans, 1990), for the texts of all three documents.

7. John Suggit, "Redemption: Freedom Regained," in *Doing Theology in Context: South African Perspectives*, ed. John de Gruchy and Charles Villa-Vicencio, Theology and Praxis 1 (Maryknoll, NY: Orbis Books, 1994), 121.

Life   131

The *kairos* of any rhetorical-theological moment is linked to the kairotic origins of Christianity: the Christ event, in whom the God of Israel, already known in the Hebrew Scriptures as the God who is "in search of man," is further revealed as in search also of gentiles.[8] In other words, the prophetic *ethos* of sin-talk is premised upon the very particular understanding that who God is, is God-for-us. The God of the Christic *kairos* is one whose being is being-for-us, inherently relational and focused on human well-being, or, as Karl Rahner reminds us, that of self-communicating grace.[9] This view of God translates into the "preferential option for the poor" of liberation theologies, the preferential option for women of feminist theologies, or the notion that "[God] is in a special way the God of the destitute, the poor and the wronged" of the South African antiapartheid confessional tradition.[10] So, when feminist theologian Serene Jones removes her treatment of sin from the doctrine of creation and the *imago Dei*, and into the realm of soteriology, she makes an implicit decision to engage in sin-talk in a prophetic way, for by doing so she locates sin-talk in the midst of talk of "God for us."[11]

As a prophetic utterance, the doctrine of sin is certainly more closely related to soteriology than it is to the doctrine of creation: it is not primarily part of a theological perspective on human nature (after all, as discussed in the previous chapter, sin is not an expression, but a distortion, of human nature)—rather, it is something that can only be rightly understood in light of God's self-revelation as God-for-us. However, at the same time one could argue that the doctrine of creation is not separable from soteriology either, not if we view creation in terms of God's overflowing love, God's "original grace." In other words, the idea of original grace is essential to any doctrine of sin, although, as I argued before, not as a replacement for the concept of original sin, but instead as the lens through which it ought to be understood. Rosemary Radford Ruether expresses something similar when she says that feminist (prophetic) sin-talk is dependent upon a vision of the good in which

---

8. See Abraham Joshua Heschel's book *God in Search of Man: A Philosophy of Judaism* (New York: Farrar, Straus and Cudahy, 1955). As an aside, while for the Christian, Christ is the decisive revelation of God, this ought not to negate the fact that the God of Christ is in the first place the God of Israel, who is fully known because of God's self-revelation that is expressed in the Torah, Prophets, and Writings.

9. Karl Rahner, *Foundations of the Christian Faith: An Introduction to the Idea of Christianity* (New York: Crossroad, 1995), 116–33.

10. The quote is from the Confession of Belhar, which was formulated in South Africa in response to the *status confessionis* created as a result of the theological justification of the apartheid system. This is somewhat distinct from liberation theologies, which respond more directly to political systems. See https://www.pcusa.org/site_media/media/uploads/theologyandworship/pdfs/belhar.pdf.

11. Serene Jones, *Feminist Theory and Christian Theology: Cartographies of Grace*, Guides to Theological Inquiry (Minneapolis: Fortress Press, 2000), 95.

the notion of relationality is central (which, I suggested in the previous chapter, is something already implied in classical sin-talk).[12]

The prophetic *ethos* of feminist discourses, rooted in the cry for life in the name of the God of life, drives toward a form of sin-talk that eschews speculation and would rather function, in the words of Alistair McFadyen, "as a distinctive theological language, speaking of concrete pathologies in relation to God."[13] As such, sin-talk is focused on concrete social issues, and aims at exposing reigning social ideas as serving not the common good but the narrow interests of a particular group. Prophetic rhetorical sin-talk, notes Don Compier, does not pursue "knowledge as such but offers a pragmatic diagnosis that aims to loosen the readers' allegiance to the oppressive status quo," thereby functioning as a critical theory of society.[14]

In light of these observations, it is clear that the sharp criticisms of classical sin-talk leveled by feminist theologians are neither simply a reaction to classical sin-talk, nor a rejection of sin-talk, and it even goes beyond structural "grammatical" similarities with the classical doctrine of original sin. Instead, the critical rhetoric of feminist theologians in response to the gender crisis at the heart of classical Christian sin-talk is expressive of the prophetic *ethos* of an emerging feminist rhetorical approach to sin. The rhetoric of oppression we encounter in these feminist critiques functions as a critical theory of society by naming concrete pathologies. The rhetoric of difference we encounter in the earliest layers of the feminist critiques of classical sin-talk exposes reigning ideas regarding sin to be serving not the common good but rather the narrow interests of a particular group. The rhetoric of reason frequently employed by feminist theologians points to the flawed philosophy that lies behind the oppressive nonsense the church has been proclaiming regarding women for centuries in support of the patriarchal status quo. In pointing to the various ways in which the flaws in classical sin-talk have played a role in the explicit and implicit justification and normalization of gender violence, feminist critical-constructive sin-talk exhibits a very concrete focus. In short, the prophetic *ethos*, being rooted in the *kairos* of the human "cry for life" and the recognition of the divine presence in concrete life situations crying out for justice, can never be content with sin-talk that stays at the level of the speculative. Prophetic sin-talk is focused on the real, physical, and emotional lives of human beings—the realities that people face and the places where death

---

12. Ruether, *Sexism and God-Talk*, 163.

13. Alistair McFadyen, *Bound to Sin: Abuse, Holocaust and the Christian Doctrine of Sin* (Cambridge: Cambridge University Press, 2000), 5.

14. Don H. Compier, *What Is Rhetorical Theology? Textual Practice and Public Discourse* (Harrisburg, PA: Trinity Press, 1999), 59.

threatens to overcome those real lives. And this is the kind of *ethos* that we see driving feminist conversations on sin.

Feminist constructive sin-talk is also characterized by a particular *logos* and *pathos*. We turn to the latter next.

PATHOS: EMBRACING THE DIVERSITY OF LIFE

Rhetoric, as we have seen, operates with a holistic anthropology, which is aware that the persuasiveness of discourse not only lies in the structure of its arguments (*logos*) or the persuasiveness of the speaker (*ethos*), but also in the way it resonates with the emotions and situation of the audience that is addressed (*pathos*). Feminists argue that the androcentrism of most classical theologians prevented them from seeing the *pathos* of audiences other than ruling-class males. As shown in chapter 3, their assumption that the universal sin to be addressed is that of an overweening sense of self led to a rhetoric of sin that intensified the internal loss of self that too often typifies the lives of women—a loss of self that, in turn, results in part from the scapegoating of women by classical sin-talk, which we discussed in chapter 4. In thinking about the element of *pathos* in prophetic feminist sin-talk, a general distinction needs to be made between, on the one hand, the sins of women, and on the other hand, the sins committed against women.

First, when it comes to the sins of women, feminist sin-talk is characterized by what Serene Jones refers to as "rhetorical scaling," that is, a "careful consideration of the audience to whom one preaches sin."[15] In classical sin-talk, says Jones, the "mirror" in which the person looks and sees sin was male, a "face wearing the spots of pride." But if a woman looks into the "mirror of unfaithfulness," the face of sin takes on different forms. Jones is well aware that this is not simply a matter of now seeing a female face in the mirror (i.e., of positing an essentialist "female sin" of self-loss). Her proposal is rather that we need to rebuild the mirror itself, and she suggests that Luce Irigaray's notion of the concave mirror might be useful as a metaphor for expressing the complexity here. In contrast to the essentialist identity conveyed by the metaphor of the flat, stable, singular reflection, Irigaray's mirror is a concave one that "gives not a single image of a stable woman but an infinite display of multiple visages reflecting the diversity of identities that exist both internally to each woman and among women as a whole."[16]

---

15. Jones, *Feminist Theory and Christian Theology*, 110.
16. Ibid., 115–16.

Such rhetorical scaling is reflective of the rhetorical principle of *decorum*, or the idea that careful consideration of the audience is needed if language is to be persuasive, and its concomitant concept of *kairos* as the doctrine of discerning what is fitting in terms of time and situation. I need to reiterate that this does not mean simply replacing patriarchal rhetoric with a gendered rhetoric of "male" and "female" sins. An essentialist understanding of gender and of sin is negated by the reality of both the cultural construction of gender and its intersection with other (often oppressive) cultural constructs, which shape our agency in more complex ways than can be seen from the vantage point of binary gender oppositions. The space one occupies within the complexity of patriarchal power relations shapes one's particular experiences and also has implications for the kind of agency one is able or inclined to exercise. In short, an "add women and stir" approach is not sufficient. Failure to recognize that women and men sin, as Mary Grey puts it, "both as individuals, in gender-specific ways and according to the degree of autonomy they possess within the power structures" of patriarchy, confines women (and men) to an individualistic and essentialist model of sin that can never serve to address concrete issues such as the problem of gender violence.[17]

In fact, when it comes to gender violence, the picture becomes particularly muddy. Even the recognition of the "female sin" of self-loss can become problematic. Mary Potter Engel notes that seeing loss of the self or "hiding" as sin can be just as problematic for victims of abuse as emphasizing sin-as-pride can be, because disassociation and hiding can be important survival techniques in situations of abuse.[18] At times, "hiding" or lack of self-assertion should be understood not as passivity but as an active response to a situation of violence. Sometimes a woman's spirit is so broken, or her situation so dangerous, that she can hardly be blamed for her lack of resistance or her inability to escape. It is not rhetorically or pastorally appropriate to accuse individual battered women of the "sin of silence," since that ignores the particular *pathos* of the individual.[19] Such an accusation would also fall back onto a Pelagian-style individualistic moralism that accomplishes little

---

17. Mary Grey, "Falling into Freedom: Searching for New Interpretations of Sin in a Secular Society," *Scottish Journal of Theology* 47, no. 2 (1994): 235.

18. Mary Potter Engel, "Evil, Sin, and the Violation of the Vulnerable," in *Lift Every Voice: Constructing Theologies from the Underside*, ed. Susan Brooks Thistlethwaite and Mary Potter Engel (San Francisco: Harper & Row, 1998), 160.

19. See Sheila Redmond, "'Remember the Good, Forget the Bad': Denial and Family Violence in a Christian Worship Service," in *Women at Worship: Interpretations of North American Diversity*, ed. Marjorie Proctor-Smith and Janet R. Walton (Louisville, KY: Westminster/John Knox Press, 1993), 77–78, for a critique of this.

beyond reinforcing negative self-esteem, thereby, ironically, once again contributing to self-negation, that is, the *pathos* and indeed the "typical" pathology (sin) of women.

On the other hand, as Carol Lakey Hess notes, "While we must be careful not to blame the victim, we must also be careful not to reinforce the victim by calling what is harmful a virtue."[20] In other words, we cannot call virtuous a lack of (oppositional) female agency in the face of violence; then we would simply be continuing the Christian tradition's advice to women to submit to the violence done to them in the name of feminine virtue. In calling this loss of self or passivity "sin" (in a more tragic sense, rather than moralistically pointing fingers at the individual), feminist theologians are saying that self-sacrifice and greater loss-of-self in the face of male violence is not a virtue (as was traditionally said or at least implied), but is the way in which women contribute to their own *hamartia*, that is, "missing the mark" of the good in their lives. In short, calling women to responsibility for their own healing (thus calling women to oppositional agency in the face of violence) is just as important as not blaming individual women if at times they choose strategic "hiding" or "passivity" for the sake of survival.

It should be clear from the above that, in their focus on the sins *of* women, feminist theologians, especially those operating with constructivist rather than essentialist understandings of gender, are guided by the realization that no universal sin, nor even a universal *female* sin, can be identified. When it comes to addressing sins *against* women, such as violence, the rhetorical principle of recognizing the particularities of the "audience" of sin-talk becomes even more complex. The difficulties with regard to addressing gender oppression are expressive of the complexities of patriarchy itself—a notion that, as noted before, refers not only to gender oppression but to a hierarchical system that places elite men over other men and all women in a complex hegemonic web. Only when we see male domination and the violent practices that go along with it as part of a broader, multilayered system of patriarchy that creates crisscrossing intersections of oppression can we start to grasp the complex picture of how issues of colonialism, racial oppression, and so on interact with the ways in which we can deal with gender oppression. Feminist critiques of some forms of gender violence that are commonly associated with Majority World cultures often fall prey to a mind-set that assumes that the only remedy for gender violence is the utilization of Western cultural

---

20. Carol Lakey Hess, "Reclaiming Ourselves: A Spirituality for Women's Empowerment," in *Women, Gender, and Christian Community*, ed. Jane Dempsey Douglas and James F. Kay (Louisville, KY: Westminster John Knox Press, 1997), 149.

ideals, especially those mined from the Enlightenment.[21] Such an imperialistic approach should be rejected by a feminism that takes seriously the intricacies of patriarchy as encompassing also the oppression of cultural or racial "others." In other words, feminism should not become "Western Patriarchal Feminism."[22] At the same time, however, feminism does not belong to white women, despite the fact that some of its prominent proponents have at times fallen prey to white hegemonic assumptions: feminism is about the rights and dignity of *all* women. Developing a global, intersectional feminism that is practiced by women around the globe, in conversation with each other—and in awareness of the ways in which feminist concerns intersect with issues of race, class, sexual orientation, global power relations, and so forth—is crucial for the future of feminist theology as part of an increasingly global Christian theological enterprise. But caution is called for, especially as it relates to cultural differences. About that, some general remarks:

As the prominent African feminist theologian Mercy Amba Oduyoye reminds us, cultural critiques should start from within, not be an imposition from without. Cultural hermeneutics, she argues, confronts one with "the challenge of struggling with one's culture while fencing off those waiting to use our culture to under-rate us."[23] She warns that culture is frequently a euphemism to protect actions that require analysis, and adds that we *all* need to interpret our own culture, engage in intercultural dialogue, and work toward cultural transformation.

Majority World women do often engage in such internal critiques, pleading for a more dynamic understanding of culture. In fact, they are often quite vocal in their embrace of feminism and their calls for cultural change, such

---

21. See, e.g., Sander L. Gilman, "'Barbaric' Rituals?" in *Is Multiculturalism Bad for Women?* ed. Joshua Cohen, Matthew Howard, and Martha C. Nussbaum (Princeton, NJ: Princeton University Press, 1999), 53–58, for an argument that the feminist outcry against female circumcision is similar to nineteenth-century anti-Semitic tirades against the circumcision of Jewish boys, and as such rests on assumptions of Western Christian cultural superiority. He is right in noting such a tone in some feminist arguments. For example, the superiority of Western culture is clearly assumed in Susan Moller Okin's essay "Is Multiculturalism Bad for Women?" in the same volume, in which she argues against the cultural defense used by some immigrants in court cases relating to gender violence. While she is correct in saying that such defenses are deeply problematic, she is insufficiently critical of her own cultural essentialism and her assumptions about the superiority of Western culture. At the same time, however, Gilman ignores the fact that many women within cultures that practice FGM themselves speak out against it—indeed, it was largely because of the lobbying of "non-Western" feminists such as Ghanaian-born feminist Efua Dorkenoo that female genital mutilation was finally condemned by the World Health Organization in 1993 (see Kirstin Olsen, *Chronology of Women's History* [Westport, CT: Greenwood Press, 1994], 394).

22. Azizah Y. Al-Hibri, "Is Western Patriarchal Feminism Good for Third World/Minority Women?" in Cohen, Howard, and Nussbaum, *Is Multiculturalism Bad for Women?* 41–46.

23. Mercy Amba Oduyoye, *Introducing African Women's Theology* (Cleveland, OH: Pilgrim Press, 2001), 13.

as when Ghanaian lawyer Rosemary Ofibea Ofei-Afboagye bluntly says, "A culture that teaches male mastery and domination over women must be altered."[24] In other words, as Bonnie Honig remarks, culture should not be understood as "patriarchal permission for powerful men to subordinate vulnerable women."[25]

Therefore, just as feminism has learned to reject *gender* essentialism, so it also needs to guard against *cultural* essentialism. Sudanese physician Nahid Toubia rightly asks, "Why is it only when women want to bring about change for their own benefit that culture and custom become sacred and unchangeable?"[26] American feminist theologian Kathryn Tanner argues for a perspective that does not define culture in terms of stasis and consensus, but rather as historically in process, as something that binds people together as a common focus for engagement, if not necessarily agreement, and as inclusive of its own alternatives.[27] Tanner's approach is not to argue for the neglecting of cultural borders, but for the recognition of what Delwin Brown would call the "porousness" of those boundaries.[28] Similarly, notable feminist theorists Nancy Fraser and Seyla Benhabib criticize the "balkanization of culture" by the type of multiculturalism that "celebrates difference uncritically while failing to interrogate its relation to equality," and point out that cultural essentialism generates coherence for the purposes of understanding and control by outsiders, whereas participants in a culture experience their traditions, stories, rituals, symbols, tools, and living conditions through shared, albeit contested and contestable, narrative accounts.[29]

Cultural essentialism ironically hides underlying Western hegemony, apart from being a cheap version of political correctness that ignores the very real pain and humiliation of women. Prominent Indian feminist philosopher Uma Narayan (who now teaches in the United States) points out that idealized and totalized notions of culture can be traced back to a colonialist *ethos* of control, which resulted in problematic pictures of both "Western culture"

24. Rosemary Ofibea Ofei-Afboagye, "Domestic Violence in Ghana: An Initial Step," *Columbia Journal of Gender and Law* 4, no. 1 (1994): 25.
25. Bonnie Honig, "My Culture Made Me Do It," in Cohen, Howard, and Nussbaum, *Is Multiculturalism Bad for Women?* 35–40.
26. Lori Heise, Kirsten Moore, and Nahid Toubia, *Sexual Coercion and Reproductive Health: A Focus on Research* (New York: Population Council, 1995), 59.
27. Kathryn Tanner, *Theories of Culture: A New Agenda for Theology* (Minneapolis: Fortress Press, 1997), esp. chs. 1–3.
28. Delwin Brown, *Boundaries of Our Habitations: Tradition and Theological Construction*, SUNY Series in Religious Studies, ed. Harold Coward (Albany: State University Press of New York, 1994), 26, 91. Brown uses this notion in connection with both religious traditions (which he argues often function like cultures) and cultures.
29. Nancy Fraser, *Justice Interruptus: Critical Reflections on the "Postsocialist" Condition* (New York: Routledge, 1997), 185; Seyla Benhabib, *The Claims of Culture: Equality and Diversity in the Global Era* (Princeton, NJ: Princeton University Press, 2002), 5.

and "indigenous culture." She suggests that these pictures are both idealized and totalized constructions, which are far from being faithful to the values that actually pervade institutional practices and social life, and which tend to posit the values and practices of the more powerful within the culture as pertaining to the culture as a whole.[30] Hence, she argues that Western acceptance of so-called cultural defenses in cases of violence against "non-Western" women is often accompanied by a "lurid exoticism" that combines with free-floating ideas about Majority World "backwardness," which functions to keep the Other comfortably foreign. For example, Western discussions of Indian dowry deaths frequently focus on perceived "cultural" explanations of this phenomenon, confusing it with the ancient, and in fact not very widespread, practice of *sati* (widow-burning) to provide a spectacle of "Indian women being burnt to death every day" because of "something strange" within Indian culture. Such discussions ignore religious, cultural, and historical differences within India—and the fact that dowry-deaths are a fairly recent phenomenon that probably have more to do with economic gain in a market economy than with anything specifically "cultural."[31] Essentialist constructs of culture all too often serve merely to resist calls for change in gender dynamics that arise from within cultures, and to hide the fact that cultural essentialism itself is often the result of Western hegemonic constructs and assumptions.

Majority World feminists furthermore call for a more *representative* understanding of human cultures. In other words, they challenge the tendency to identify cultures in terms of dominant male voices within it. These dominant male voices often dismiss the politics of feminists in their midst as a symptom of Westernization. But, says Uma Narayan, Majority World feminists' experiences within their own contexts inform their politics, and their feminist analyses are the result of political organizing and political mobilization, initiated and sustained by women within these Majority World contexts.[32] A more representative perspective on culture would include these voices instead of dismissing them.

Narayan also shows how the charge of Westernization is rooted in the struggle against colonialism, where the "sound and fury of these 'my culture is better than your culture' conflicts between male-dominated colonial governments and male-dominated Third-World nationalist movements often

---

30. Uma Narayan, *Dislocating Cultures: Identities, Traditions, and Third-World Feminism* (New York: Routledge, 1997), 3–39.
31. Ibid., 101–4.
32. Ibid., 13. As a matter of fact, she says, many Majority World feminist criticisms bear resemblance to the criticisms voiced by nonfeminist women in the same contexts, with the difference that feminists tend to see the problems they criticize as systemic rather than as rooted in personal, individual pathologies.

served to obscure the fact that women were clearly second-class citizens in *all* these cultural contexts."[33] Narayan is not equating the sexist discourse of both groups, and recognizes that there were obviously good reasons for colonized women to prefer nationalist discourse over that of colonialism—including that of "Western imperial feminism," which most often shared the racist and colonialist assumptions of Western men. Her point is merely that gender played an ideological role in both colonial empires and Majority World nationalist movements, and that this legacy has placed "Western" and "non-Western" women against each other as "competing cultural embodiments of appropriate femininity and virtue." Ironically, Narayan says, it is often the very same people who have embraced other aspects of "Western" culture who evoke the charge of Westernization against Majority World feminists. For example, the same men who are comfortable wearing Western styles of dress (and do not see that as compromising their culture) might protest heavily in the name of cultural integrity if women were to do the same. Thus Narayan concludes that the depiction of certain changes and not others as examples of Westernization, assumes that the latter has an obvious meaning that needs no discussion. She therefore argues that one important strategy for Majority World feminists accused of Westernization, is to point to the fluid, fractured, selective, and changing deployment of this "labeling."[34]

In short, a strong argument is to be made for a more dynamic and representative perspective on cultures, if we are to hear and address the plurality of the *pathos* of women, while steering clear of both white Western feminist hegemony, on the one hand, and a value-free multiculturalism that ignores women's real suffering, on the other hand. A prophetic *ethos*, combined with the willingness to learn more about the *pathos* of women from various contexts, ought to lead feminists, even Western feminists, to "side with the underdogs."[35] This implies that, although rhetoric is so often associated with the act of speaking, attention to *pathos* means that listening is integral to the art of rhetoric—and Western feminists in particular should do some listening. After all, only the engaged rhetor can discern the *kairos*—and I would add that the rhetor at best does not work alone but is part of a broader engaged conversational group of rhetors. In other words, instead of either making essentialist assumptions about cultures from the perspective of a hegemonic Western feminism, or, conversely, abandoning all criticism of gender violence in the name of "cultural sensitivity," which paradoxically hides Western patriarchal perspectives on other peoples' cultures, a listening, open, intersectional

---

33. Ibid., 18.
34. Ibid., 29.
35. Yael Tamir, "Siding with the Underdogs," in Cohen, Howard, and Nussbaum, *Is Multiculturalism Bad for Women?* 47–52.

feminist conversation should be the starting point of theological rhetoric in an increasingly global and especially Majority World church.

Therefore, when it comes to talking about the sins perpetrated against women, including that of gender violence, the reality of culture needs to be kept in mind yet not absolutized. Gender violence is a multiheaded hydra that takes many forms and has multiple causes. It is often culturally specific and needs to be addressed within specific contexts. This would include the potential use of local traditions to address gender violence (e.g., "Circle Sentencing" in Canada's Yukon Territory or *salishe* in India and Bangladesh).[36] But it is also a global phenomenon, linked to various gender stereotypes (some Christian in origin, some not) that have one thing in common: they devalue women. These stereotypes include those images of ideal and defiled womanhood advanced by classical Christian sin-talk. Intersectional feminist theology should not hesitate to participate in a global approach toward combating gender violence, based on an understanding of sisterhood that does not negate the differences between women, but recognizes and works with these differences, while white Western feminists in particular ought to adopt a respectful listening attitude rooted in a rejection of Western hegemonic ideas. The racist and essentialist assumptions that often accompanied the notion of sisterhood have rightly been challenged, but this does not negate the fact that feminism draws significant strength from the rhetoric of sisterhood, as African American feminist theorist bell hooks notes.[37] Feminist sin-talk that addresses gender violence therefore needs, in the words of Serene Jones, a "rhetoric of commonality," while also being aware of the reality of difference.[38]

In short, then, feminist rhetorical sin-talk recognizes the complex *pathos* of women and particularly asks about the implications of women's situations (both psychological and cultural) for speaking of the sins of women as well as the sins committed against women, with sensitivity to the complexity of discerning the *kairos* that gives rise to the feminist rhetorical situation. At the same time the prophetic *ethos* that drives feminist sin-talk, and the seriousness of the exigence of the feminist rhetorical situation, call for a loud and clear theological denunciation of death-dealing discourses in cultures and theologies—a denunciation we find at the heart of the *logos* of feminist sin-talk. But more than the denunciation of death needs to happen. While the prophetic

---

36. Match International Centre, "The Circle of Healing: Aboriginal Women Organizing in Canada," in *Women and Violence: Realities and Responses around the World*, ed. M. Davies (London: Zed Books, 1994), 231–39; B. Datta and R. Motihar, *Breaking Down the Walls: Violence against Women as a Health and Human Rights Issue* (New Delhi: Ford Foundation, 1999), 32.

37. See bell hooks, "Sisterhood: Political Solidarity between Women," in *Feminist Social Thought*, ed. Diana Tietjens-Meyers (New York: Routledge, 1997), 485–500.

38. Jones, *Feminist Theory and Christian Theology*, 41.

ethos might call for a strong denunciation of death, it also, especially in conjunction with the Wisdom tradition, calls for an affirmation of life—and that means recognition of the diverse realities of women's lives, of women's *pathos*.

We now turn an examination of the contours of the *logos* that drives feminist constructive sin-talk.

LOGOS: DENOUNCING DEATH

The prophetic *ethos* of feminist sin-talk, rooted in the affirmation of life by the God of life, and the *pathos* of women, which is partially shaped by widely occurring gender oppressions, particularly widespread gender violence, call for sin-talk in which the *logos* is, first of all, aimed at denouncing death.[39] We have already seen an implicit denunciation of death in the feminist argument that the slow death of self-loss is contrary to the divine will and is not virtuous self-sacrifice, and in the feminist call for the overcoming of death-dealing dualism and its rhetoric of death. In the previous chapter I argued that, in their exposure of the patriarchal rhetoric of life-denial and of death found in classical sin-talk, feminist theologians ironically use the same theological "grammar" found in classical sin-talk to point to the patriarchal system as the "original sin" that leads to death. Here I outline that argument in more detail by arguing that the actual content or *logos* of feminist sin-talk, driven by a prophetic *ethos*, and in recognition of the complex *pathos* of women, denounces death by making three basic interrelated moves: it names particular sins in relation to God, situates those sins within systemic distortion, and points out how classical sin-talk itself plays a role in such systemic distortion and its resultant particular sins.

Here, too, the emphases found in feminist sin-talk are not entirely novel, since there are particular moments in the Christian tradition when Christian sin-talk was "cleaning house," so to speak—that is, in prophetic moments in the history of doctrine. What is new is the fact that feminist theologians are utilizing the language of sin in the interests of women, something that has rarely occurred in Christian history.

---

39. This phrase, which resonates well with María Pilar Aquino's starting point in the "cry for life," is from the original title of Don Compier's dissertation, "Denouncing Death: John Calvin's Critique of Sin and Contemporary Rhetorical Theology" (Ph.D. diss., Emory University, 1992). The findings of his dissertation were later published as *John Calvin's Rhetorical Doctrine of Sin*, Text and Studies in Religion 86 (Lewiston, NY: Edwin Mellen Press, 2001). We have already encountered Compier's work on rhetorical theology and the task of sin-talk. His rhetorical-political reading of Calvin's sin-talk plays a central role in structuring the arguments of this section.

One example of a classical theologian whose rhetoric on sin has some surprising similarities with feminist sin-talk is John Calvin, whose practical-rhetorical, rather than speculative sin-talk has been of interest to several theologians in recent decades, including rhetorical theologians Serene Jones and Don Compier. Jones notes that "a rhetorical reading of [Calvin's] *Institutes* throws light on the pastoral and political character of Calvin's writings."[40] According to Jones, Calvin "uses his rhetorical skills to construct doctrines that produce in his readers a certain play of mind, a play of mind that has as its final goal the inculcating of a faithful disposition."[41] An important clue in reading Calvin, she says, is to realize that the political nature of his writing is not limited to the overtly political sections of his work, but can be seen in discussions of doctrines that may at first appear nonpolitical.[42] This same principle is at work in Don Compier's analysis of Calvin's practical sin-talk, which does not focus on Calvin's formal treatment of the doctrine of sin (which is largely a repetition of Augustine), but instead looks at Calvin's practical sin-talk in the form of denunciations of the medieval penitential system (which is best seen as sociopolitical rather than simply anti-Catholic critique). This analysis is particularly helpful in highlighting the dynamics of the kind of moves we see in feminist sin-talk.

I am not suggesting that Calvin is the only or even necessarily the best figure from the classical Christian traditions to retrieve for feminist purposes. However, Calvin is an excellent example of a classical theologian who is best read as a rhetorical theologian whose focus was on the practical effects of doctrines. Calvin stood in the tradition of Renaissance French humanism and was overtly interested in rhetoric. Theologians who emphasize Calvin's continuity with humanism, including humanism's emphasis on rhetoric, find in Calvin an engaged mode of theological praxis, pointing out that his criterion for right doctrine was "that it could produce practical results, that it could engender the warmth, enthusiasm and action appropriate to the needs of the time."[43] He was influenced by the Roman rhetorical tradition of Cicero and Quintilian, and in particular the key concept in that tradition, that of *decorum*. The latter, I have argued, is closely related to the concept of *kairos*, understood

---

40. Serene Jones, *Calvin and the Rhetoric of Piety*, Columbia Series in Reformed Theology (Louisville, KY: Westminster John Knox Press, 1995), 5.
41. Ibid., 30.
42. Ibid., 5.
43. William J. Bouwsma, "Calvinism as Renaissance Artifact," in *John Calvin and the Church: A Prism of Reform*, ed. Timothy George (Louisville, KY: Westminster/John Knox Press, 1990), 37. For Calvin's "practical sin-talk," see, for example, books 3 and 4 of the *Institutes of the Christian Religion*, ed. John T. McNeill, trans. Ford Lewis Battles (Philadelphia: Westminster Press, 1960). For Calvin's more traditional treatment of sin, see Book 2 (especially section 1) of the *Institutes*.

as emphasizing the particular context, its revelation, and its call for justice. Serene Jones points out that Calvin followed Cicero and Petrarch in accommodating his theology to the needs of his audience, with an eye toward making them "good."[44] There is therefore a partial methodological compatibility between Calvin's theology and that of modern rhetorical theologians, including feminist theologians, who for the most part tend to be rhetorical theologians in practice if not in theory.

Moreover, Compier's analysis shows Calvin making the kind of moves that I see feminist theologians making as well, even if their language is quite different. In general, Compier identifies several characteristics in Calvin's sin-talk that are typical of a rhetorical approach to doctrine, such as a concern for practical affairs and concrete applications, rather than abstract speculations; a focus on a specific public, with attention to the principle of *decorum*; an air of tentativeness and contingency; a polemical tone; and a holistic anthropology that recognizes the proper place of human passions.[45] Compier's analysis furthermore points to three elements in Calvin's rhetoric of denunciation (of death) that are of particular significance for our purposes: the use of the *imago Dei* concept as an argument for social justice, an attack on structures that hold absolute power over people's lives, and criticism of the misuse of the concept of sin. Let me briefly elaborate on each of these, before showing how this correlates with feminist sin-talk.

First, from a perspective that sees an intimate link between love of God and love of neighbor, says Compier, Calvin "equates sins against humans with sacrilege against the supreme ruler of heaven and earth."[46] In the *Institutes*, Calvin remarks that God finds "the marks and features of his own countenance" in humans, and in his commentary on Genesis 9:6, Calvin claims that violence against the neighbor indeed wounds God himself, for "since they bear the image of God engraven on them, He deems himself violated in their person."[47] Therefore, says Compier, one could say that in the Reformer's mind all human beings are icons of the divine, and he "equates sins against humans with sacrilege against the supreme ruler of heaven and earth."[48]

Here Compier builds upon the foundation of those scholars, such as Ronald Wallace, David Cairns, and Nicholas Wolterstorff, who have argued that Calvin's treatment of the image of God also functions as an argument for

---

44. Jones, *Calvin and the Rhetoric of Piety*, 28.
45. Compier, *John Calvin's Rhetorical Doctrine of Sin*, 39–41.
46. Ibid., 103.
47. Calvin, *Institutes* 3.17.5; *Commentary on Genesis*, 9:6, available at https://biblehub.com/commentaries/calvin/genesis/9.htm. See also Nicholas Wolterstorff, "The Wounds of God: Calvin's Theology of Social Injustice," *Reformed Journal* 37, no. 6 (1987): 16.
48. Compier, *John Calvin's Rhetorical Doctrine of Sin*, 103.

social justice. Compier points to what he calls the "cord binding love of God and love of neighbor," arguing that Calvin's zeal for God's honor should always be understood as functioning within the whole of the double love command, that is, as linked to "love of neighbor." Thus, Compier points out, Calvin's argument for the critical importance of piety immediately appeals to its social utility as "source and spirit" of properly ordered human relations. He quotes Calvin as enjoining people to do all within their power to promote the welfare of others because every person "is both image of God, and our flesh," and therefore "we ought to hold our neighbor sacred."[49] Compier furthermore suggests that Calvin's insistence that we must love our neighbor because we love God is not only reflective of a theocentric emphasis but also has a persuasive goal, in that he knows that external considerations can provide pretexts to evade moral obligations to others, but if people were to look at others as the image of God, those external considerations should not apply. Similarly, South African Reformed theologian John de Gruchy, writing in response to the *kairos* of South African apartheid, argues that the *imago Dei* is "the doctrine which brings together not only our knowledge of God and of ourselves but also our relationship to others," and that we are therefore "to relate to other people on the basis of our all having been made in the 'image of God.'"[50]

Second, Compier argues that Calvin's attacks on the primacy of the pope and the control that the medieval church had over people's lives should be read as a rejection of absolute power over every detail of individuals' lives.[51] In principle, Calvin affirmed the freedom of human beings to organize for themselves at least those aspects of life that are not firmly spelled out in Scripture, in accordance with local needs and customs. Of course the problem is that local practices can be just as oppressive as large systems of power. This was perhaps well illustrated in the tight control Calvin himself sometimes held over Geneva in response to the threatening situation in which the new Protestants found themselves. Compier's point here, though, is well taken, namely that Calvin rejected the systemic injustice of top-down power that does not take into account the real needs of people on the grassroots level.

Third, Compier points out that Calvin rejected the misuse of the concept of sin in his attacks on the elaborate late-medieval penitential system because in his view it served to bind and not free people.[52] Calvin was not alone in this emphasis: the Protestant Reformation was to a large extent rooted in a rejection

---

49. Ibid., 95.
50. John W. de Gruchy, *Liberating Reformed Theology: A South African Contribution to an Ecumenical Debate* (Grand Rapids: Eerdmans, 1991), 136.
51. Compier, *John Calvin's Rhetorical Doctrine of Sin*, 106ff.
52. Ibid., 116ff.

of the medieval penitential system, as well as the concomitant nominalist and popular distortions in the doctrines of sin and grace of the era (which did not necessarily reflect the broader Catholic theological heritage). According to Jane Dempsey Douglass, these distortions led to a "religiousness pervaded by anxiety and scrupulosity."[53] Douglass notes that Calvin was deeply opposed to nominalist ideas regarding the human ability to produce perfect unselfish love of God as prerequisite for grace. Luther and Calvin biographers indicate that it was a spirituality of anxiety that led to the young Luther's search for a gracious God and Calvin's search for a certainty that lies beyond human imperfections.[54] Calvin did not see such certainty of redemption as forthcoming in the penitential system. In not presenting people with the certainty of grace, he saw it as psychologically abusive, and hence as oppressive of human beings. Calvin therefore attacked the penitential system as a misuse of the concept of sin—in part because it obscured God's grace and added to people's misery.

In Compier's reading, then, we see Calvin launching a "rhetoric of delegitimation" in the name of defending humans who are made in God's image, against the legitimation of tyranny, and against the use of penance as disciplinary technology by the medieval church.[55] In short, Compier sees Calvin as making a strong case for justice in the name of a God who is intimately involved in human life and personally offended by the exploitation and violation of human beings. Compier's description of "Calvin's God" resonates strongly with the emphasis noted earlier in María Pilar Aquino's work on the God who is near, and who shares in daily struggles. As such, Calvin exhibits something of the prophetic *ethos* that also drives feminist sin-talk. Second, in light of the way oppressive systems perpetuate themselves via quasi-religious mystification, Compier finds Calvin's link between idolatry and domination, and his recognition of the persuasive power of images and rites, to be very suggestive.[56] From this it follows that the doctrine of sin "involves rhetorical critique that discovers the unquestioned and questionable assumptions that

---

53. Jane Dempsey Douglass, *Women, Freedom, and Calvin* (Philadelphia: Westminster Press, 1985), 19. For a further discussion, see also Paul Tillich, *A History of Christian Thought: From Its Judaic and Hellenistic Origins to Existentialism*, ed. Carl Braaten (New York: Simon & Schuster, 1976), 214.

54. See, for example, Roland H. Bainton, *Here I Stand: A Life of Martin Luther* (Nashville: Abingdon-Cokesbury, 1950), and William J. Bouwsma, *John Calvin: A Sixteenth-Century Portrait* (New York: Oxford University Press, 1988), 32–48.

55. Compier, *John Calvin's Rhetorical Doctrine of Sin*, 106, 116. Regarding the latter, Compier refers here to Michel Foucault's argument that modern psychiatry learned from the "disciplinary technology" developed by the church (Michel Foucault, *The History of Sexuality*, vol. 1, trans. Robert Hurley [New York: Vintage Press, 1980], 61). Although Foucault argued that this satisfied the needs of many, Compier points out that there is evidence of widespread popular animosity toward the penitential system during the time of Calvin.

56. Compier, *What Is Rhetorical Theology?* 67. Compier here refers to insights from Kenneth Burke, whose contributions to modern rhetorical theory were mentioned in chapter 1.

permit a destructive system to continue."[57] Third, in Calvin's attack on the medieval penitential system (i.e., his attack on rival understandings of how to deal with sin), Compier finds a classical example of a theologian pointing to the "sins of sin-talk." Compier thus concludes that Calvin's "heated accusations aimed to expose the many ways in which the reigning religious regime denied persons made in God's image their due, while imprisoning them in tyrannical institutions and destructive and intrusive penitential practices."[58] One may differ with much of what Calvin had to say, and Compier is correct in warning against any oversimplifications of the affinities between past Christian polemic and critical discourses today. Nevertheless, in Calvin we find a fascinating example of how critique of oppressive rhetoric on sin is an inherent part of Christian sin-talk itself. Given the provocative moves Compier finds in Calvin's sin-talk, I have to agree with him that "it does not seem farfetched to postulate that the prophetic tradition of Christian hamartiology and contemporary intellectual praxis share a common spirit."[59] The naming of the "sins of sin-talk" that we encounter in feminist critiques of classical sin-talk, while focusing on women's experiences in a way not done in the classical traditions, is therefore not something entirely new. It is, indeed, a classical move.

The prophetic *ethos* and complex perspective on *pathos*, when coupled with the theocentric gaze upon human relationships and structures that characterize specifically theological language, shape the *logos* of feminist sin-talk in a similar way as it did those of Calvin and of other prophetic discourses on sin in the Jewish and Christian traditions. Although feminist theologians will be critical of the androcentric myopias of classic male prophetic forms of sin-talk, common elements in their *ethos* lead to moves that are very similar to those noticed in Calvin: a radical critique of a dominant hamartiological tradition (naming the "sins of sin-talk"); an emphasis on the dignity of humans as icons of the divine, with this now claimed equally for women; and a focus on systemic-structural sin, with its concomitant complex understanding of human agency. Let me outline each of these emphases in more detail.

As we have seen, in the first place, feminist sin-talk is very critical of classical sin-talk and the kinds of rhetoric found in the latter, because of the detrimental effects that these rhetorical practices have had on women's lives. Within this feminist critique we already encounter constructive feminist sin-talk that utilizes the grammar of original sin in order to denounce death. In Calvin's denunciations of the penitential system, we have seen how attacking a rival doctrine of sin in the name of human dignity can be part of a

---

57. Ibid.
58. Compier, *John Calvin's Rhetorical Doctrine of Sin*, ii.
59. Compier, *What Is Rhetorical Theology?* 70.

constructive, prophetic doctrine of sin, not antithetical to it. Likewise, feminist sin-talk ultimately does not consist of two separate moves, one critical and one constructive. Rather, what we see is that the constructive already encompasses the critical, that the critical already presupposes the constructive. One is reminded of Peter Hodgson's approach to theology: "In order to construct, we must deconstruct. But because of deconstruction, we must construct."[60] It is precisely in critiquing classical sin-talk that feminist theologians are engaging in constructive prophetic sin-talk of their own.

Second, we have also seen that feminist theologians, in their focus on systemic oppression of women, engage in a clear critical retrieval of classical hamartiological perspectives. More so than one finds in the classical doctrine of original sin, however, and somewhat akin to Calvin's prophetic denunciation of systems of oppression, one finds in feminist sin-talk a clear denunciation of sinful structures and cultural systems. This systemic focus is not only structurally similar to the doctrine of original sin, but also taps into prophetic, rhetorical modes of sin-talk—such as those found not only in modern liberation theologians but also in some classical theologians such as Calvin. Moreover, this systemic focus enables us to view moral agency in a more nuanced manner than would be possible if individual agency is viewed either in isolation, or in terms of gender dualism.

Finally, the doctrine of the *imago Dei* is central to this prophetic form of sin talk, because, as Calvin suggests, God is violated in the violation of the human person as divine image. But, like classical sin-talk, the doctrine of the *imago Dei* has been caught up in patriarchal thought patterns, so much so that the World Council of Churches, recognizing the critiques of feminist theologians, has concluded that "the doctrine of God's image (imago Dei) has by tradition been a source of oppression and discrimination against women."[61] The question whether women are the image of God occupied some prominent classical theologians, many of whom concluded that women are not the image of God, or are so only in connection with their husbands.[62] Three speculative approaches to the *imago Dei* in the Christian tradition may be identified, and all three are problematic from a feminist perspective. The so-called *substantive* approach, which sees the *imago Dei* in terms of a

---

60. Peter C. Hodgson, *Winds of the Spirit: A Constructive Christian Theology* (Louisville, KY: Westminster John Knox Press, 1994), 39.

61. Mary Catherine Hilkert, "Cry Beloved Image: Rethinking the Image of God," in Ann O'Hara Graff, ed., *In the Embrace of God: Feminist Approaches to Theological Anthropology* (Maryknoll, NY: Orbis Books, 1995), 193.

62. Abelard, for example, concluded that, according to St. Paul, men and not women are the image of God. Gratian, whose canon law allowed for the "chastising" of wives, likewise concluded that women are not made in the image of God. Augustine concluded that women are the image God only in connection with their husbands.

property of human nature, usually reason, often played into views of women as ontologically inferior or lacking in reason. The result was that women were classically seen as less in the image of God than men. The *functional* interpretation of the *imago Dei* focuses on the dominion of humans over the earth as God's representatives. When understood in terms of dominion over the earth, the doctrine of the *imago Dei* not only resembles the patriarchal *ethos* of control, but it would also subtly exclude those who have not traditionally been seen by the church as having authority—including, in particular, women.[63] According to the *relational* view of the *imago Dei*, which became prominent in the twentieth century, human beings resemble the Trinitarian God in their ability to enter into relationship. Despite the similarities between this view and the emphasis on relationality often encountered in feminist theologies, this approach has frequently been used to argue for a "subordinate but equal" role for women. The argument is based on an interpretation of intra-Trinitarian relationships that simultaneously emphasizes the equality of the Father and the Son, and the latter's obedience and subservience to the Father.[64] Here we see speculative theology at its worst. Although the doctrine of the Trinity is not simply Christian metaphysics, but is rooted in the Christian experience of the dynamic presence of God in the *kairos* of the Christ event and in the continuing presence of the Spirit of Christ in the community of faith, it can become very speculative when it comes to intra-Trinitarian relationships.[65] More importantly, as Catherine LaCugna notes, "there is no intrinsic reason why men should be correlated with God the Father and women with God the Son."[66]

Yet, despite their critiques of the doctrine of the *imago Dei*, feminist theologians are also using it constructively. As is the case with their approach to the doctrine of sin, feminist theologians' approach to the doctrine of the *imago Dei* is concrete rather than speculative. They tend to use it as a metaphor for the affirmation of human dignity, instead of focusing on the locus or nature of the *imago Dei* in human beings. This is not entirely new to the Christian tradition, as can be seen in the emphasis in Calvin mentioned earlier. In the Roman Catholic tradition, too, the doctrine of the *imago Dei* "undergirds the social teaching of the church protecting the most vulnerable members of

---

63. There is theological potential in the view of the *imago Dei* as representatives of God, when understood in the sense of responsibility for, rather than dominion over, the earth. But this volume is not the place to explore that topic.

64. Hilkert, "Cry Beloved Image," 199.

65. For more on this dynamic perspective on the Trinity, see Catherine M. LaCugna, *God for Us: The Trinity and the Christian Life* (San Francisco: HarperSanFrancisco, 1991), 21–52.

66. Catherine Mowry LaCugna, "God in Communion with Us," in *Freeing Theology: The Essentials of Theology in Feminist Perspective*, ed. Catherine Mowry LaCugna (San Francisco: HarperSanFrancisco, 1993), 98.

society from extinction or harm."[67] Yet feminist theologians add their own emphasis by "simply drawing out the implications of affirming that women are fully human beings made in the image of God."[68]

Behind the protests against forms of sin-talk that are harmful to women, then, is a strong affirmation of women's dignity, and of women's status as *imago Dei*. Feminist reappropriations of this doctrine argue against versions of the *imago Dei* that dehumanize women instead of recognizing the divine image in them. Such dehumanization of women includes the patriarchal dual feminine symbols of Mary and Eve—neither is fully human and hence neither is *imago Dei*, and both play a role in the justification and normalization of a culture of routine gender violence.[69] The matter is clearer in the case of Eve, as symbol of fleshly carnality and evil, than in the case of Mary. But classical Mary symbolism is intertwined with the Eve symbol, and thus participates in the dehumanization of women by emphasizing a feminine ideal of self-sacrifice and humility even to the point of self-negation. Moreover, where classical Mary symbolism is combined with the notion of the *imago Dei*, women are usually depicted in terms of complementarity to men. In a subtle way, then, men remain the true image of God, and women only derivatively so. To the extent that classical sin-talk participates in casting women in the patriarchal images of Eve and Mary, it therefore also participates in the dehumanization of women.

In the time when Calvin talked about the violation of the "neighbor" as a violation of God, the generic "neighbor" was still primarily imagined as male (not to mention white and European). Christians have traditionally managed to escape the radical implications of the *imago Dei* symbol by simply classifying some (ruling males) as truly or "more so" the image of God than others (women, people of color, etc.). One might even say that the radicalism of feminist theology lies in its insistence that women are fully the image of God, and that the ethical implications of this doctrine should be taken to its conclusion: that the subjugation, oppression, or violation of women is indeed the subjugation, oppression, or violation of the very image of God—and therefore, as Calvin might have suggested, the violation of God's own self. In a prophetic feminist rhetoric of sin aimed at addressing gender violence and other forms of gender oppression, then, one central affirmation might be that, given the full human dignity of women, their "iconicity," the

---

67. Hilkert, "Cry Beloved Image," 192.
68. Janet Kalven in Hilkert, "Cry Beloved Image," 192.
69. Of course in some "high" Mariologies, especially those leaning toward declaring her co-redemptrix, Mary is *imago Dei*, but that does not negate the fact that the patriarchal-cultural Mary symbol is ultimately dehumanizing to regular women, and in her relation to the Eve symbol further robs women of being seen as fully *imago Dei*.

violation of women *is* the violation of the divine—not because women are now declared divine, but because the God who shares in daily struggles is violated in the violation of those who are *imago Dei*. In contrast to forms of sin-talk that participated in systemic gender violence by casting women as deserving of punishment and implicitly encouraging women to accept it, feminist sin-talk proclaims that gender violence is sin, and as such a rejection of the divine presence in the world.

This is no mere flowery theological talk. Rather, it is a radically theocentric—or rather, as Mary McClintock Fulkerson would say, *theacentric*—mode of sin-talk. From a theological perspective, gender violence is a central aspect of that fundamental tear in the fabric of the world that Christians have traditionally named "original sin," and as such a symptom of estrangement from the Divine and hence of our brokenness. Gender violence does not only follow upon a rhetoric of dehumanization—it also dehumanizes. All the classical metaphors for sin, such as corruption, defilement, or alienation, are, from various angles, descriptive of the way gender violence and other forms of gender oppression rip into the good in human life.[70] To call this a violation of the divine is therefore not farfetched.

Compier's analysis suggests that Calvin's prophetic sin-talk is critical, theocentric, and systemic. Similarly, but with explicit awareness of gender injustice, rooted in a prophetic *ethos*, and aware of the complex *pathos* of women within the feminist rhetorical situation, the arguments (*logos*) of feminist sin-talk can be described as critical, *theacentric*, and systemic. Like Calvin and other prophets of old, but with their own focus on the particular *pathos* of women, feminists engage in a concrete, prophetic—and thus rhetorical—form of sin-talk in order to attack a "rival" doctrine of sin. This feminist sin-talk is *theacentric* because at its heart stands the radical affirmation of women's full humanity and iconicity, as classically expressed in the doctrine of the *imago Dei* and loudly and fully reaffirmed for women. Having "expanded" (or rather, completed) the symbol of the *imago Dei* in this way, feminist theologians might well follow, yet transcend, Calvin in using this doctrine to argue that gender violence is not merely displeasing or problematic, or an ethical problem to be addressed, but constitutes the violation of the divine in this world. Finally, feminist sin-talk has a systemic element, as we saw in the previous chapter,

---

70. See Marjorie Hewitt Suchocki, *The Fall to Violence: Original Sin in Relational Theology* (New York: Continuum, 1995), for an emphasis on sin *as* violence. Rejecting, alongside Saiving et al., the traditional description of sin as prideful rebellion against God, Suchocki instead sees sin as rebellion against creation, which primarily takes the form of violence. Violence is sin because it describes actions that should not have happened, for which there is human responsibility, and for which there is an alternative vision (ibid., 45). By telling various stories of violence, Suchocki brings home the dehumanizing reality of the sin of violence.

in that its focus is not only on personal or individual actions, although that is part of it, but because it knows that sinful agency is located within broader matrixes of oppression.

AFFIRMING LIFE

Our critical rhetorical inquiry has taken us into the depths of feminist critiques of classical Christian sin-talk. Making use of various feminist rhetorical strategies, feminist theologians have pointed to serious flaws in classical Christian sin-talk. Rooted in a patriarchal *ethos* characterized by a drive toward control, characterized by a *logos* of female defilement and subjugation, which I have argued echoes the Eve/Mary dichotomy, and excluding the *pathos* of its female audiences, much of classical sin-talk ultimately fails the test of praxis by helping to normalize gender violence. But, I have argued, in launching critiques of the rhetorical practices discernible in the sin-talk of classical theologians, feminist theologians are themselves engaging in constructive sin-talk, and this constructive sin-talk transcends merely proposing a "female sin," or showing how women have been the victims of men's sin. In sketching the depth dimension of the failings of classical sin-talk, feminist theologians are already moving toward such a constructive form of feminist sin-talk, because they point to an understanding of sinful agency as embedded in patriarchy as "original," systemic sin. The *ethos* driving feminist sin-talk is a prophetic one, rooted in the living God and the human cry for life. Feminist sin-talk, whether talking about the sins of women or the sins perpetrated against women, is (or should be) characterized by rhetorical scaling and an analogical imagination that can hold together both the differences among, and the unity of, women within the complex feminist rhetorical situation. In attacking rival doctrines of sin, sketching its depth dimension, and denouncing the dehumanization of women and the concomitant violence against women, feminist theologians construct a rhetorical, prophetic form of sin-talk that may help to address concrete issues such as gender violence.

At its heart, what feminist sin-talk does is to denounce death. It denounces the rhetoric of death found in the classical theme of blaming women for sin, and it denounces the rhetoric of life-denial easily conjured up by an over-emphasis on pride. It denounces the exigence in the rhetorical situation of women's lives, the various forms of oppression that women face every day, and in particular gender violence, which, although it also takes forms that target men (especially men who are "feminized" through various kinds of rhetoric), particularly targets women. It denounces systemic gender oppression, even speaking of it with the language of original sin. This denunciation of death is rooted in a prophetic *ethos* that derives from the human cry for life in the name of the God of life. It speaks to the diversity of life experienced by women, and accommodates to their varying needs. And it affirms the dignity of women as it denounces the violation of God's image in women, and thereby of God as well.

Because it speaks in the name of the God of life, feminist sin-talk also pushes forward, toward an affirmation of life. Sin-talk has a negative connotation, because it speaks of human pathologies—so the aspect of denunciation of death is central to it. But it is also a liberating form of theological rhetoric, because it speaks in the name of God. It speaks not only of what is wrong, but presupposes and pushes toward that which is right. It does not only denounce death, but it wants to affirm life. Perhaps the most important thing to take from Augustine's classical perspective on sin is that pride and concupiscence are fundamentally antidivine dispositions: sin is therefore what separates us from the source of life and flourishing, and it is a matter of broken relationships with God, the self, and the other. As such, as I have suggested earlier in this chapter, sin needs to be understood in light of two intertwined theological claims: it is theocentric, and it is soteriocentric. As theocentric language, sin-talk cannot be divorced from how we think about God. Sin-talk becomes negative, moralistic rhetoric if it is divorced from solid God-talk. If God is the stern taskmaster, the patriarchal father, then sin-talk almost by definition becomes harsh. If God is understood as the One who wills our well-being, who wills our life, then sin-talk becomes grace-talk. The God who is In-Search-of-Humanity, who becomes One-of-Us, who is God-for-Us, the God who is known in the overflowing love that creates the world, who speaks through Torah and Prophets in the religion of Israel, who for Christians is known by the foundational *kairos* event of Christ, such a God is defined by grace, and any talk of human pathology therefore needs to be both theocentric and soteriocentric. To speak of sin, then, is to speak of human lostness, of broken relationality, of the malaise that often has no name. In his famous sermon, *You Are Accepted*, Paul Tillich wrote,

> There are few words more strange to most of us than "sin" and "grace." They are strange, just because they are so well-known. During the centuries they have received distorting connotations, and have lost so much of their genuine power that we must seriously ask ourselves whether we should use them at all, or whether we should discard them as useless tools. But there is a mysterious fact about the great words of our religious tradition: they cannot be replaced. All attempts to make substitutions, including those I have tried myself, have failed to convey the reality that was to be expressed; they have led to shallow and impotent talk. There are no substitutes for words like "sin" and

"grace." But there is a way of rediscovering their meaning, the same way that leads us down into the depth of our human existence. In that depth these words were conceived; and *there* they gained power for all ages; *there* they must be found again by each generation, and by each of us for himself. Let us therefore try to penetrate the deeper levels of our life, in order to see whether we can discover in them the realities of which our text speaks.[71]

Feminist theology, in its various manifestations, constitutes one of the ways in which modern theology tries to rediscover the meaning of words like "sin" and "grace." But after all is said and done, perhaps the most important thing we can say is that sin and grace should never be separated. Sin-talk is diagnostic talk—it identifies the illness for which the medicine already exists. It ought not to be reduced, as it so often has been, to judgment talk for which punishment already exists. Even if the possibility of punishment remains part of Christian rhetoric, it needs to be put into perspective. Authentic sin-talk is not the same as moralistic talk, as Augustine, despite his own gender blindness, reminded us so long ago. Individual moralism is indeed the language of death. Authentic sin-talk is the language of *pathos* and not only of pathology, born from a prophetic *ethos*, aimed at denouncing that which is death-dealing, and at affirming life. The unfortunate participation of much of classical sin-talk in the patriarchal rhetoric of death and life-denial does not mean that we should abandon all sin-talk, but indeed calls us to internal critique, and to the firm, prophetic denunciation of death and the affirmation of life in the name of the God of life. Feminist theologians, in a now almost sixty-year-old conversation on sin, do exactly this.

The language of sin is not really about good and evil, but about the brokenness of the world. We have to speak this language if we are to embrace the task, as Judaism teaches us, of *Tikkun Olam*, the task of healing the world. The God of Life, the God of the prophets, the God of the Christ, is not the God of the patriarchal rhetoric that dehumanizes women into the patriarchal feminine that is doubly associated with death, but is the God of humanization, of healing the world, of human flourishing, of the resurrection from the dead.

---

71. Paul Tillich, *The Shaking of the Foundations* (New York: Charles Scribner's Sons, 1948), 153–54.

Bibliography

Al-Hibri, Azizah Y. "Is Western Patriarchal Feminism Good for Third World / Minority Women?" In *Is Multiculturalism Bad for Women?* ed. Joshua Cohen, Matthew Howard, and Martha C. Nussbaum, 41–46. Princeton, NJ: Princeton University Press, 1999.
Ansell, Nicholas John. *"The Woman Will Overcome the Warrior": A Dialogue with the Christian/Feminist Theology of Rosemary Radford Ruether.* New York: University Press of America, 1994.
Aquinas, Thomas. *Summa Theologiae.* Trans. Fathers of the English Dominican Province. New York: Benziger Brothers, 1946.
Aquino, María Pilar. *Our Cry for Life: Feminist Theology from Latin America.* Maryknoll, NY: Orbis Books, 1993.
Aquino, María Pilar, and Elisabeth Schüssler Fiorenza, eds. *In the Power of Wisdom: Feminist Spiritualities of Struggle.* London: SCM Press, 2000.
Ardener, Shirley. *Perceiving Women.* London: J. M. Dent & Sons, 1975.
Aristotle. *On Rhetoric: A Theory of Civic Discourse.* Trans. George A. Kennedy. New York: Oxford University Press, 2007.
———. *Politics.* Trans. George A. Kennedy. New York: Oxford University Press, 2007.
Asad, Talal. *Genealogies of Religion: Discipline and Reasons of Power in Christianity and Islam.* Baltimore: Johns Hopkins University Press, 1993.
Augustine. *The City of God.* Trans. Henry Bettenson. New York: Penguin Books, 1984.
———. *The Confessions.* In *The Works of Saint Augustine: A Translation for the 21st Century*, vol. 1, book 1, trans. Maria Boulding. New York: New City Press, 2001.
———. *On Continence.* In *The Nicene and Post-Nicene Fathers* 3, ed. Philip Schaff. Grand Rapids: Eerdmans, 1988.
———. *Teaching Christianity (De Doctrina Christiana).* Trans. Edmund Hill, O.P. In *The Works of Saint Augustine*, ed. John E. Rotelle, O.S.A. New York: New City Press, 1996.
———. *The Trinity.* Ed. John E. Rotelle. Trans. Edmund Hill, O. P. New York: New City Press, 1991.
Baard, Rachel Sophia. "Original Grace, Not Destructive Grace: A Feminist Appropriation of Paul Tillich's Notion of Acceptance." *Journal of Religion* 87 (July 2007): 411–34.
———. "Responding to the Kairos of HIV/AIDS." *Theology Today* 65 (2008): 368–81.
Bainton, Roland H. *Here I Stand: A Life of Martin Luther.* Nashville: Abingdon-Cokesbury, 1950.
Baldwin, Claude-Marie. "John Calvin and the Ethics of Gender Relations." *Calvin Theological Journal* 26 (1991): 133–43.

Barkai, Avraham. "*Volksgemeinschaft*, 'Aryanization,' and the Holocaust." In *The Final Solution: Origins and Implementation*, ed. David Cesarani, 34–43. London: Routledge, 1994.

Barth, Karl. *Church Dogmatics*, I/2, *The Doctrine of the Word of God*. Ed. G. W. Bromiley and T. F. Torrance. Trans. G. T. Thomson and Harold Knight. Edinburgh: T&T Clark, 1956.

———. *Church Dogmatics*, III/4, *The Doctrine of Creation*. Ed. G. W. Bromiley and T. F. Torrance, various translators. Edinburgh: T&T Clark, 1961.

———. *Church Dogmatics*, IV/2, *The Doctrine of Reconciliation*. Ed. G. W. Bromiley and T. F. Torrance. Trans. G. W. Bromiley. Edinburgh: T&T Clark, 1958.

Benhabib, Seyla. *The Claims of Culture: Equality and Diversity in the Global Era*. Princeton, NJ: Princeton University Press, 2002.

Bhabha, Homi K. *The Location of Culture*. London: Routledge, 1994.

Bieler, André. *L'homme et la femme dans la morale calviniste*. Geneva: Labor et Fides, 1963.

Bitzer, Lloyd. "The Rhetorical Situation." *Philosophy and Rhetoric* 1 (January 1968): 1–14.

Bizzell, Patricia, and Bruce Herzberg, eds. *The Rhetorical Tradition: Readings from Classical Times to the Present*. Boston: Bedford Books, 1990.

Bloch, Maurice. *Prey into Hunter: The Politics of Religious Experience*. Lewis Henry Morgan Lecture Series 1984. Cambridge: Cambridge University Press, 1992.

Boff, Leonardo. *The Maternal Face of God*. San Francisco: Harper & Row, 1987.

Bohner, Gerd, and Norbert Schwarz. "The Threat of Rape: Its Psychological Impact on Nonvictimized Women." In *Sex, Power, Conflict: Evolutionary and Feminist Perspectives*, ed. David M. Buss and Neil M. Malamuth, 162–75. New York: Oxford University Press, 1996.

Bonhoeffer, Dietrich. *Discipleship*. Dietrich Bonhoeffer Works 4. Minneapolis: Fortress Press, 2001.

Booth, Wayne C. *The Company We Keep: An Ethics of Fiction*. Berkeley: University of California Press, 1988.

Bouwsma, William J. "Calvinism as Renaissance Artifact." In *John Calvin and the Church: A Prism of Reform*, ed. Timothy George, 28–41. Louisville, KY: Westminster/John Knox Press, 1990.

———. *John Calvin: A Sixteenth-Century Portrait*. New York: Oxford University Press, 1988.

Brock, Rita Nakashima. *Journeys by Heart: A Christology of Erotic Power*. New York: Crossroad, 2000.

Brown, Delwin. *Boundaries of Our Habitations: Tradition and Theological Construction*. SUNY Series in Religious Studies, ed. Harold Coward. Albany: State University of New York Press, 1994.

Brown, Joanne Carlson, and Rebecca Parker. "For God So Loved the World?" In *Christianity, Patriarchy, and Abuse: A Feminist Critique*, ed. Joanne Carlson Brown and Carole R. Bohn, 1–30. Cleveland: Pilgrim Press, 1989.

Brown, Robert McAfee, ed. *Kairos: Three Prophetic Challenges to the Church*. Grand Rapids: Eerdmans, 1990.

Bunting, Alyce B., and Joy B. Reeves. "Exploring Belief Relationships in the Areas of Sex Roles, Religion, and Rape." *Journal of Pastoral Counseling* 16, no. 1 (Spring/Summer 1981): 53–64.

Burke, Kenneth. *A Rhetoric of Motives*. Berkeley: University of California Press, 1969.

———. "Rhetoric—Old and New." *Journal of General Education* 5 (1951): 203–5.

Burt, Martha R. "Cultural Myths and Supports for Rape." *Journal of Personality and Social Psychology* 38, no. 2 (1980): 217–30.
Calvin, John. *Commentary on the Book of the Prophet Isaiah*. Vol. 1, ed. William Pringle. Grand Rapids: Baker Book House.
———. *Commentary on the Book of the Prophet Jeremiah*. Vol. 1, ed. John Owen. Grand Rapids: Baker Book House.
———. *Commentary on Genesis*, 9:6. https://biblehub.com/commentaries/calvin/genesis/9.htm.
———. *Institutes of the Christian Religion*. Library of Christian Classics 20 and 21. Ed. John T. McNeill. Trans. Ford Lewis Battles. Philadelphia: Westminster Press, 1960.
———. *Ioannis Calvini opera quae supersunt omnia*. Ed. G. Baum et al. Braunschweig, Germany: C. A. Schwetschke, 1863–1900.
Carr, Ann. *Transforming Grace: Christian Tradition and Women's Experience*. New York: Continuum, 1998.
Centers for Disease Control and Prevention. *Morbidity and Mortality Weekly Report*, September 5, 2014. http://www.cdc.gov/mmwr/preview/mmwrhtml/ss6308a1.htm?s_cid=ss6308a1_e.
Charry, Ellen T. "Augustine of Hippo: Father of Christian Psychology." *Anglican Theological Review* 88, no. 4 (Fall 2006): 575–89.
Chopp, Rebecca S. *The Power to Speak: Feminism, Language, God*. New York: Crossroad, 1989.
———. "Theological Persuasion: Rhetoric, Warrants, and Suffering." In *Worldview and Warrants: Plurality and Authority in Theology*, ed. William Schweiker, 17–31. Lanham, MD: University Press of America, 1987.
Christ, Carol P. "Why Women Need the Goddess: Phenomenological, Psychological, and Political Reflections." In *Womanspirit Rising: A Feminist Reader in Religion*, ed. Carol Christ and Judith Plaskow, 273–87. San Francisco: Harper & Row, 1979.
Cicero. *De finibus bonorum et malorum*. Loeb Classical Library 40, ed. G. P. Goold, trans. Harris Rackham. New York: Macmillan, 1914.
———. *De Officiis*. Loeb Classical Library 21, ed. G. P. Goold, trans. Walter Miller. Cambridge, MA: Harvard University Press, 1975.
Clark, Elizabeth, and Herbert Richardson, eds. *Women and Religion: A Feminist Sourcebook of Christian Thought*. New York: Harper & Row, 1977.
Cone, James H. *The Cross and the Lynching Tree*. Maryknoll, NY: Orbis Books, 2017.
Consigny, Scott. "Rhetoric and Its Situations." *Philosophy and Rhetoric* 7, no. 3 (1974): 175–86.
Compier, Don H. "Denouncing Death: John Calvin's Critique of Sin and Contemporary Rhetorical Theology." Ph.D. diss., Emory University, 1992.
———. *John Calvin's Rhetorical Doctrine of Sin*. Texts and Studies in Religion 86. Lewiston, NY: Edwin Mellen Press, 2001.
———. *What Is Rhetorical Theology? Textual Practice and Public Discourse*. Harrisburg, PA: Trinity Press, 1999.
Confession of Belhar, September 1986. https://www.pcusa.org/site_media/media/uploads/theologyandworship/pdfs/belhar.pdf.
Cooper-White, Pamela. *The Cry of Tamar: Violence against Women and the Church's Response*. Minneapolis: Fortress Press, 1995.
Costin, Frank, and Norbert Schwarz. "Beliefs about Rape and Women's Social Roles: A Four-Nation Study." *Journal of Interpersonal Violence* 2 (1987): 46–56.

Cudd, Ann E. *Analyzing Oppression.* Studies in Feminist Philosophy. New York: Oxford, 2006.
Cunningham, David S. *Faithful Persuasion: In Aid of a Rhetoric of Christian Theology.* Notre Dame, IN: University of Notre Dame Press, 1991.
Daly, Mary. *Beyond God the Father: Toward a Philosophy of Women's Liberation.* Boston: Beacon Press, 1973.
———. *Gyn/Ecology: The Metaethics of Radical Feminism.* Boston: Beacon Press, 1978.
Datta, B., and R. Motihar. *Breaking Down the Walls: Violence against Women as a Health and Human Rights Issue.* New Delhi: Ford Foundation, 1999.
de Gruchy, John W. *Liberating Reformed Theology: A South Africa Contribution to an Ecumenical Debate.* Grand Rapids: Eerdmans, 1991.
Didache. In *Early Christian Fathers*, ed. Cyril C. Richardson, 161–79. Louisville, KY: Westminster John Knox Press, 2006.
Dijkstra, Bram. *Idols of Perversity.* New York: Oxford University Press, 1986.
Dingle, Adele, ed. *Domestic Violence and the Churches: Train the Trainer Manual.* Queensland, Australia: Joint Churches Domestic Violence Project.
Dobash, R. Emerson, and Russell P. Dobash. *Violence against Wives: A Case against the Patriarchy.* New York: Free Press, 1979.
Douglass, Jane Dempsey. *Women, Freedom, and Calvin.* The 1983 Annie Kinkead Warfield Lectures. Philadelphia: Westminster Press, 1985.
Duck, Ruth C. "Sin, Grace, and Gender in Free-Church Protestant Worship." In *Women at Worship: Interpretations of North American Diversity*, ed. Marjorie Proctor-Smith and Janet R. Walton, 55–69. Louisville, KY: Westminster/John Knox Press, 1993.
Dunfee, Susan Nelson. "The Sin of Hiding: A Feminist Critique of Reinhold Niebuhr's Account of the Sin of Pride." *Soundings* 65 (Fall 1982): 316–27.
Eliade, Mircea. *The Sacred and the Profane: The Nature of Religion.* Trans. Willard R. Trask. New York: Harcourt, Brace & World, 1959.
Elizondo, Virgilio. "Mary and the Poor: A Model of Evangelizing Ecumenism." In *Mary in the Churches*, ed. Hans Küng and Jürgen Moltmann, 59–65. New York: Seabury Press, 1983.
Engel, Mary Potter. "Evil, Sin, and Violation of the Vulnerable." In *Lift Every Voice: Constructing Theologies from the Underside*, ed. Susan Brooks Thistlethwaite and Mary Potter Engel, 152–64. San Francisco: Harper & Row, 1998.
———. "Historical Theology and Violence against Women: Unearthing a Popular Tradition of Just Battery." In *Revisioning the Past: Prospects in Historical Theology*, ed. Mary Potter Engel and Walter E. Wyman Jr., 51–75. Minneapolis: Fortress Press, 1992.
Ess, Charles. "Reading Adam and Eve: Re-Visions of the Myth of Woman's Subordination to Man." In *Violence against Women: A Christian Theological Sourcebook*, ed. Carol J. Adam and Marie M. Fortune, 92–120. New York: Continuum, 1995.
Evangelical Lutheran Church in America. "Gender-Based Violence." http://www.elca.org/Our-Work/Publicly-Engaged-Church/Justice-for-Women/Social-Issues/Gender-Based-Violence.
Exum, J. Cheryl. *Fragmented Women: Feminist (Sub)versions of Biblical Narratives.* Journal for the Study of the Old Testament Supplement Series 163. Guildford, UK: Sheffield Academic Press—JSOT Press, 1993.
Faus, José Ignacio González. "Sin." In *Systematic Theology: Perspectives from Liberation Theology*, ed. Jon Sobrino and Ignacio Ellacuriá, 194–204. Maryknoll, NY: Orbis Books, 1996.

Fontaine, Petrus. *The Light and the Dark: A Cultural History of Dualism.* 13 vols. Amsterdam: J. C. Gieben, 1986.
Fortune, Marie. "The Church and Domestic Violence." *TSF Bulletin* 8, no. 2 (1984): 17.
———. *Sexual Violence: The Unmentionable Sin.* Cleveland: Pilgrim Press, 1983.
Foucault, Michel. *The History of Sexuality.* Vol. 1, trans. Robert Hurley. New York: Vintage Press, 1980.
Francesco, Roberto. *The Dictionary of Moral Theology.* London: Burns & Oates, 1962.
Fraser, Nancy. *Justice Interruptus: Critical Reflections on the "Postsocialist" Condition.* New York: Routledge, 1997.
Fraser, Nancy, and Linda J. Nicholson. "Social Criticism without Philosophy: An Encounter between Feminism and Postmodernism." In *Feminism/Postmodernism*, ed. Linda J. Nicholson, 19–38. New York: Routledge, 1990.
Fulkerson, Mary McClintock. *Changing the Subject: Women's Discourses and Feminist Theology.* Minneapolis: Fortress Press, 1994.
———. "Sexism as Original Sin: Developing a Theacentric Discourse." *Journal of the American Academy of Religion* 59, no. 4 (Winter 1991): 653–75.
Gaventa, Beverly Roberts, and Cynthia L. Rigby. *Blessed One: Protestant Perspectives on Mary.* Louisville, KY: Westminster John Knox Press, 2002.
Geertz, Clifford. "Religion as a Cultural System." In *A Reader in the Anthropology of Religion*, ed. Michael Lambek, 61–82. Malden, MA: Blackwell, 2002.
Gerhardt, Elizabeth. *The Cross and Gendercide: A Theological Response to Global Violence against Women and Girls.* Downers Grove, IL: IVP Academic, 2014.
Gil, Rosa Maria, and Carmen Inoa Vazquez. *The Maria Paradox: How Latinas Can Merge Old-World Traditions with New-World Self-Esteem.* New York: Putnam, 1996.
Gilligan, Carol. *In a Different Voice: Psychological Theory and Women's Development.* Cambridge, MA: Harvard University Press, 1982.
Gilman, Sander L. "'Barbaric' Rituals?" In *Is Multiculturalism Bad for Women?* ed. Joshua Cohen, Matthew Howard, and Martha C. Nussbaum, 53–58. Princeton, NJ: Princeton University Press, 1999.
Girard, René. *Things Kept Secret from the Foundation of the World.* Trans. Stephen Bann and Michael Metteer. Stanford, CA: Stanford University Press, 1987.
Gramsci, Antonio. *Selections from the Prison Notebooks.* Ed. and trans. Quinton Hoare and Geoffrey Nowell Smith. New York: International Publishers, 1971.
Grey, Mary. "Falling into Freedom: Searching for New Interpretations of Sin in a Secular Society." *Scottish Journal of Theology* 47, no. 2 (1994): 223–43.
Gudorf, Christine E. *Victimization: Examining Christian Complicity.* Philadelphia: Trinity Press, 1992.
Gutiérrez, Gustavo. *A Theology of Liberation: History, Politics and Salvation.* Rev. ed. Trans. Sister Caridad Inda and John Eagleson. Maryknoll, NY: Orbis Books, 2001.
Halkes, Catharina. "Mary and Women." In *Mary in the Churches*, ed. Hans Küng and Jürgen Moltmann, 66–73. New York: Seabury Press, 1983.
Hartsock, Nancy. "Rethinking Modernism: Minority vs. Majority Theories." *Cultural Critique* 7 (Fall 1987): 187–206.
Hawkesworth, M. E. *Beyond Oppression: Feminist Theory and Political Strategy.* New York: Continuum, 1990.
Heggen, Carolyn Holderread. "Religious Beliefs and Abuse." In *Women, Abuse, and the Bible*, ed. Catherine Clark Kroeger and James R. Beck, 15–27. Grand Rapids: Baker Books, 1996.

Helliwell, Christine. "'It's Only a Penis': Rape, Feminism, and Difference." *Signs: The Journal of Women and Culture and Society* 15, no. 3 (Spring 2000): 789–816.

Heise, Lori, Mary Ellsberg, and Megan Gottemoeller. "Ending Violence against Women." Johns Hopkins University School of Public Health, Series L, number 11. *Population Reports*. Baltimore, MD: Population Information Program, 1999.

Heise, Lori, Kirsten Moore, and Nahid Toubia. *Sexual Coercion and Reproductive Health: A Focus on Research*. New York: Population Council, 1995.

Heschel, Abraham Joshua. *God in Search of Man: A Philosophy of Judaism*. New York: Farrar, Straus and Cudahy, 1955.

Hess, Carol Lakey. "Reclaiming Ourselves: A Spirituality for Women's Empowerment." In *Women, Gender and Christian Community*, ed. Jane Dempsey Douglass and James F. Kay, 141–50. Louisville, KY: Westminster John Knox Press, 1997.

Hilkert, Mary Catherine. "Cry Beloved Image: Rethinking the Image of God." In *In the Embrace of God: Feminist Approaches to Theological Anthropology*, ed. Ann O'Hara Graff, 190–205. Maryknoll, NY: Orbis Books, 1995.

Hodgson, Peter C. *Winds of the Spirit: A Constructive Christian Theology*. Louisville, KY: Westminster John Knox Press, 1994.

Honig, Bonnie. "My Culture Made Me Do It." In *Is Multiculturalism Bad for Women?* ed. Joshua Cohen, Matthew Howard, and Martha C. Nussbaum, 35–40. Princeton, NJ: Princeton University Press, 1999.

hooks, bell. "Sisterhood: Political Solidarity between Women." In *Feminist Social Thought*, ed. Diana Tietjens Meyers, 485–500. New York: Routledge, 1997.

Hughes, P. E., ed. *The Register of the Company of the Pastors of Geneva in the Time of Calvin*. Grand Rapids: Eerdmans, 1966.

Jarratt, Susan C., and Nedra Reynolds. "The Splitting Image: Contemporary Feminisms and the Ethics of Éthos." In *Ethos: New Essays in Rhetorical and Critical Theory*, ed. James S. Baumlin and Tita French Baumlin, 37–63. Dallas, TX: Southern Methodist University Press, 1994.

Johnson, Elizabeth A. *She Who Is: The Mystery of God in Feminist Theological Discourse*. New York: Crossroad, 1995.

———. *Truly Our Sister: A Theology of Mary in the Communion of Saints*. New York: Continuum, 2006.

———. "Wisdom Was Made Flesh and Pitched Her Tent among Us." In *Reconstructing the Christ Symbol*, ed. Maryanne Stevens, 95–117. New York: Paulist Press, 2004.

Jones, Serene. *Calvin and the Rhetoric of Piety*. Columbia Series in Reformed Theology. Louisville, KY: Westminster John Knox Press, 1995.

———. "Cultural Labor and Theological Critique." In *Converging on Culture: Theologians in Dialogue with Cultural Analysis and Criticism*, ed. Delwin Brown, Sheila Greeve Davaney, and Kathryn Tanner, 158–75. New York: Oxford University Press, 2001.

———. *Feminist Theory and Christian Theology: Cartographies of Grace*. Guides to Theological Inquiry. Minneapolis: Fortress Press, 2000.

Jost, Walter, and Michael J. Hyde, eds. *Rhetoric and Hermeneutics in Our Time: A Reader*. New Haven, CT: Yale University Press, 1997.

Kanyoro, Musimbi. "Feminist Theology and African Culture." In *Violence against Women: Reflections by Kenyan Women Theologians*, ed. Grace Wamue and Mary Getui, 4–12. Nairobi: Acton Publishers, 1996.

Kassian, Mary A. *Women, Creation, and the Fall*. Westchester, IL: Crossway, 1990.

Keener, Craig S. "Some Biblical Reflections on Justice, Rape, and an Insensitive Society." In *Women, Abuse, and the Bible*, ed. Catherine Clark Kroeger and James R. Beck, 117–30. Grand Rapids: Baker Books, 1996.
Keller, Catherine. "Of Swallowed, Walled, and Wordless Women." *Soundings* 65 (Fall 1982): 328–39.
Kennedy, George A. *Classical Rhetoric and Its Christian and Secular Tradition from Ancient to Modern Times*. Chapel Hill: University of North Carolina Press, 1980.
Kinneavy, James L. "*Kairos*: A Neglected Concept in Classical Rhetoric." In *Rhetoric and Praxis: The Contribution of Classical Rhetoric to Practical Reasoning*, ed. J. D. Moss, 79–105. Washington, DC: Catholic University of America Press, 1986.
———. "*Kairos* in Classical and Modern Rhetorical Theory." In *Rhetoric and Kairos: Essays in History, Theory, and Praxis*, ed. Phillip Sipiora and James S. Baumlin, 58–76. Albany: State University of New York Press, 2002.
Klasen, Stephan, and Claudia Wink. "Missing Women: Revisiting the Debate." *Feminist Economics* 9 (2003): 263–99.
Kneidel, Gregory. "Rhetoric in the Age of Reformation and Counter-Reformation." In *Encyclopedia of Rhetoric*, ed. Thomas O. Sloane, 690–94. New York: Oxford University Press, 2001.
Kristof, Nicholas D., and Sheryl WuDunn. *Half the Sky: Turning Oppression into Opportunity for Women Worldwide*. New York: Vintage Books, 2010.
Kroeger, Catherine Clark, and James R. Beck, eds. *Women, Abuse, and the Bible*. Grand Rapids: Baker Books, 1996.
LaCugna, Catherine Mowry. *God for Us: The Trinity and the Christian Life*. San Francisco: HarperSanFrancisco, 1991.
———. "God in Communion with Us." In *Freeing Theology: The Essentials of Theology in Feminist Perspective*, ed. Catherine Mowry LaCugna, 83–114. San Francisco: HarperSanFrancisco, 1993.
Lee, Sang Hyun. *From a Liminal Place: An Asian American Theology*. Minneapolis: Fortress Press, 2010.
Lindbeck, George A. *The Nature of Doctrine: Religion and Theology in a Postliberal Age*. Philadelphia: Westminster Press, 1984.
Luther, Martin. "Lectures on Genesis." In *Luther's Works*. Vol. 1, ed. Jaroslav Pelikan. St. Louis, MO: Concordia Publishing House, 1955.
Mananzan, Mary John. "Feminine Socialization: Women as Victims and Collaborators." In *Violence against Women*, ed. Elisabeth Schüssler Fiorenza and Mary Shawn Copeland, 44–52. Concilium 1994/1. Maryknoll, NY: Orbis Books, 1994.
Manne, Kate. *Down Girl: The Logic of Misogyny*. New York: Oxford University Press, 2018.
Match International Centre. "The Circle of Healing: Aboriginal Women Organizing in Canada." In *Women and Violence: Realities and Responses around the World*, ed. M. Davies, 231–39. London: Zed Books, 1994.
McBride, James. *War, Battering, and Other Sports: The Gulf between American Men and Women*. Atlantic Highlands, NJ: Humanities Press, 1995.
McFadyen, Alistair. *Bound to Sin: Abuse, Holocaust, and the Christian Doctrine of Sin*. Cambridge: Cambridge University Press, 2000.
McKerrow, Raymie E. "Critical Rhetoric: Theory and Praxis." *Communication Monographs* 56 (1989): 91–111.
McLaughlin, Eleanor Commo. "Equality of Souls, Inequality of Sexes: Woman in Medieval Theology." In *Religion and Sexism: Images of Woman in the Jewish and*

Christian Traditions, ed. Rosemary Radford Ruether, 213–66. Eugene, OR: Wipf and Stock, 1998.

Meyer-Wilmes, Hedwig. "Persecuting Witches in the Name of Reason: An Analysis of Western Rationality." In *The Fascination of Evil*, ed. Herman Häring and David Tracy, 11–17. Concilium 1998/1. Maryknoll, NY: Orbis Books, 1998.

Migliore, Daniel. "Sin and Self-Loss: Karl Barth and the Feminist Critique of Traditional Doctrines of Sin." In *Many Voices, One God: Being Faithful in a Pluralistic World*, ed. Walter Brueggemann and George W. Stroup, 139–54. Louisville, KY: Westminster John Knox Press, 1998.

Miles, Margaret R. *Augustine on the Body*. Eugene, OR: Wipf and Stock, 1979.

Narayan, Uma. *Dislocating Cultures: Identities, Traditions, and Third World Feminism*. New York: Routledge, 1997.

Neumann, Erich. *The Great Mother*. Princeton, NJ: Princeton University Press, 1955.

Niebuhr, Reinhold. *The Nature and Destiny of Man: A Christian Interpretation*. New York: Charles Scribner's Sons, 1948.

Noddings, Nel. *Women and Evil*. Berkeley: University of California Press, 1989.

Oduyoye, Mercy Amba. *Introducing African Women's Theology*. Cleveland, OH: Pilgrim Press, 2001.

Ofei-Afboagye, Rosemary Ofibea. "Domestic Violence in Ghana: An Initial Step." *Columbia Journal of Gender and Law* 4, no. 1 (1994): 25.

Okin, Susan Moller. "Is Multiculturalism Bad for Women?" In *Is Multiculturalism Bad for Women?* ed. Joshua Cohen, Matthew Howard, and Martha C. Nussbaum, 9–24. Princeton, NJ: Princeton University Press, 1999.

Olsen, Kirstin. *Chronology of Women's History*. Westport, CT: Greenwood Press, 1994.

Palmer, Richard E. "What Hermeneutics Can Offer Rhetoric." In *Rhetoric and Hermeneutics in Our Time: A Reader*, ed. Walter Jost and Michael J. Hyde, 108–31. New Haven, CT: Yale University Press, 1997.

Pannenberg, Wolfhart. *Anthropology in Theological Perspective*. Edinburgh: T&T Clark, 1985.

Panofsky, Dora, and Irwin Panofsky. *Pandora's Box*. New York: Pantheon, 1962.

Pelikan, Jaroslav. *The Growth of Medieval Theology (600–1300)*. Vol. 3 of *The Christian Tradition: A History of the Development of Doctrine*. Chicago: University of Chicago Press, 1978.

Perelman, Chaim, and Lucie Olbrecths-Tyceta. *The New Rhetoric: A Treatise on Argumentation*. Trans. John Wilkinson and Purcell Weaver. Notre Dame, IN: University of Notre Dame Press, 1969.

Phan, Peter C. "Betwixt and Between: Doing Theology with Memory and Imagination." In *Journeys at the Margin: Toward an Autobiographical Theology in American-Asian Perspective*, ed. Peter Phan and Jung Young Lee, 113–34. Collegeville, MN: Liturgical Press, 1999.

Plantinga, Cornelius, Jr. *Not the Way It's Supposed to Be: A Breviary of Sin*. Grand Rapids: Eerdmans, 1995.

Plaskow, Judith. *Sex, Sin, and Grace: Women's Experience and the Theologies of Reinhold Niebuhr and Paul Tillich*. New York: University Press of America, 1980.

Plato. *Gorgias and Phaedrus*. Trans. James H. Nichols Jr. Ithaca, NY: Cornell University Press, 1998.

Potter, Mary. "Evil, Sin, and the Violation of the Vulnerable." In *Lift Every Voice: Constructing Theologies from the Underside*, ed. Susan Brooks Thistlethwaite and Mary Potter Engel. San Francisco: Harper & Row, 1998.

———. "Gender Equality and Gender Hierarchy in Calvin's Theology." *Signs* 11, no. 4 (Summer 1986): 725–39.

———. "Historical Theology and Violence against Women: Unearthing a Popular Tradition of Just Battery." In *Revisioning the Past: Prospects in Historical Theology*, ed. Mary Potter Engel and Walter E. Wyman Jr., 51–75. Minneapolis: Fortress Press, 1992.

Presbyterian Church (U.S.A.), *Turn Mourning into Dancing! A Policy Statement on Healing Domestic Violence*. https://www.pcusa.org/resource/turn-mourning-dancing-policy-healing-dom/.

Rahner, Karl. *Foundations of the Christian Faith: an Introduction to the Idea of Christianity*. New York: Crossroad, 1995.

Ray, Stephen G., Jr. *Do No Harm: Social Sin and Christian Responsibility*. Minneapolis: Fortress Press, 2003.

Recovering Grace. "How 'Counseling Sexual Abuse' Blames and Shames Survivors." April 18, 2003. http://www.recoveringgrace.org/2013/04/how-counseling-sexual-abuse-blames-and-shames-survivors/.

Redmond, Sheila. "'Remember the Good, Forget the Bad': Denial and Family Violence in a Christian Worship Service." In *Women at Worship: Interpretations of North American Diversity*, ed. Marjorie Proctor-Smith and Janet R. Walton, 71–82. Louisville, KY: Westminster/John Knox Press, 1993.

Reik, Theodore. *Myth and Guilt*. New York: G. Brazilier, 1970.

Reis, Elizabeth. *Damned Women: Sinners and Witches in Puritan New England*. Ithaca, NY: Cornell University Press, 1997.

Riggins, Stephen Harold. "The Rhetoric of Othering." In *The Language and Politics of Exclusion: Others in Discourse*, ed. S. H. Riggins, 1–30. Communication and Human Values. Thousand Oaks, CA: Sage Publications, 1997.

Romero, Joan Arnold. "Karl Barth's Theology of the Word of God: Or, How to Keep Women Silent and in Their Place." In *Women and Religion*, rev. ed., ed. Judith Plaskow and Joan Arnold Romero, 63–73. Missoula, MT: Scholars Press, 1974.

Ruether, Rosemary Radford. "The Cult of True Womanhood." *Commonweal* 99 (November 9, 1973): 130.

———. "Dualism and the Nature of Evil in Feminist Theology." *Studies in Christian Ethics* 5, no. 1 (1992): 30–31.

———. "Ecofeminism: Symbolic and Social Connections of the Oppression of Women and the Domination of Nature." In *Ecofeminism and the Sacred*, ed. Carol J. Adams, 13–23. New York: Continuum, 1993.

———. "Goddesses and Witches: Liberation and Countercultural Feminism." *Christian Century*, September 10–17, 1980, 842–47.

———. "Home and Work: Women's Roles and the Transformation of Values." *Theological Studies* 36 (December 1975): 647–59.

———. "Male Clericalism and the Dread of Women." In *Women and Orders*, ed. Robert J. Heyers, 1–13. New York: Paulist Press, 1974.

———. *New Woman, New Earth: Sexist Ideologies and Human Liberation*. New York: Seabury Press, 1975.

———. *Sexism and God-Talk: Toward a Feminist Theology*. Boston: Beacon Press, 1993.

———. "Virginal Feminism in the Fathers of the Church." In *Religion and Sexism: Images of Woman in the Jewish and Christian Traditions*, ed. Rosemary Radford Ruether, 150–83. Eugene, OR: Wipf and Stock, 1998.

———. "The Western Religious Tradition and Violence against Women in the Home." In *Christianity, Patriarchy, and Abuse: A Feminist Critique*, ed. Carole

Carlson Brown and Carole R. Bohn, 31–41. Cleveland, OH: Pilgrim Press, 1989.
Saiving, Valerie. "The Human Situation: A Feminine View." In *Womanspirit Rising: A Feminist Reader in Religion*, ed. Carol P. Christ and Judith Plaskow, 25–42. San Francisco: Harper & Row, 1992.
Sanday, Peggy Reeves. "The Socio-Cultural Context of Rape: A Cross-Cultural Study." *Journal of Social Issues* 37, no. 4 (1981): 5–27.
Schleiermacher, Friedrich. *The Christian Faith*. Ed. H. R. Mackintosh and J. S. Stewart. Edinburgh: T&T Clark, 1989.
Schüngel-Straumann, Helen. "'From a Woman Sin Had Its Beginning, and Because of Her We All Die.' (Sir 25:24)." *Theology Digest* 45, no. 3 (Fall 1998): 203–10.
Schüssler Fiorenza, Elisabeth. *But She Said: Feminist Practices of Biblical Interpretation*. Boston: Beacon Press, 1992.
———. "Challenging the Rhetorical Half-Turn: Feminist and Rhetorical Biblical Criticism." In *Rhetoric, Scripture, and Theology: Essays from the 1994 Pretoria Conference*, ed. Stanley E. Porter and Thomas H. Olbricht, 28–53. Journal for the Study of the New Testament Supplement Series 131. Sheffield, UK: Sheffield Academic Press, 1996.
———. "Introduction." In *Violence against Women*, ed. Elisabeth Schüssler Fiorenza and Mary Shawn Copeland, vii–xxiv. Concilium 1994/1. Maryknoll, NY: Orbis Books, 1994.
———. *Jesus and the Politics of Interpretation*. New York: Continuum, 2000.
Schüssler Fiorenza, Francis. *Foundational Theology: Jesus and the Church*. New York: Crossroad, 1984.
Sheridan, David, Tony Michel, and Jim Ridolfo. "*Kairos* and New Media: Toward a Theory and Practice of Visual Activism." *Enculturation: A Journal of Rhetoric, Writing, and Culture* 6, no. 2 (2009), http://enculturation.net/6.2/sheridan-michel-ridolfo.
Smith, Christine M. "Sin and Evil in Feminist Thought." *Theology Today* 50, no. 2 (July 1993): 208–19.
Sprenger, J., and H. Kramer. *Malleus Maleficarum*. Trans. Montague Summers. New York: Dover Publications, 1971.
Stephen, Lynn. *Women and Social Movements in Latin America: Power from Below*. Austin: University of Texas Press, 1997.
Suchocki, Marjorie Hewitt. *The Fall to Violence: Original Sin in Relational Theology*. New York: Continuum, 1995.
Suggit, John. "Redemption: Freedom Regained." In *Doing Theology in Context: South African Perspectives*, ed. John de Gruchy and Charles Villa-Vicencio, 113–24. Theology and Praxis 1. Maryknoll, NY: Orbis Books, 1994.
Tamir, Yael. "Siding with the Underdogs." In *Is Multiculturalism Bad for Women?* ed. Joshua Cohen, Matthew Howard, and Martha C. Nussbaum, 47–52. Princeton, NJ: Princeton University Press, 1999.
Tanner, Kathryn. *Theories of Culture: A New Agenda for Theology*. Minneapolis: Fortress Press, 1997.
Tertullian. *De Cultu Feminarum* 1.1. In *The Ante-Nicene Fathers*, vol. 4, ed. Alexander Roberts and James Donaldson, trans. S. Thelwall. Grand Rapids: Eerdmans, 1986.
Thistlethwaite, Susan Brooks. "Battered Women and the Bible: From Subjection to Liberation." *Christianity and Crisis* 41, no. 18 (1981): 308–13.

———. "Every Two Minutes: Battered Women and Feminist Interpretation." In *Feminist Interpretation of the Bible*, ed. Letty M. Russell, 96–107. Philadelphia: Westminster Press, 1985.
———. *Sex, Race, and God: Christian Feminism in Black and White*. New York: Crossroad, 1989.
Thompson, Roger. "Kairos Revisited: An Interview with James Kinneavy." *Rhetoric Review* 19, no. 1–2 (Autumn 2000): 73–88.
Tillich, Paul. "Basic Principles of Religious Socialism." In *Political Expectation*, ed. James Luther Adams, 58–88. New York: Harper & Row, 1971.
———. *A History of Christian Thought: From Its Judaic and Hellenistic Origins to Existentialism*. Ed. Carl Braaten. New York: Simon and Schuster, 1976.
———. *The Interpretation of History*. New York: Charles Scribner's Sons, 1936.
———.*The Shaking of the Foundations*. New York: Charles Scribner's Sons, 1948.
———. *Systematic Theology*. Volume 1. Chicago: University of Chicago Press, 1951.
———. *Systematic Theology*. Volume 2. Chicago: University of Chicago Press, 1957.
Tracy, David. *The Analogical Imagination: Christian Theology and the Culture of Pluralism*. New York: Crossroad, 1981.
———. "Lindbeck's New Program for Theology: A Reflection." *The Thomist* 49 (1985): 460–72.
———. *Plurality and Ambiguity: Hermeneutics, Religion, Hope*. Chicago: University of Chicago Press, 1987.
Trevor-Roper, Hugh. *Religion, the Reformation, and Social Change*. London: Macmillan, 1967.
United Methodist Women. "Domestic Violence Awareness." https://www.united methodistwomen.org/domestic-violence.
United Nations. United Nations Population Fund, "Sex Imbalances at Birth—Current Trends, Consequences, and Policy Implications," August 2012. http://www.unfpa.org/public/home/publications/pid/12405.
UN Women. "Facts and Figures: Ending Violence against Women." http://www.unwomen.org/en/what-we-do/ending-violence-against-women/facts-and-figures.
United States Conference of Catholic Bishops. "When I Call for Help: A Pastoral Response to Violence against Women." http://www.usccb.org/issues-and-action/marriage-and-family/marriage/domestic-violence/when-i-call-for-help.cfm.
Van Huyssteen, J. Wentzel. *The Shaping of Rationality: Toward Interdisciplinarity in Theology and Science*. Grand Rapids: Eerdmans, 1999.
Vatz, Richard. "The Myth of the Rhetorical Situation." *Philosophy and Rhetoric* 6 (1973): 154–61.
Warren, Karen J. "The Power and the Promise of Ecological Feminism." In *Environmental Ethics: Readings in Theory and Application*, ed. Louis P. Pojman, 173–83. Belmont, CA: Wadsworth, 1998.
Weems, Renita. *Battered Love: Marriage, Sex, and Violence in the Hebrew Prophets*. Minneapolis: Fortress Press, 1995.
West, Angela. *Deadly Innocence: Feminist Theology and the Mythology of Sin*. London: Cassel, 1995.
White, Erin, and Marie Tulip. *Knowing Otherwise: Feminism, Women, and Religion*. Melbourne, Australia: David Lovell Publishing, 1991.
Wiley, Tatha. *Original Sin: Origins, Developments, Contemporary Meanings*. New York: Paulist Press, 2002.

Williams, Delores. "The Color of Feminism, or, Speaking the Black Woman's Tongue." In *Feminist Theological Ethics: A Reader*, ed. Lois K. Daly, 42–58. Louisville, KY: Westminster John Knox Press, 1994.

———. "Sin, Nature, and Black Women's Bodies." In *Ecofeminism and the Sacred*, ed. Carol J. Adams, 24–29. New York: Continuum, 1993.

———. "A Womanist Perspective on Sin." In *A Troubling in My Soul: Womanist Perspectives on Evil and Suffering*, ed. Emilie M. Townes, 130–49. Maryknoll, NY: Orbis Books, 1993.

Williams, Patricia A. *Doing without Adam and Eve: Sociobiology and Original Sin*. Minneapolis: Fortress Press, 2001.

Wolterstorff, Nicholas. "The Wounds of God: Calvin's Theology of Social Injustice." *Reformed Journal* 37, no. 6 (1987): 14–22.

Young, Iris Marion. *Justice and the Politics of Difference*. Princeton, NJ: Princeton University Press, 1990.

Index

abuse. *See also* gender violence
  in church (*see* gender violence, church's role in)
  domestic (*see* domestic abuse)
  dowry death, 138
  genital mutilation, 46, 136n21
  global, 45, 140
  harassment, 47
  matricide, 92–94, 100, 105
  oppression (*see* oppression)
  rape (*see* rape)
  sexual, prevalence of, 45–46
  silencing, of women, 47, 134
Adam and Eve story, 84–85, 95–96, 113. *See also* Eve
agency
  human, 113–17, 123, 126, 147
  sinful, 112, 114, 151
  women's, 76
"Ain't I a Woman?" (Truth), 104
androcentrism
  in Augustinian thought, 60
  defined, 37
  Mary/Eve symbols as, 105
  patriarchy as, 115
  and pride, 68, 70–71
  of theologians, 62–64
anger, 75–77, 125
Aquino, María Pilar, 6, 129, 141n39, 145
Ardener, Shirley, 94
Aristotle, 12, 14–18
art, rhetoric as, 32–34
Asad, Talal, 21–22
audiences. *See pathos* (of audiences)
Augustine of Hippo, 58–62
  androcentrism in, 60
  on Eve, 88
  on pride, 86, 112–13
  on rhetorical theology, usefulness of, 18
  and sexuality, 60, 85
  on sin, origin of, 85–86
  on subordination of women, 99, 99n50
  and threefold movement, sin as, 59, 112, 125

Barth, Karl, 20, 63–64, 80
being, of women, 90–91
Benhabib, Seyla, 137
Beyond God the Father (Daly), 90
Bible and gender violence, 50–54, 129
biological, women's experiences as, 65, 69
Bitzer, Lloyd, 32–34
blame, of men, 117–18
blame, of women. *See also* blame critique
  biblical, 50–53
  and human nature, 120
  vs passivity, 135
  and rape, 51, 51n51
  Tillich on, 71
blame critique. *See also* blame, of women
  body condemnation, church history of, 85–88
  and Eve, 84–85, 89–90
  and the Mary/Eve dichotomy, 102–7
  rhetoric of oppression (*see* rhetoric of oppression)
  rhetoric of reason (*see* rhetoric of reason)
  theologians on, 88–89

Index

body, women's. *See also* gender violence
   abuse of (*see* abuse *for individual types*)
   church condemnation of, 85–88
   male control of, 99, 116
   /mind dualism, 98
   and seduction, 51–52, 89–90
   and sexuality (*see* sexuality)
   and sin, origin of, 85–86
   sins of, 112
   value of, 26, 85–86, 98, 124
Boff, Leonardo, 79
Bonhoeffer, Dietrich, 2
Booth, Wayne, 15
Brock, Rita Nakashima, 77, 119–20, 122n25, 124
brokenheartedness, 119–20, 124–25
brokenness
   divine, 120, 124–25
   and gender violence, 150
   inner, 112, 119–20, 124
   relationality, 60, 74, 109, 112, 119–20, 124–25
   and sin, 60, 153
Brown, Delwin, 1, 137
Burke, Kenneth, 12–13

Calvin, John
   on death denunciation, 143–45
   on domestic abuse, 50, 92
   and sin-talk, 145–51
Campbell, Harry, 105
Carr, Ann, 79–80
Center for Health and Gender Equity (CHANGE), 45
chaos/order myth, 94–96
Charry, Ellen, 61
choice, human, 74, 112–15, 117–18
Chopp, Rebecca, 23
Christ, Carol P., 19
Christ event, 35, 131
church. *See also* theologians, classical; theologians, modern; theology, Christian
   and blame, of women, 50–52, 91–92
   and body condemnation, 85–88
   and domestic abuse, 49–52, 52nn54–55, 91–92
   on gender violence, 52–54, 129
   male dominance in, 53–54
   and oppression, 91

   patriarchy in, 79
   power of, 144
   and rape, 50–53
   and rhetoric of oppression, 90–92, 96
Cicero, 12, 16, 18, 60, 142–43
City of God, The (Augustine), 59, 85–86, 88
Clark, Elizabeth, 94
classes, social. *See* Others (cultural groups)
Classical Rhetoric, 12–16. *See also ethos; logos* (death denouncing); *pathos* (of audiences)
communicability (as sin-talk characteristic), 122–23
compensation gap, 41
Compier, Don, 110–11, 132, 141n39, 142–46, 150
complementarity, gender, 76, 115–16
concupiscence, 59–60, 67–68, 83, 86
Confessions (Augustine), 86, 125
consciousness/unconsciousness dualism, 100–101
consent, to oppression, 75–76
Consigny, Scott, 32–34, 36
constructive rhetorics
   about, 10
   in feminist sin-talk critique, 111
   and patriarchal *ethos*, 128
   and theology, 1
constructivism, 69–70
context, of rhetoric. *See* rhetorical situation
contextual judgment, 15
contingency (as sin-talk characteristic), 122–23
control, men over women. *See* dominance, male
Cooper-White, Pamela, 47, 53
corporate moral agency, 114–15
creation
   doctrine of, 131
   narratives, 94–96
creationism, 87
critical-constructive model, rhetorical theology, 10, 146–47
critical rhetorical inquiry, 10, 14, 18–19, 22–23
crypto-foundationalism, 20, 20n32
Cult of True Womanhood, 103–4

Index

cultural
  constructs, 69–70
  critiques, 136–37
  essentialism, 38, 137–38
  exclusion, 39–40
  groups (race, class, gender, etc.) (*see* Others (cultural groups))
  imperialism, 43
  patterns, 20–21
  realities, 19–20
  -wide issues (*see* systemic issues)
Cunningham, David, 19–20

Daly, Mary
  on the fall, 91, 115
  on Mary/Eve dichotomy, 103
  and rhetoric of oppression, 24, 90–91
  on victimization, 73
death denouncing. *See logos* (death denouncing)
death outcome (as sin-talk characteristic), 124
decorum, 15–16, 134, 142
de Gruchy, John, 144
dehumanization, of women
  and body sins, 112
  as distortion of human nature, 122–23
  Mary/Eve symbols, 105, 149
  Noddings on, 101
  and violence, 106, 150, 150n70
dialectical reasoning, 18, 20–22
Dictionary of Moral Theology (Francesco), 50–51
dignity, human, 146–49
disassociation, with self, 68, 70, 79, 134
discerning, doctrine of, 134
discipline, domestic, 49–51, 92
distortion
  of grace, pre-Reformation, 145
  of human nature, 112, 120–23
  of relationality, 115–16
  of self-other relationship, 97
  of sin, and sin-talk, 110–11
  of sin, pre-Reformation, 145
  of sociality, 123
diversity, 135–41
divine-human relationship, 58–60, 74, 120, 124–25, 150
divine revelation, 130
doctrinal symbols. *See* symbols, faith

doctrine
  of creation, 131
  of discerning, 134
  of *imago Dei*, 97, 143–44, 147–50, 147n62
  of love, 66, 70, 82
  of original sin (*see* original sin, doctrine of)
  rhetorical approaches to, 143
  rhetorical effects of, 19–20
  of sin (*see* sin-talk, classical (Christian); sin-talk, feminist)
domestic abuse
  biblical, 49–51, 129
  church role in, 49–52, 52nn54–55, 91–92
  as discipline, 49–51, 92
  and economic exploitation, 41
  and female submissiveness, 64
  global, 45
  in history, 50
  and homicide, 46
  just cause, 103
  justification for, 105
  rape, 45–46, 105, 116
dominance, male. *See also* subjugation, of women
  global, 39–40, 138
  over nature, 94
  and power, patriarchal, 134
  as sexual access, 116
  as systemic, 37–38
Douglass, Jane Dempsey, 145
Down Girl (Manne), 37
dowry deaths, 138
dualism, 97–101, 105, 105n71
Duck, Ruth, 61
Dunfee, Susan Nelson
  introduction to, 57–58
  on pride, 72
  on sensuality, 67–68
  and sins, of women, 25

economic consequences, of oppression, 40–42
Eliade, Mircea, 102
Elizondo, Virgilio, 78
"Enemy, The" (Daly), 24
Engel, Mary Potter, 76–77, 103, 134
Enuma Elish, 94–95

Eros, 100–101
Ess, Charles, 96
essentialism, 38–39, 134, 137–38
ethics
  kairos, 17, 34–36
  love, 66
  relativism, 32, 34
  in rhetoric, 16–17
  and rhetorical situations, 32
ethos
  about, 14–16
  of control, 94
  prophetic, 128–33
  and sin-talk, 14
Eve
  Augustine on, 88
  as dehumanizing, 105
  as evil, 98, 102, 149
  Mary/Eve dichotomy, 102–3
  as sin, symbol of, 83–85, 88–92, 95–96
  as temptress, 72, 89–90
evil. *See also* sin
  Augustine on, 59
  body as, 86
  choices of, 125
  female as, 73, 93, 97–99, 101, 115
  and Pandora myth, 84–85, 84n2
exploitation, 40–41, 99, 103–4
Exum, Cheryl, 51–52

fall, the (of humanity into sin)
  Daly on, 91, 115
  and oppression, 109–10
  and original sin, 119 (*see also* original sin, doctrine of)
  Tillich on, 71
Faus, José Ignacio González, 114
feminine principle (*Eros*), 100–101
feminism
  global, 4–5, 135–41
  patriarchy as, 37–38
  positions, 90
  radical, 90–91
feminist
  classifications, 24
  concepts, 35–44
  criticism, 109–10, 115, 146–47
  sin-talk (*see* sin-talk, feminist)
  social change, responsibility for, 128, 133

  strategies, 24–27
First World cultures. *See* Majority
  World cultures
Fortune, Marie, 54
Foucault, Michel, 13
Fraser, Nancy, 43, 137
freedom, human, 67–68, 70, 112
Fulkerson, Mary McClintock, 38, 111, 121

Geertz, Clifford, 19, 21–22
gender. *See also* gender violence; gender violence, church's role in
  complementarity, 76, 115–16
  essentialism, 38, 134
  of God, 19, 97, 101–2
  mortality bias, 46–47
  and race, 5, 42, 103–4
  sin, differences in, 65, 68, 134
gendercide, 46–47
gender violence. *See also* abuse; gender violence, church's role in
  in creation narratives, 94–95
  as culturally specific, 45, 140
  as divine violation, 149–50
  and dualism, 101
  global, 45–47, 135, 138, 140
  human nature of, 112, 120, 123
  nonresistance to, 64, 76, 134
  prevalence of, by form, 45–47
  from self-hatred, 73
  and social class and race, 5, 36, 42, 103–4
  as systemic, 43, 47–49
  Western cultural ideals of, 135–40
gender violence, church's role in
  blame, of women, 50–52, 91–92
  domestic abuse, 49–52, 52nn54–55, 91–92
  marriage hierarchy, 53–54, 76, 122
  neglect of issues, 52–54
  silence on, 125
genital mutilation (FGM), 46, 136n21
genocide, 106
Gerhardt, Elizabeth, 54
Gil, Rosa Maria, 79
Gilligan, Carol, 25
global
  abuse, 45–47, 140
  feminism, 4–5, 135–41

Index

rhetoric, 79, 79n58, 81
sexism, 138–39
sin-talk, 140
God
  broken relationship with, 120, 124–25
  Calvin on, 145
  as divine violation, 149–50
  estrangement from, 62–63, 71, 150
  -for-us, 131
  gender representation of, 19, 97, 101–2
  -human relationship, 58–60, 74, 150
  image of, 97, 143–44, 147–50, 147n62
  of life, 129–30
  Mary's obedience to, 79
  masculine rhetoric of, 97, 101–2
  of the poor and wronged, 131
  in prophetic *ethos*, 131
  rebellion against, 59, 112, 150n70
  Trinitarian, 148
Goddess, in feminism, 19, 24, 91, 128, 128n1. *See also* Tiamat
Good Wife, 103
governments, colonial, 138
grace
  as an original state, 119–20, 124
  destructive, 74
  and self-loss, 70
  and sin, 2, 68, 76, 131, 152–53
grammar, of doctrine of original sin. *See also* original sin, doctrine of
  about, 109–10
  contradictions in, 112–14
  and feminist sin-talk, 121–26
  feminist sin-talk vs classical sin-talk, 111–12
  patriarchy, as original sin, 115–21
  sin-talk retrieval, 110–11
  structural sin, 114
Gramsci, Antonio, 13, 43
Greece, ancient, and language, 12
greed, 59
Grey, Mary, 134
Gudorf, Christine, 75
guilt, 72, 88, 117–18
Gutiérrez, Gustavo, 18, 114
Gyn/Ecology (Daly), 91

Halkes, Catharina, 78
hamartiosphere, 114, 122

harassment, sexual, 47
Hartsock, Nancy, 38–39
Hawkesworth, Mary, 24, 26–27, 90–91
healing, for sin, 118–19, 124–25
Heggen, Carolyn Holderread, 53
Hess, Carol Lakey, 75, 135
hiding, sin of, 67, 72–73, 134
Hodgson, Peter, 147
Holocaust, 101, 106
Holy Spirit, 35
Honig, Bonnie, 137
hubris, 59, 63
human dignity, 146–49
humanism, 142
human nature, distortion of, 112, 120–23
"Human Situation: A Feminine View, The" (Saiving), 57
humility
  in confession, 61
  and consent, to oppression, 75–76
  destructive language of, 70–71
  and guilt, 72
  in Mary symbol, 79
  as pathology, female, 61
  St. Benedict's ladder to, 75
  and submissiveness, female, 64
  as victim quality, 73–74

identification, rhetoric as, 12–13
identities, diversity of, 133
imagination, in struggle, 26
imago Dei, 97, 143–44, 147–50, 147n62
immanence, 35
In a Different Voice (Gilligan), 25
individual vs structural sin, 74, 112, 114–16, 122, 122n25
inferiority, of women, 84, 88, 93, 97
inheritance, of sin, 87, 112, 119–20
inner logic. *See* grammar, of doctrine of original sin
Institutes of the Christian Religion (Calvin), 142, 142n43, 143
interstitial perspective, 5, 36, 42, 103–4
Irigaray, Luce, 133

Jarratt, Susan, 14
Johnson, Elizabeth A., 5, 19, 78–79

Index

Jones, Serene
  on audiences, 133
  as author influence, 6
  on Calvin, 142–43
  on feminist sin-talk, 110
  on labor division, 41
  on Lindbeck, 19–20
  on oppression, social, 117–18
  and strategic essentialism, 39
justice, 16–17, 34, 36, 129–30, 129n3, 143–45

kairic law, 17
kairos
  about, 33–34
  and decorum, 16, 142
  discerning, 139–40
  and ethics, 17, 34–36
  feminist concepts, 35–41
  gender violence (*see* gender violence)
  gender violence, church's role in (*see* gender violence, church's role in)
  Kinneavy on, 33–34
  oppression, of women, 109
  and *pathos* (of audiences), 134
  of revelation, divine, 130–31
  rhetorical situation (*see* rhetorical situation)
  and time, 17
Kanyoro, Musimbi, 39
Keener, Craig S., 52–53
Keller, Catherine, 95
Kinneavy, James L., 16–17, 33–34
Klasen, Stephan, 47
Kristof, Nicholas, 46

labor division, 41
LaCugna, Catherine, 148
Lady of Guadalupe, 78
language. *See also* rhetoric
  20th century interest in, 9
  in classical era, 12
  influence of, 13–14
  morality in, 16
  persuasiveness of, 134
  and praxis, 21
Latin America, and Mary symbol, 79, 81
laws, and violence, 43–44
lexis, 16

liberation theology, 18–19, 114–15
life, cry for, and prophetic *ethos*, 128–33, 141n39
Lindbeck, George, 19–21
logos
  about, 14–15
  as masculine principle, 100–101
  of sin-talk, 101
logos (death denouncing)
  and Calvin, 142–45
  and feminist sin-talk, 150–51
  rhetoric of, elements, 143–45
  sin-talk, critique of, 145–46
loss of self, 68, 70, 79, 134
love
  doctrine of, 66, 70, 82
  ethics, 66
  for God, 143–45
  of material world, 59–60
  for neighbor, 143–44
  self, Augustine on, 58–59
  self-sacrificial, 61, 70–76
Luther, Martin, 50, 88–89, 92

Majority World cultures, 135–41
male sin-talk elements, 146–50
Malleus Maleficarum [Hammer of Witches] (Kramer, Sprenger), 93
Mananzan, Mary John, 75
Manne, Kate, 37
marginalization, 41–42. *See also* androcentrism
Mariology, 78–79
marriage
  church on, 92
  discipline in, 49–51, 92
  hierarchy in, 53–54, 76, 122
  and Mary symbol, 105
  submission, female, in, 53–54, 64, 80, 84, 105
Mary, the Virgin-Mother
  as dehumanizing, 105
  and Lady of Guadalupe, 78
  as life-denial symbol, 78–82
  Mary/Eve dichotomy, 102–3
  obedience of, 79, 105
  Protestantism on, 80
  Second Vatican Council on, 79–80
  virtues of, 79–80

matricide, as witch hunts, 92–94
McFadyen, Alistair, 61, 76, 121–23, 132
McLaughlin, Eleanor, 105
men
  as the enemy, 24
  as *imago Dei*, 97
Meyer-Wilkes, Hedwig, 94
Middle Ages, wifely discipline, 49–50
Miles, Margaret, 85
mind/body dualism, 98
Miriam of Nazareth, 78–79
mirror of unfaithfulness, 133
misinformation, exposing. *See* rhetoric of reason
misogyny. *See* sexism
modern rhetorical theory, 12–19
mood, 19
moralism, 153
morality
  Aristotle on, 18
  human agency, 113–17, 123, 126, 147
  pathology, 126
  responsibility, 118–19
  and rhetoric, 15–18
  and rhetorical situations, 32
  transgressions, 125
mortality biases, 46–47
motivation, 19, 21–22
murder, of women, 46–47, 92–94

Narayan, Uma, 137–39
nature, 65, 69, 94–95
Nature of Doctrine, The (Lindbeck), 21
neighbors, love of, 143–44
Neumann, Erich, 101
New Rhetoric, 12–19
Niebuhr, Reinhold, 62, 67–68, 70, 72
Noddings, Nel, 100–101

Oduyoye, Mercy Amba, 136
Ofei-Afboagye, Rosemary Ofibea, 137
oppression, of women. *See also* rhetoric of oppression
  as a choice, 117–18
  collective character of, 117–18
  as divine violation, 149–50
  faces of, 41–44
  imago Dei as, 147

and original sin language, 109–10
as systemic, 116, 147
original sin, doctrine of
  Augustine on, 59–61, 112, 125
  as condition, 113–14
  in feminist rhetoric, 109–10
  and grace, 119–20, 124
  grammar of (*see* grammar, of doctrine of original sin)
  as historical event, 113
  patriarchy as, 115–21
  sexism as, 115
  and sexuality, 87
  source of, 85–87
  tensions in, 112–14
Ortner, Sherry, 69
othering, rhetoric of, 13
Others (cultural groups)
  class, 103–4, 104n66
  demonization/idealization paradox, 98–100
  and essentialism, 39
  global, 39, 136
  interstitial perspective, 5, 36, 42, 103–4
  marginalization of, 41–42
  racial, 38, 40, 42–44, 103–4
  term exclusivity, 36
  women as, 103, 105

Pandora, 84–85, 84n2, 96, 98
passivity, 69, 76, 79, 105, 134–35
pathology
  and gender violence, 48–49
  humility, 61
  morality, 126
  and pride, 57
  self-sacrifice, 57, 61, 68
  and sin, 114
  sin-talk on, 122–23, 126
pathos (of audiences)
  about, 14–16
  and cultural essentialism, 137–38
  feminism, global, 135–37
  and rhetorical scaling, 133–34
  and sins of women, 133
  Westernization, 138–39
  and women's sins, 134–35
patriarchal *ethos*, 129

patriarchy
  about, 37–38
  biblical, 50–51, 53–54
  Daly on, 24
  and essentialism, 38–39
  as feminist concept, 37–38
  and gender violence, 47–48
  global, 39–40, 136
  grand narrative of, 39–41
  hierarchy of, 135
  as original sin, 115–21 (*see also* original sin, doctrine of)
  perpetuation of, 70, 81
  power relations of, 134
  reality of, questioning, 123
  as a religion, 91
  as universal, 123
Pelagianism, 60, 74, 112, 117, 135
penitential system, medieval, 144–45, 145n55
personhood, 38–39, 123
persuasiveness, 1, 12–15, 22, 133–34
piety, 10, 20, 22, 144
Plaskow, Judith
  introduction to, 57–58
  sensuality, 67–68, 67n27
  and sins, of women, 25
  on Tillich, 71
  on women's experience, 69
Plato, 12, 17
poverty, 41–42
power
  of church over individuals, 144
  patriarchal, 134
  and religion, 21–23
  social, 19–20, 42
powerlessness, 42–43
praxis, 9, 18–19, 21, 23
prejudice, against women. *See* sexism
pride. *See also* pride critique
  as androcentric, 68, 70–71
  Augustine on, 58–62, 86, 112–13
  Barth on, 63–64
  and concupiscence, 60–61
  as destructive to women, 72–74
  and humility, 64
  as tension in doctrine of original sin, 112–13
  Tillich on, 62–63
pride critique. *See also* pride
  Augustinian history of, 58–62
  modern history of, 62–64
  and rhetoric of difference, 64–69
  and rhetoric of oppression, 69–72
professions, of women, 41
prophetic *ethos*, 128–33
prostitution, 104
punishment, 153
purity, sexual, 51, 53, 78–79, 104

Quintilian, 12, 16, 142

racial issues, 38–40, 42–44, 103–4
radical critique, 146
radical feminism, 90–91
radicality (as sin-talk characteristic), 122–23
rape
  biblical, 50–53
  justification of, 81
  and dehumanization, 106
  domestic, 45–46, 105, 116
  and Lady of Guadalupe, 78
  prevalence of, 45–46
  racial, 104, 104n66
  victims of, blaming, 51, 51n51 (*see also* blame, of women)
Ray, Stephen, 42
reasoning, logical, 12–13
redemption, 130
relationality, brokenness of, 60, 74, 109, 112, 115–16, 119–20, 124–25
relationships, and *imago Dei*, 144
repentance, 130, 144–45
resistance, to violence, 76–77
responsibility, for sin, 112, 115–19
retrieval, hermeneutic of, 110–12
revelation, 17, 20, 35, 130
Reynolds, Nedra, 14
rhetoric
  about, 9–11
  as art, 32–34
  and Calvin, 142
  classical vs modern, 11–18
  defined, 9
  feminist, as sin-talk, 109–10
  feminist strategies, 24–27
  justice in, 16–17
  and listening, 139
  origin of, 32–34

Index

persuasion of, 12–14
and power, 22
rhetorical theory, 11–18
theological, 18–23 (*see also* rhetorical theology)
rhetorical scaling, 133–34
rhetorical situation
  about, 31–33
  feminist, 111
  and oppression, 74–75
  prophetic in, 130
  and rhetorical theology, 33–35
  Saiving on, 66–67
  and sociality conditions, 123
rhetorical strategies, 24–27. *See also individual strategies*
  rhetoric of difference, 64–69
  rhetoric of oppression, 69–72, 90–96
  rhetoric of reason, 97–107
rhetorical theology
  defined, 10
  and dialectical reasoning, 18, 20–22
  and doctrines, 19–20
  and *kairos*, 34
  persuasive task of, 22
  and social reality, 19–20
rhetorical theory
  classic vs new, 12–14
  ethics of, 15–17
  and persuasive argument elements, 14–15
  postmodern, 20
  rhetorical situation, 32
rhetoric of death, 102–7
  church's role in, 91–92, 100
  Eve as symbol of (*see* Eve)
  as justification for violence, 27
  and sexism, 37
rhetoric of difference, 64–68
  about, 25, 27
  and patriarchal *ethos*, 132
  Saiving on, 65–66
rhetoric of life-denial, 73–82
  about, 28
  and androcentric sin-talk, 75–76
  and complementarity, gender, 76
  and denouncing death, 141, 151
  and Mary symbol, 78–81
  and pride, 73–74

and resistance, to violence, 76–77
and submissiveness, female, 74–75
rhetoric of oppression, 69–72, 90–96
  about, 24, 27, 83
  church role in, 90–92, 96
  and creation narratives, 94–96
  matricide, 92–94
  and patriarchal *ethos*, 132
  Ruether on, 97
  Saiving on, 66
rhetoric of othering, 13
rhetoric of reason
  about, 25–27, 97
  control, by male, 99
  dualism, 98–101
  evil, female as, 98
  nature, female association with, 99
  Other/self distortion, 97–100
  and patriarchal *ethos*, 132
  Ruether on, 97
rhetoric of vision, 26–27
rhetoric scaling, 134
Richardson, Herbert, 94
Roman, ancient, on language, 12
Roman Catholic Church, 52
Romero, Joan Arnold, 80
Ruether, Rosemary Radford
  about, 99n49
  on agency, 116
  as author influence, 6
  on blame critique, 91–92
  and body, devaluing of, 26
  on constructive feminist sin-talk, 128
  on creation narratives, 95
  dualistic *logos* in patriarchal rhetoric, 97, 101
  on evil, female as, 98
  on exploitation, 41, 99
  on feminist sin-talk, 110
  on Mary/Eve dichotomy, 102–3
  on rhetoric of oppression, 97
  on rhetoric of reason, 97
  on sexism, 115
  on wifely insubordination, Middle Ages, 50
  on witch hunts, 92

Saiving, Valerie, 25, 57, 64–65
scapegoating, 13, 91, 93–94, 98–99, 106, 117

Schleiermacher, Friedrich, 114
Schüssler Fiorenza, Elisabeth
  as author influence, 6
  on critical rhetorics, 10
  on gender violence, 44–45
  on patriarchy, 40
  on religion and power, 22–23
  on submission, female in marriage, 53–54
seduction, 51–52, 72, 89–90
self-actualization, 71
self-esteem, 43
self-hatred, 73. *See also* rhetoric of life-denial
self-loss, 68, 70, 79, 134
self-love, 58–59
self-other relationship, 97–98
self-sacrifice, 61, 70–76
Sen, Amartya, 46–47
sensuality, 62, 67–68, 72. *See also* self-loss
sexism
  about, 37
  blame critique (*see* blame critique)
  in the church, 52, 79, 88
  culturally-specific, 138–39
  defined, 37, 49
  evil of, 26
  grammar, of doctrine of original sin (*see grammar*, of doctrine of original sin)
  kairos (*see kairos*)
  life, affirmation of (*see logos* (death denouncing))
  in Mary/Eve, 104–5
  as original sin, 115–17
  pride paradigm (*see* pride critique)
  rhetoric (*see* rhetoric)
  rhetorical practices of, 27
  in sin-talk, Christian, 96
sexual harassment, 47
sexuality
  in Adam and Eve story, 84–85
  and Augustine, 60, 85
  and guilt, of women, 72
  and original sin, 87
  purity, 51, 53, 78–79, 104
She Who Is (Johnson), 5
silencing, of women, 47, 134
sin
  accountability for, 113–14
  Augustine view on, 58–62
  and body, origin of, 85–86
  and brokenness, 60, 153
  as choice, 117
  corporate, 114–15
  and death, 110
  doctrine of (*see* sin-talk, classical (Christian); sin-talk, feminist)
  gender differences, 65, 68, 134
  generational transfer of, 87, 112, 119–20
  and grace, 2, 68, 76, 131, 152–53
  healing of, 118–19, 124–25
  of hiding, 67, 72–73, 134
  and human nature, 120
  individual, 74, 112, 114–19, 122, 122n25
  and marginalization, 42
  modern view of, 113–14
  Niebuhr on, 62
  original (*see* original sin, doctrine of)
  and penitential system, medieval, 144–45
  pride as (*see* pride critique)
  relationality of, 59–60, 120
  responsibility for, 112, 114–17, 119
  roots of, Augustine on, 59–60, 84, 86, 88
  significance of, 2–3, 11
  source of, 85–87
  as systemic, 114–18, 122n25
  Tillich on, 62–63
  as tragic, 112
  and women, 25, 65, 67–68, 89, 93, 98, 116, 133, 135, 140
sinful agency, 112, 114, 151
sin of weakness, 62, 71
sin-talk, classical (Christian)
  Adam and Eve story, 84–85, 95–96, 113
  androcentric, 75, 77–78
  Augustinian trajectory of, 58–62, 58n2, 73
  Calvin as critique example, 145–50
  characteristics of, 121–24
  creation narratives, 94–96
  as critical, 146–47
  early, 86, 88–89
  vs feminist sin-talk, 111–12, 121–26
  God in, 101, 131
  history with feminist theology, 10–11
  on human moral evils, 125

humility in confession, 61
logos of, 101
male, elements of, 146–50
misogyny in, 96
oppressive rhetoric critique in, 146
pride critique of (*see* pride critique)
as prophetic, 128
retrieval of, 110–11
sins of, 146
and social issues, 132
as systemic, 147
as theocentric, 147–50
victim qualities idealized in, 73–74
in witch hunter's handbook, 93
sin-talk, feminist
about, 111
and Calvin, 150–51
vs classical sin-talk, 111–12, 121–26
criticism as, 109–11, 115
elements of, 150
grammar of, 121–26
Jones on, 110
as prophetic, 128
Ruether on, 110, 128
and societal change, 128, 132
situations, rhetor created, 32
slavery, 101
social
change, 128, 133, 136–37
issues, 132
positioning, 19–20, 42
reality, 19–20
sin, 116
Socrates, 12, 17
Sojourner Truth, 104
soteriology, 131
soul, 85–87
speaker, as *ethos*. *See ethos*
sphere of sin, 114, 122
St. Benedict's ladder to humility, 75
Stephens, Lynn, 81
stereotypes
culture, 137–38
female, 103
strategic essentialism, 39
structural sin, 114–18, 146–47
subjugation, of women
Augustine on, 99, 99n50
as divine violation, 149–50
in marriage, 53–54
during Middle Ages, 49–50

as punishment for sin, 84, 88–89
in Renaissance era, 103
in theological rhetoric, 75
submissiveness, female, 53–54, 64, 74–76, 80, 84, 105
Suggit, John, 130
symbols, faith
cultural, 41
Eve, as sin, 95–96
as language, 23
Mary, 78–82
and power relations, 10, 13, 21
and reality, social, 13, 19–21
and rhetorical theology, 21–22
theological, 9
in theology definition, 1
Systematic Theology (Tillich), 62–63
systemic issues
dehumanization of women, 112
gender violence, 44, 47–49
oppression, 116, 147
patriarchy (*see* patriarchy)
scapegoating, 93–94
sin, 60, 114–18, 122n25, 146–47
sin-talk, 147, 150–51
violence, 43, 47–49

tact. *See* decorum
Tamar, 53
Tanner, Kathryn, 137
temptress, women as, 51–52, 72, 89–90
Tertullian, 88
theologians, classical
androcentrism in, 60, 62–64
Calvin, John (*see* Calvin, John)
on domestic discipline, 50
on inferiority of women, and Eve, 88–89
on rape, 50–51
theologians, modern
on Adam and Eve story, reality of, 113
androcentrism in, 62–63
Barth, Karl, 63–64
Niebuhr, Reinhold, 62
Tillich, Paul, 62
theology, Christian. *See also* church; sin-talk, classical (Christian); theologians, classical; theologians, modern
about, 1
cultural differences in, 136–37, 136n21

theology, Christian (*continued*)
  on human moral evils, 125
  liberation, 18–19, 114–15
  praxis, 9, 18–19 (*see also* rhetorical theology)
  rhetorical (*see* rhetorical theology)
  and rhetorical situation, 33–35
Thistlethwaite, Susan Brooks, 76–77
Thomas Aquinas (saint), 5, 88
threefold movement (doctrine of original sin), 59, 112, 125
Tiamat, 94–95
Tillich, Paul, 62–63, 71, 152–53
time, 17, 34
Toubia, Nahid, 137
Tracy, David, 21, 36
traducianism, 87
transgender population, inclusivity of, 36
Trevor-Roper, Hugh, 93–94
Trinitarian God, 148
Trinity, The (Augustine of Hippo), 59
truth, 12–14, 16, 21–22

unconsciousness, 100–101
universality (as sin-talk characteristic), 122–23

Van Huyssteen, Wentzel, 20
Vasquez, Carmen Inoa, 79
Vatz, Richard, 32–34
victimization, of women, 24, 73, 116, 118, 134
violence. *See* gender violence; gender violence, church's role in
virginity, 51, 53, 78–79

wage gap, 41
Warren, Karen J., 94
Weems, Renita, 51
Westernization, 39–40, 135–40
Wiley, Tatha, 113
Williams, Delores, 42–43
Wink, Claudia, 47
Wisdom tradition, 129, 129n3
witch hunts, 92–94, 100, 105
women
  classification of, 102, 104
  of color, 42–43
  as image of God, 147–50, 147n62
  sins of, 65, 67–68, 88, 116, 133–35, 140
women's experience
  about, 15, 27
  aspects of, 37–38
  biological vs culturally constructed, 69–70
  as feminist theology source, 35
  inclusivity of, in term, 36, 40
  in rhetoric of difference, 65–66
work environments, for women, 41–42
WuDunn, Sheryl, 46

You Are Accepted (Tillich), 152–53
Young, Iris Marion, 41, 49

www.ingramcontent.com/pod-product-compliance
Lightning Source LLC
Chambersburg PA
CBHW071923290426
44110CB00013B/1451